Ties That Bind:

Life Together in the Baptist Vision

Edited by
Gary Furr and Curtis W. Freeman

Smyth & Helwys Publishing, Inc.
Macon, Georgia

ISBN 1-880837-77-3

Ties That Bind:
Life Together in the Baptist Vision

Edited by Gary A. Furr and Curtis W. Freeman

Printed in the United States of America.

The paper used in this publication meets the minimum requirements of American Standard for Information Sciences—Permanence of paper for Printed Library Materials, ANSI Z39.48–1984.

Library of Congress Cataloging-in-Publication Data

Ties that Bind : life together in the Baptist vision / Gary A. Furr and Curtis W. Freeman, editors.
viii + 248 pp. 6 x 9" (15 x 23 cm.)
Includes bibliographical references.
ISBN 1-880837-77-3
1. Baptists. 2. Conversion. 3. Spiritual formation—Baptists. 4. Church and social problems—Baptists. I. Furr, Gary.
BX6332.T54 1994
286—dc20 94-8325
CIP

Contents

Preface ix

Life Together in the Baptist Vision 1

Part 1: The Conversionist Tie

The Conversionist Tie: Our Hearts in Christian Love 5

1. Southern Baptists and Conversion:
   An Evangelical Sacramentalism 9
   Bill Leonard

2. Toward a Conversionist Spirituality 23
   James Wm. McClendon, Jr.

3. The Hermeneutics of Conversion 33
   Randy Hatchett

4. Horace Bushnell, Spiritual Formation, and Conversion 49
   James Reed

Part 2: The Contemplative Tie

The Contemplative Tie: The Fellowship of Kindred Minds 65

5. The Contemplative Roots of Baptist Spirituality 69
   E. Glenn Hinson

6. A Confession for Catholic Baptists 83
   Curtis W. Freeman

7. Spiritual Direction and the Baptist Tradition 99
   Thomas B. Turner

8. Spiritual Discernment, the Community, and Baptists 109
   Wm. Loyd Allen

9. "The Road of Ashes": Prospects for Disillusioned Baptists 127
   Gary Furr

Part 3: The Corporate Tie

The Corporate Tie: The Fellowship . . . Is Like to That Above 151

10. Music in the Spiritual Life of Baptists 153
Robert Reid

11. "Something Old, Something New":
Worship Styles for Baptists in the Nineties 171
Paul Basden

12. Walter Rauschenbusch on Prayer and Social Action 191
Philip LeMasters

13. Spiritual Transcendence in the Black Experience in America . . . 205
Samuel Proctor

14. Holy Insecurity: The Practice of Piety
and the Politics of the Spirit 217
Barry Harvey

Postscript 243

Contributors 245

"Blest Be the Tie That Binds;
Our Hearts in Christian Love;
The Fellowship of Kindred Minds
Is Like to That Above."

—*John Fawcett*

To Debra and Vickie,

and to the ties that bind our hearts

in Christian love and friendship

Preface

This book began when I entered a two-year program with the Upper Room in which I worshiped, prayed, studied, and befriended an ecumenical community of fifty or so fellow Christians at Mercy Center in Burlingame, California. We studied the history of Christian spirituality and learned to appreciate the ways that others worshiped, prayed to, thought about, and felt God.

I also began to ask in a fresh way, "What is distinctive in my own heritage? Is there a Baptist spirituality?"

As longtime friends, this new direction naturally entered into our frequent long-distance conversations. It resulted in a presentation to a gathering of the Baylor Theology Group in 1992 in Fort Worth, Texas. After two days of presentation and discussion together, we parted again, but continued to run up large phone bills and keep the idea alive.

When I had to choose a project for the second year in the Academy, the time had come for the present volume. I called on Curtis to join me in the project. Every edited work is the product of many efforts. The title of this book comes from two original suggestions, one from Jim McClendon to utilize "life together" and the other from Curtis Freeman based on John Fawcett's hymn "Blest Be the Tie That Binds." Curtis also devised the structural divisions in the book as it now stands. Glenn Hinson was a great help in directing the initial stages. When we approached Scott Nash at Smyth & Helwys, he was immediately interested. He and Jackie Riley have shown great help and support for the project throughout.

Naturally, because we are Baptists, we do not expect agreement from our readers. We feel it might be an evidence of loss of identity if we *did* all agree. We do, however, accept responsibility for the contents. We allowed the contributors both to speak for themselves and to accept the criticism that comes with their presentations. We hope that this volume is a starting point and an encouragement for other Baptists to reflect on our own peculiar and rich spirituality.

This work has been a labor of love. There are many people to thank, more than can be mentioned. Our wives—Debra Freeman and Vickie Furr—and our children—Heather, Erin, and Katie Furr and Cole and Lauren Freeman—deserve our love and thanks and have shown incredible support as we plodded through this effort. The Academy community #7 at Mercy Center, Danny Morris, Nancy Thurston, and especially my covenant group—Wendy, Larry, Genevieve, Lois, Mike, and Susan (and not a Baptist in the lot)—deserve thanks for their encouragement.

Thanks are due each contributor who not only showed interest in the book, but without exception expressed enthusiasm for its aim. Finally, our secretaries, Nancy Garst at Houston Baptist University and Pat Quinn at Vestavia Hills Baptist Church, did an enormous amount of typing, correcting, and formatting. Without them we would not have completed the task. Thanks are also due Lora Ann Sassnett at First Baptist Church in Blakely, Georgia, who gave initial assistance in this work.

Above all, thanks be to God, whose loving, joyful Presence makes every labor potentially one of love. And thanks to those churches in our lives where both of us witnessed the pains and joys of living out the Christian life in the Baptist vision.

Gary Furr

Life Together in the Baptist Vision

Gary Furr and Curtis W. Freeman

The desire to find that life is meaningful and has a purpose is one of the most basic spiritual needs felt by Americans. Regrettably, according to pollster George Gallup, seventy percent of the public does not believe that churches are effective in helping people satisfy this longing.[1] A growing number of people are consequently searching elsewhere for spiritual help and guidance. An article in *Newsweek* magazine surprisingly observed that "the current edition of *Books in Print* lists nearly 2,000 titles on prayer, meditation, and techniques for spiritual growth—more than three times the number devoted to sexual intimacy and how to achieve it."[2]

One need only brouse the selection in the local bookstore at the mall to find a montage of writings on spirituality. Yet it is disconcerting to discover that the books on Christian spirituality are displayed together with works on mysticism, new-age, Jungian analysis, and the occult. We are reminded of the biblical injuction to "test the spirits to see whether they are from God" (1 John 4:1).

The contemporary attraction to things spiritual surely reflects the motto of our age that "novelty is vitality." Some would thus infer that the interest in spirituality is simply a trend in the nineties like the fascination with secularity was a fad in the seventies. We believe, however, that the turn to spirit is deeper evidence, not of a spiritual vitality, but of a secular pathology. Our souls have grown sick from secularism.[3] Still, we take the current interest in spirituality to be a hopeful sign. The ethos of spiritual longing suggests a cultural gesture that deserves a thoughtful response. Our purpose here is not simply to explore new trends but to examine old truths, or rather to consider old truths made new.

Walter Capps in *The Monastic Impulse* examines the frequent charge that the recent fascination with monasticism and monastic spirituality grows out of narcissism and the loss of meaningful communal structures in contemporary life. In a chapter entitled "Contemplation and Narcissism" Capps answers that this interest is instead "a compelling desire to uncover a religiously sanctioned, unified perspective on the world."[4]

As the exponential forces of change and disintegration unravel the fabric of these structures that render meaning for individuals, the hunger for spirituality is inevitable. Karl Rahner once said that the "theologian of the future will be a mystic or he or she will not exist at all."[5] While much current spirituality *is* faddish and self-serving, it is also evidence of a powerful hunger, one that is universal and undeniable. The church has a profound opportunity for witness and learning—this includes Baptists.

Nevertheless, the disciplines and practices described in the literature cannot be welcomed uncritically or received indiscriminantly. Those who intentionally name themselves Baptists must give these texts a close reading. They must seek to discover what it means to live under the influence of the Holy Spirit from the perspective of the Baptist vision.[6] The notion of a spiritual vision is instructive because it emphasizes that spirituality is not simply a matter of prayer, contemplation, and meditation. It is seeing things in a particular way that is rooted in shared convictions that enable us to make sense of the Christian life with all its hopes and contradictions.[7] We have been inspired by the efforts of Christian scholars within other confessional traditions to articulate a particular vision by offering serious reflection on the shared convictions of a believing community.[8] These essays attempt to reflect on the Baptist vision in interaction with the spiritual traditions of the whole church.

To the extent that we can speak of a Baptist way of seeing things we do so first with a story. For many years, Dr. John Gill served as pastor of the Carters Lane Baptist Church in London. When he became infirmed and unable to minister, the congregation invited a younger man, Rev. John Fawcett, to preach. When Dr. Gill died, the church extended a call for Fawcett to be its pastor at an annual salary of forty pounds. At the time, Fawcett was the pastor of a struggling congregation in Wainsgate that could barely afford a salary of twenty-five pounds. Because he had four small children and a wife to provide for, Fawcett reluctantly accepted the call to Carters Lane. After selling some of his books and furniture in preparation for the move, however, he decided not to go. It is believed that out of experience, and with the people of Wainsgate in mind, he penned these words:

> Blest be the tie that binds
> Our hearts in Christian love.
> The fellowship of kindred minds
> Is like to that above.[9]

We have taken the image of the Spirit as the tie that binds to be a central metaphor for this book. As Fawcett's song wonderfully gives witness, the Baptist vision arises out of the life in the Spirit, a shared life that is bound together in a common faith, love and hope. A *communion in the Spirit* creates a *community of the Spirit*. But, we might ask, just how does the Spirit bind us together? The essays in this collection attempt to point in the direction of an answer. In the first section, the writers suggest that the reconciling work of the Spirit is evident in the call to be converted through the gospel that confronts us in word and sacrament. We call this *the conversionist tie*. In the second section of essays, the binding activity of the Spirit is described as an invitation to become enlightened in holiness through the disciplines of prayer and devotion. We call this *the contemplative tie*. In the final section, the transforming movement of the Spirit is perceived as one learns to envision the coming of God's peaceable reign in history and community. We call this *the corporate tie*.

Through puritan and revivalist influences, the Baptist vision has been significantly shaped by conversionist spirituality. It is thus common to understand life together in the Spirit as *a fellowship of the word*. In isolation, however, this perspective can be distorted and become a gnostic caricature of the gospel, without spiritual transformation or historical location.[10] Baptists have also been influenced by contemplative spirituality, and thus it is understandable to describe life together in the Spirit as *a communion of prayer*. Contemplation alone, however, can mutate into rationalistic quietism or legalistic perfectionism.[11] Baptists have also been guided by a corporate spirituality and an awakened social consciousness, thus life together in the Spirit may be characterized as *a community of the kingdom*. Experience-oriented worship can become narcissistic, however, and an exclusive focus on social justice without the spiritual transformation of conversion and the spiritual formation of holiness can degenerate into a works righteousness.[12]

We, therefore, understand these three accounts of the tie that binds to be reciprocally complementary rather than mutually exclusive. The essays themselves reflect this tension and interaction as they draw from all three traditions. The editors also experience the mutuality of influences. Both of us are products of (and still attempt to remain true to) a largely conversionist heritage. One of us, however, is currently part of an ecumenical academy for spiritual formation that occasionally lives in semi-monastic community and the other serves as a pastor of an inner city, multi-ethnic congregation with a strong emphasis on social ministry. We hope that this collection of essays will stimulate a growing conversation about the nature and shape of a shared spiritual life for others who wish to see things from the Baptist vision.

Notes

[1]George H. Gallup, Jr., "Six Basic Spiritual Needs of Americans," in *Yearbook of American and Canadian Churches 1992*, ed. Kenneth B. Bedell and Alice M. Jones (Nashville: Abingdon Press, 1992) 15-16.

[2]Cited by Timothy Jones in *Christianity Today* (8 November 1993): 23.

[3]Eugene H. Peterson, "Spirit Quest," *Christianity Today* (8 November 1993): 27.

[4]Walter Capps, *The Monastic Impulse* (New York: Crossroads, 1983) 143.

[5]Schneiders, Sandra, "Theology and Spirituality: Strangers, Rivals or Partners?" *Horizons* 13/2 (1986): 253-74.

[6]We have adopted the phrase "the baptist vision" from James William McClendon who uses the little b to denote a distinctive perspective and guiding stimulus that grew out of the radical reformation and consequently has shaped the life and thought of a host of believers' church people. McClendon, *Systematic Theology: Ethics* (Nashville: Abingdon Press, 1986) 27.

[7]Simon Tugwell borrows the notion of spirituality as "a way of viewing things" from the eighteenth-century Jesuit priest Jean-Pierre de Caussade, in *Ways of Imperfection: An Exploration of Christian Spirituality* (Springfield IL: Templegate Publishers, 1985) vii-viii.

[8]For example, Esther De Waal, *Living with Contradiction: Reflections on the Rule of St. Benedict* (San Francisco: HarperSanFrancisco, 1989).

[9]The story may well be apocryphal as William J. Reynolds notes in *Companion to Baptist Hymnal* (Nashville: Broadman Press, 1976) 43-44

[10]Harold Bloom argues that "Southern Baptists call themselves Christians, but like most Americans they are closer to ancient Gnostics than to early Christians," in *The American Religion: The Emergence of the Post-Christian Nation* (New York: Simon and Schuster, 1992) 22. Although we disagree with Bloom's assertion that the gnostic grip on American religion is a good thing, we nevertheless agree with his assessment of the gnostic trajectory of what we have called conversionist spirituality.

[11]The unitarianism proclivity of eighteenth-century General Baptists and the Hicksite schism in nineteenth century Quakerism are examples of the rationalistic tangent in contemplative spirituality. The pietistic tendency to conceive of a little church within the big church or the more modern trend to distinguish between spiritual and carnal Christians are examples of legalistic perfectionism.

[12]Some expressions of the social gospel movement and protestant liberalism might be construed as works righteousness, that is, to conceive of good works as the means whereby one becomes virtuous and spiritual.

The Conversionist Tie: Our Hearts in Christian Love

A man clothed in rags stood with his face from his house. He held a book in his hand and bore a great burden on his back. As he read from the book, the man wept and cried out, "What shall I do to be saved?" Directly, one called Evangelist instructed him to "fly from the wrath to come" (Matt 3:7). "Whither must I fly?" the man asked. Evangelist pointed toward the wicket gate (Matt 7:13-14), and thus the man began his journey away from the City of Destruction.

Along the way his neighbors, Obstinate and Pliable, sought to dissuade him. He fell into the Slough of Despond. Mr. Worldly Wiseman almost succeeded in turning him back, but he eventually arrived at the house of Interpreter who, with the aid of the Spirit, guided him until they came to a wall called Salvation. In that place stood a cross. When he came to the foot of the cross, his burden rolled away. Afterward, three shining ones appeared to give witness to his conversion. The first messenger pronounced his sins to be forgiven, the second clothed him in new raiment, and the third marked his forehead and gave him a roll with a seal that testified to the assurance of salvation. As Christian continued on his journey he sang,

> Thus far did I come loaden with my sin,
> Nor could ought ease the grief that I was in,
> Till I came hither: What a place is this!
> Must here be the beginning of my bliss?
> Must here the burden fall from off my back?
> Must here the strings that bound it to me, crack?
> Blest Cross! blest Sepulcher! blest rather be
> The Man that there was put to shame for me.[1]

Bunyan's autobiographical account of his own conversion in *Grace Abounding to the Chief of Sinners* recalls an experience that is strikingly parallel to the Christian in *Pilgrim's Progress*. Bunyan describes how his preparation for the new birth came through the witness of a group of poor women in his town of Bedford. As he considered their testimony, he was tempted by rogues and ranters to reject the foolishness of the gospel. Instead, he began to read the Bible with new eyes. A short time later he had a vision in which he saw the poor Christians of Bedford on the sunny side of a high mountain and himself shivering in the cold. Between him and the mountain there was a wall, and in the wall was a narrow gap through which he made his way into the light. This vision was the beginning of his conversion, but Bunyan's real life journey through the gap and into the light was protracted and tortuous. With the spiritual guidance of the Bedford church and his pastor, John Gifford, Bunyan was finally converted as he declared to his wife, "I must go to Jesus."[2]

Bunyan's narratives display the economy of a conversionist spirituality. With the guidance of spiritual illumination and the instruction of Christian education he discovered the way of salvation. Through the witness of the gospel and the word of Scripture he came under the conviction of sin, and by the agency of grace he was converted to faith in Christ. The emphasis of conversionist spirituality thus falls on the transformation of "Our hearts in Christian love" which is epitomized in a personal conversion experience. A. D. Nock has described conversion as

> the reorientation of the soul of an individual, his deliberate turning from indifference or from an earlier form of piety to another, a turning which implies a consciousness that a great change is involved, that the old was wrong and the new is right.[3]

To be sure, Baptists and other evangelicals have maintained the indispensability of a conversion experience, but there is no theological consensus about the nature of the "reorientation" and the "great change" or the relationship of conversion and spirituality. The story is told that J. B. Gambrell was once asked by a zealous revivalist if conversion was the end of the Christian life. Gambrell is said to have replied, "Yes—the front end." Conversionist spirituality attempts to give voice to the conviction that the Christian life cannot be formed by spiritual discipline until it is first transformed by radical conversion. But conversionist spirituality also recognizes that conversion is germinal not terminal. The Christian life that begins with the new birth is nourished by the spiritual food of scripture, prayer, and worship and is enacted into the social practices of baptism, eucharist, and discipleship.

Since Baptists have ascribed great significance to conversion, it is important to ask about its nature and role in developing spiritual life. Bill Leonard's essay traces the theology of conversion through six distinct traditions in American Baptist history. As Leonard carefully shows, Baptists have given divergent accounts of conversion. For some, it is a long struggle, for others it is an instantaneous event, and for still others it is the result of education and nurture. James McClendon sketches a conversionist spirituality by exploring four transformative stages in the Christian life and the corresponding formative practices: preparation-catechesis, conversion-baptism, discipleship-Lord's supper, and the unpredictable element-congregational discernment. Randy Hatchett suggests that the analogies of conversion and community enable the hermeneutical imagination to read the Bible with a sense of immediacy. James Reed challenges the spirituality of instantaneous and dramatic conversion through an examination of Horace Bushnell's theology of Christian nurture. We hope that these essays will stimulate serious reflection about the importance of conversion for the transformation and formation of the spiritual life.

Notes

[1]John Bunyan, *The Pilgrim's Progress,* ed. N. H. Keeble (New York: Oxford University Press, 1984) 32.

[2]John Bunyan, *Grace Abounding to the Chief of Sinners,* 262, ed. W. R. Owens (London: Penguin Books, 1987) 7-67.

[3]Arthur Darby Nock, *Conversion: The Old and the New in Religion From Alexander the Great to Augustine of Hippo* (Oxford: Clarendon Press, 1933) 7.

Southern Baptists and Conversion: An Evangelical Sacramentalism

Bill J. Leonard

Conversion and Baptism

It is Sunday night in a "typical" Southern Baptist Church somewhere between Tupelo, Mississippi, and El Paso, Texas. The lights dim and the curtains part across the fiberglass baptistry to reveal a pastor in white robe and hip boots, standing in front of a mural of the river Jordan that strangely resembles the landscape of South Alabama or East Texas. One by one the candidates enter the water and are immersed, each reflecting the diverse elements of Southern Baptist theology and practice regarding conversion and baptism.

They might easily include:

- A seven-year-old girl, the child of active church members, nurtured to faith through the life of the congregation,
- A twenty-seven-year-old man dramatically converted through the church's direct witness of personal evangelism,
- A deacon in the congregation who, "not satisfied" with the validity of his earlier profession of faith, receives baptism as a new convert,
- A former Methodist and exemplary Christian for twenty years receiving baptism by immersion as a prerequisite to membership in the local Baptist congregation.

These brief case studies reflect situations that occur weekly in Southern Baptist churches. They demonstrate the significance that Southern Baptists place on the conversion of sinners to faith and the baptism of believers into Christ and his church. They also reveal something of the diversity, indeed, the confusion that Southern Baptists face in the theology and practice of that most basic Baptist imperative, evangelism. They raise innumerable questions that Southern Baptists, whether so-called fundamentalists or moderates, must confront on the way to the twenty-first century.

First, what about the children? When is the "proper" age for conversion? In a denomination that claims to take its baptismal cues only from the New Testament, is the baptism of children consistent with the practice of the New Testament church? What is the nature of childhood faith? Will the seven-year-old girl conclude at age sixteen that she did not really understand what she was doing in childhood and request rebaptism so as to get it right this time? Is her conversion through Christian nurture as acceptable within the community of faith as the dramatic adult experience? Will she always feel a little "outside" or "doubtful" because she cannot testify to a dramatic salvation?

Second, what about the rebaptism of those whose conversion to faith occurred years before? From a New Testament perspective, is the former Methodist and long-time disciple receiving the same baptism as the new believer?

Third, what does the growing number of rebaptisms for Southern Baptist church members suggest about Southern Baptist evangelistic theology and methodology? Will the rebaptized deacon request a third or fourth baptism when doubts and sin again descend upon him or when he has a new and "better" religious experience? How do Southern Baptists distinguish between justification and sanctification, between conversion as entering in and as going on in faith? What does the growing number of rebaptisms say about the theology and methodology of Southern Baptist evangelism?

Each of the persons mentioned here would no doubt be counted among the total number of "baptisms" performed in Southern Baptist churches in a given year. By implication, each represents a new convert to Christian faith. Yet one has been a convert for many years, and another has been baptized and therefore counted at least once before by the SBC. Thus, of the 351,071 baptisms in SBC churches in 1985, how many were administered to persons from other traditions who were converted long ago? How many were second, third, or fourth time baptisms of Southern Baptist church members? How many were children ages five to ten, and how many were adult converts?

Ron Lewis, former staff member of the Southern Baptist Sunday School board, suggested that, "In ninety-two percent of your (SBC) churches, the only real growth you've had in the last five years has been from baptizing the children of your members and from transfers of members from other churches."[1] One might also ask what portion of that number included those rebaptized Southern Baptists who had already claimed conversion and baptism in SBC churches at least once before.

Thus the dilemma. Southern Baptists face a crisis in their understanding of evangelism and conversion. They must ask the hard questions about the nature of Christian faith in Jesus Christ and the continuing life of the gospel.

This chapter represents an attempt to provide some historical and theological perspective on the nature of conversion and evangelism in Southern Baptist life. It reflects two basic and rather obvious theses: First, Southern Baptists are heirs of a variety of theological and practical traditions regarding conversion. While most congregations share a common concern for evangelism, many demonstrate a diversity of theological perspectives and methods, combining numerous historic traditions in varied ways.

Second, given that diversity, Southern Baptists have sought to develop ways of institutionalizing and popularizing the process of conversion in order to evangelize the masses in some systematic method. In so doing, they created a kind of evangelical sacramentalism by which an internal, subjective religious experience might be verified through certain objective criteria. While proclaiming conversion as an intensely personal, individual experience, they also developed elaborate plans, programs, and prayers for fulfilling the necessary salvific transaction. With time, confusion developed over the relationship of saving faith and salvific event.

Southern Baptist concern for personal conversion is consistent with that of the earliest Baptist groups that originated in Holland and England during the seventeenth century. Like the English Puritans from whence they came, these Baptists insisted that the true church was composed of believers only. For Baptists, the "visible" church on earth was identical with the "invisible" church in heaven. The church in this world and the next was made up of true believers alone. Entrance into Christ and his church was based on a regenerative experience of grace in the heart of every believer. Only those who had experienced such a conversion were qualified for baptism and church membership.

All Baptists agreed that personal conversion was necessary for those who would claim Christian faith and membership in the church. In their concern for evangelism and conversion, Baptists were both biblicists and pietists. As biblicists, they believed that the Holy Scripture taught the necessity for and means of conversion. As pietists, they believed that salvation was a mysterious activity of divine grace experienced in the heart of the true believer. It was not found in external works or dogmas, creeds or sacraments, but by personal experience with God. Conversion required a personal encounter with Jesus Christ, not merely intellectual assent to certain doctrines about him.

Conversion and Tradition

While affirming the biblical and personal nature of conversion, Baptists have not always agreed on when or how a person is actually converted. Indeed, they interpreted the Bible and experience in light of numerous traditions, each of which, in its own way, represents a genuinely historic Baptist position.[2] Efforts at uniting these diverse, and sometimes contradictory, traditions have created considerable debate and controversy in Southern Baptist life.

The Regular Baptist Tradition

One conversion tradition was that of the Calvinistic or Regular Baptists who entered the South in the 1690s to found such congregations as First Baptist Church, Charleston, South Carolina. As thoroughgoing Calvinists, the Regulars believed that all persons were totally depraved and therefore had no free will whereby to move toward conversion. God alone brought his irresistible grace to those sinners whom he had elected unconditionally to salvation before the foundation of the world. Only after receiving regeneration from God was the human will free to experience repentance and faith. Conversion was most often a lengthy process of struggling against God and ultimately casting all on his sovereign will. The idea that any person might freely choose to pray one prayer and immediately receive salvation was completely foreign to Regular Baptist evangelism. Since salvation begins with divine initiative, the sinner must wait on God to bring about regeneration and new birth. Free will was considered only operative in the individual after salvation occurs. The irresistible grace that drew persons to salvation would enable them to persevere in the faith. Indeed, the grace to persevere was a sure sign of the reality of the salvation of the elect.

The Regular Baptist view of conversion is evident in the article on election found in Southern Baptists' first statement of faith, the Abstract of Principles of the Southern Baptist Theological Seminary, 1859. It reads:

"Election is God's eternal choice of some persons unto everlasting life—not because of foreseen merit in them, but of His mere mercy in Christ—consequence of which choice they are called, justified and glorified."[3] Those words reflect the impact of Reformed (Calvinist) theology transported into SBC life through the Westminster Confession of English Puritans and the Philadelphia Confession of colonial Baptists. Salvation was given to those whom God had chosen from before the foundation of the world.

During this century, Southern Baptists generally have moved away from this Calvinist understanding of election and conversion. They have, however, retained the terminology of Calvinism—election, depravity, sovereignty—but redefined it considerably with a greater emphasis on free will and human participation in the salvation process. In a sense, Southern Baptists talk like Calvinists but act like Arminians, at least where conversion is concerned. That brings us to another important influence.

The Separate Baptist Tradition

A second theological tradition that shaped Southern Baptist theology of conversion came from the Separate Baptists who appeared in the South in the 1750s, founding the Sandy Creek Church in North Carolina, mother church of over forty other congregations. The Separates were revivalistic Baptists who modified their Calvinism considerably. They suggested that all persons were potentially elected to salvation, but only those who accepted Christ freely through repentance and faith were actually numbered among the elect. God's sovereign grace and human free will cooperated together to accomplish salvation.

Separate Baptists were given to bold, enthusiastic preaching that demanded dramatic, often emotional, encounter with the living Christ.[4] They "got saved" hard with experiences characterized by shouts, tears, groans, and other emotional outbursts. Yet even Separates described a conversion process that might extend over months, even years before the light of salvation broke through. In one such testimony, a Separate Baptist preacher related how his earliest religious "impressions" began at age eight and intensified at age thirteen. Conversion was not completed, however, until he was eighteen when—after weeks of spiritual distress and mourning—"I then began to cherish a little hope that I had passed from death into life."[5] This testimony is consistent with others expressed by frontier Baptists. It is also evidence that conversion was a serious process that could occur in childhood but more likely was evident in adolescence.

The Separate Baptist tradition led Southern Baptists in the direction of a modified Calvinist, eventually, perhaps, a kind of modified Arminian theology, with greater emphasis on free will and human participation in the salvific process. It stressed that all persons had the free will to choose, reject, or ignore salvation. Grace could be resisted by the free choice of the individual. Like their Separate Baptist forebears, however, Southern Baptists have generally repudiated the Arminian emphasis on "falling from grace," the idea that true believers could exercise their free will and turn from faith later on, thereby "losing" their salvation. Southern Baptists, therefore, retained the Calvinist belief in perseverance of the saints, insisting—in the words of the Baptist Faith and Message—that "all true believers endure to the end" and "will never fall away from the state of grace."[6] Those who received grace were kept to the end. They could not fall away. Those who did so had never been true recipients of grace. Many agreed with the old theological tongue twister: "The faith that fizzles at the finish was faulty from the first."

With time, however, this doctrine of the eternal security of the believer was popularized into the slogan, "Once saved, always saved," a catchy homiletical response to a complex theological issue. While the idea was meant to give encouragement to the faithful, it could also deteriorate into a kind of cheap grace and an easy ticket to heaven, promoting a salvific transactionalism and undermining the cost of discipleship.[7] It implied that justification—entering into salvation—was the primary concern of Christianity. This popularized view of perseverance often undermined the doctrine of sanctification in Southern Baptist life. Getting in was so important that going on in grace seemed secondary and even less significant. Historically Southern Baptists have been very good at introducing persons to faith but not so good in guiding them on in grace.

The Landmark Tradition

A third tradition that influenced Southern Baptist theology of conversion came from the Old Landmark movement of the 1850s, the effort to trace Baptist churches back to John the Baptist and the Jordan River. Landmarkers insisted on the need for personal faith in Christ but united the conversion experience with certain doctrines about baptism and the church.

Baptist churches, they believed, were the only true churches of Christ, a succession of local congregations that had endured from the first century.[8] While all persons who accepted Christ through repentance and faith might be saved, they could only receive the true baptism, Lord's Supper, and church membership in fellowship with the Baptists. Landmark Baptists unashamedly sang this song of faith:

Not at the Jordan River
But in that flowing stream,
Stood John the Baptist preacher
When he baptized Him.

John was a Baptist preacher
When he baptized the Lamb,
So Jesus was a Baptist
And thus the Baptists came.[9]

Landmarkers rejected "alien immersion," the baptism of believers in non-Baptist churches (societies they called them) and required rebaptism of all who were not of "like faith and order." Thus long-time Christians could be baptized alongside new converts in Landmark churches. To protect the integrity of their tradition, the Landmarkers modified, dare we say changed, the New Testament practice of baptism as profession of faith for new Christians to baptism as the way converts old and new could join a Baptist church. In so doing they created two types of baptism: baptism into Christ and baptism into a Baptist church. External doctrines about baptism came to inform the way Baptists understood the internal experience of conversion.

The legacy of Landmarkism has created significant confusion among Southern Baptists regarding the nature of baptism. Serious attention needs to be given to a theology of baptism so as to recover its biblical and historic meaning for children and adults, new converts and long-time believers. Particular attention must also be given to the issue of rebaptism. One thing seems certain, to continue to count new converts and rebaptized believers from other traditions as if they were all new Christians is to confuse evangelism and the baptismal symbol for the sake of yearly statistics.

The issue of rebaptism has become increasingly problematic in many SBC churches due to the influx of persons from other denominations. Many of these individuals wish to join Baptist churches but refuse or resent the requirement of immersion or in some cases reimmersion. Should persons who have been Christians for years be compelled to receive an ordinance that in the New Testament is given to new converts? How can Baptist churches continue to claim the uniqueness of New Testament immersion if they accept as members those who have not received it? Can a community of faith claim to have a "New Testament baptism" when it practices the baptism of children, a practice nowhere evident in the New Testament? These are serious questions that confront Southern Baptist churches across the theological spectrum.

The Revivalist Tradition

A fourth tradition that had tremendous impact on Southern Baptist theology of conversion is revivalism. Revivalism became the means that Southern Baptists used most frequently to carry their evangelical imperative to the masses. Through revivals, Baptists and other American evangelicals institutionalized the process of conversion. Beginning with the spontaneity of the frontier camp meetings, the revivalistic method was soon institutionalized into protracted meetings held periodically in Baptist churches, often seasonally after spring planting and fall harvest (an interesting way in which churches accommodated cultural and economic realities). Revivals shaped Southern Baptist understanding of the nature and process of conversion in several important ways.

(1) Revivals shortened the process of conversion significantly. The lengthy struggles with sin and self that characterized early Regular and Separate Baptist conversions were reduced to sign posts on the way to instantaneous regeneration. As H. Richard Niebuhr observed, salvation became less an extended process than an immediate event. Niebuhr suggested that in many churches revivalism institutionalized conversion in such a way that,

> Regeneration, the dying to the self and the rising to new life, now apparently sudden, now so slow and painful, so confused, so real, so mixed, becomes conversion that takes place on Sunday morning during the singing of the last hymn or twice a year when the revival preacher comes to town. There is still some reality in it for some converts but, following a prescribed pattern for the most part in its inception and progress, the life has gone out of it.[10]

(2) Revivals produced a powerful set of symbols that dramatized the need for and possibility of an immediate, conscious conversion event. Frontier revivalists utilized the anxious bench or mourner's bench as a

place where persons under conviction of sin might secure prayer and spiritual encouragement. By the late nineteenth and early twentieth centuries, coming forward to the anxious bench, inquiry room, or to shake the preacher's hand became an integral part of conversion in SBC churches. Such an act created what might be called the sacrament of walking the aisle, an outward and visible sign of an inward and evangelical grace. Converts began to describe salvation in terms appropriate to the invitation—"when I shook the preacher's hand," "when I went forward," "when I walked the aisle." In many churches, walking the aisle replaced baptism as public profession of faith in Christ. Indeed, many testified that salvation seemed to come in the very act of moving from pew to aisle.[11] In this way Southern Baptists created an outward symbol, an objective verification, of an inner spiritual experience.

(3) Perhaps without realizing it, revivalism helped turn conversion from a process of experience with grace to an transaction that fulfills a salvation requirement. Today, many church aisles are filled with people who never seem quite satisfied with their salvation event. At every life crisis many people return to repeat the transaction and reclaim salvation, hoping against hope they will get it right this time. For them, Christianity is less a life of spiritual growth and struggle than a perpetual return to the beginning. Such persons have created a potential for generations of immature Christians who never go beyond the initial stage of faith and who live on the edge of doubt that they may not have prayed the right prayer or said the right words in order to complete the necessary transaction.[12]

Revivalism brought significant spiritual renewal to Southern Baptist congregations. It also created a way in which Southern Baptists understood, articulated, and dramatized the process of conversion. Can a new generation find the grace to create a new method for bringing spiritual awakening to a culture not conducive to revivalistic techniques?

The Sunday School Tradition

A fifth tradition I would call the catechetical or Sunday School tradition of Southern Baptist church life. In the early church, the catechumen, or learners, were those who were being instructed in Christian life and faith in preparation for baptism and church membership. Southern Baptists, like others in the Calvinist tradition, have approached the question of children and conversion with hesitation, given the absence of specific biblical texts and the early Baptist practice of adult believer's baptism. The prevailing twentieth-century view is that children were born, not with

Adamic guilt, but with "a nature predisposed to sin" when faced with moral choice. Children who died before reaching the "age of (moral) accountability" were "covered by the atoning work of Christ."[13] When that mysterious age is reached is the cause of uncertainty. Baptist leader L. R. Scarborough concluded that "most children have a sense of sin between seven and ten years of age."[14] Thus, the imperative for child evangelism developed as early as the 1930s, with denominational publications urging the conversion of children in the elementary (junior) years. One manual declared, "We cannot too earnestly insist that boys and girls should be won to Christ before they leave the junior (elementary) department."[15] Children were to be nurtured in faith and led toward conversion in the formative years when their hearts and wills were yet pliable.

Today the church continues to instruct persons, particularly children, through Sunday School classes, denominational literature, and loving parents and teachers that "Jesus loves me this I know" from the moment they are brought to church. Responding to that nurture, many children make faith their own, less as a result of profound moral crisis, but as a willing confirmation of simple trust in God's love. For the last fifty to sixty years, more Southern Baptist have come to Christian faith through this evangelical method than any other. To this day a majority of the candidates for baptism in Southern Baptist churches come from children ages six to twelve.[16]

If Southern Baptists are going to baptize children and nurture them to salvation they must take the responsibility for helping them grow up to experience new "stages of faith," as James Fowler describes those diverse periods of Christian commitment.[17] We must exercise what my colleague Frank Tupper calls "mediated memory" in which churches and parents help children remember their childhood experiences of grace when their own recollection seems cloudy or uncertain. Thus when they confront the moral dilemmas of adolescence, they do not feel compelled to reject the validity of childhood grace simply because they have grown to new understanding of life. If grace only works when we "understand," it has ceased to be grace. What Christians are ever fully "satisfied" with their salvation experience? Through its teaching ministry the church leads persons, particularly children, to conversion through basic instruction and gentle nurture in the faith.

The Fundamentalist Tradition

A sixth and final tradition (this could go on indefinitely given Baptist diversity) comes from the fundamentalist tradition of nineteenth- and twentieth-century America. Most scholars agree that the absence of a significant modernist element minimized damage from fundamentalist-liberal disputes during the 1920s. Indeed, Southern Baptists maintained their strong conservative theology while avoiding efforts to institutionalize fundamentalist dogma in convention life.[18] If biblical criticism and liberal theology had limited impact on Southern Baptists before 1930, so did the dispensationalism and Princeton theology characteristic of early fundamentalism.[19]

More recently, however, Southern Baptist fundamentalists have succeeded in extending this theological and political agenda into the convention mainstream. This fundamentalist trend has had significant influence on the way some Southern Baptists understand conversion. While claiming to be the protectors of evangelism within the SBC, fundamentalists have linked "heart religion" with a propositional theology bound to such dogmas as biblical inerrancy, virgin birth, and substitutionary atonement. Often in their rhetoric, SBC fundamentalists sound as if "simple faith" in Christ is not enough. Certain doctrines about his nature are prerequisite to conversion. While basic Christian doctrines are significant for all who claim faith, the relationship between such dogmas and basic faith is a significant question for those who call persons to salvation.

For example, older conversion manuals warned the witness not to become entangled in theological questions that distract the sinner from the real issue. C. E. Autrey, noted Baptist teacher and evangelist, wrote in 1961 that "soul winners" should not "argue questions like the virgin birth and related doctrines." Autrey suggested that, "Where the soul-winner hands a lost man who is confused about some doctrinal difficulty, if he will tell him that it is not required that he understand that particular problem in order to be saved, it will help greatly."[20]

This approach is in contrast with that of prominent pastor and convention president, Adrian Rogers, who declared in a recent sermon that "If you don't believe in the virgin birth of Christ, not only do you have difficulty with the character of Mary, . . . the character of Jesus, . . the character of God, but you've got a big difficulty in your own character. And I'm gonna tell you something else, I wouldn't give you half a hallelujah for your chance of heaven if you don't believe in the virgin birth of Jesus Christ."[21]

For Rogers, conversion seems dependent on assent to particular fundamentalist ideology regarding the nature of Christ and the atonement. He insists: "No virgin birth, no deity; no deity, no sinlessness; no sinlessness, no atonement; no atonement, no hope" (of salvation).[22]

Thus the fundamentalist agenda continues to shape Southern Baptist understanding of conversion less as a dramatic, mystical experience than as assent to certain propositions regarding the nature of the Christ and the atonement.

Questions and Answers

These are but a few of the historic traditions that inform the way Southern Baptists read the Bible and proclaim the gospel. Each tradition helps Baptists understand who they are and why they act as they do. Each holds the potential to enliven or entrap us in evangelical renewal or confusion. Conclusions involve more questions than answers.

First, each of these traditions reflects the way in which a conversionist denomination sought to describe, objectify, and dare we say "tangibilify" (Albert Clege's word) an essentially subjective, existential, even mystical experience. Whether in nurture, instruction, propositional theology, or revivalistic transactionalism, some procedure for understanding and securing salvation was necessarily developed. Can Southern Baptists acknowledge diversity of conversionist traditions without trying to make one type normative for all believers?

Second, can a denomination that demands certain conceptual maturity for "understanding" sin and faith continue to baptize children? If so, can churches find ways of confirming childhood faith in adolescence or adulthood without requiring rebaptism and the repudiation of earlier, less mature but no less valid response to grace?

Third, what is the place of those—the handicapped, the mentally retarded, those with learning disabilities—who cannot adequately conceptualize? Are they still appropriate recipients of baptism and the Lord's Supper? What is the nature of conversion for those who cannot conceptualize normatively?

Fourth, what is the relationship between theological proposition and conversion faith? By transactionalizing conversion, reducing it to a series of ready-made propositions, do Southern Baptists risk undermining the mystery of biblical faith and personal encounter? Conversion is a paradox by which we enter into faith and by which faith is ever entering into us. To discover new areas of life that require conversion does not mean we must be converted all over again.

Finally, is it possible that Southern Baptists need to remythologize the nature of conversion for fulfilling an evangelical imperative in the increasing pluralism of southern society, urban church life, and secular American culture? Perhaps then they might become a renewed community, bound by certain biblical imperatives, diverse traditions to a common calling within the church of Jesus Christ.

Notes

[1]Jim Newton, "Most Churches Grow because of Transfers of Memberships," *Western Recorder*, 18 February 1986.

[2]Robert Torbet, *A History of the Baptists*, 3d ed. (Valley Forge: Judson Press, 1978) 223-34. Torbet discusses both the Regular and Separate traditions, schism and reunion.

[3]"Abstract of Principles," The Southern Baptist Theological Seminary.

[4]Walter B. Shurden, "The Southern Baptist Synthesis. Is It Cracking?" in the 1980-1981 Carver Barnes Lectures, Southeastern Baptist Theological Seminary, 1981, 5-6. Also published in *Baptist History and Heritage* 16/2 (April 1981).

[5]William Warren Sweet, *Religion on the American Frontier, 1783-1830* (New York: Henry Holt and Company, 1931) 234.

[6]*The Baptist Faith and Message*, Article V (Nashville: Sunday School Board of the SBC, 1963) 12.

[7]James Leo Garrett, E. Glenn Hinson, James E. Tull, *Are Southern Baptists "Evangelicals"*? (Macon GA: Mercer University Press, 1983) 88-90; and Bill J. Leonard, "Getting Saved in America: Conversion Event in a Pluralistic Culture," *Review & Expositor* 72/1 (Winter 1985): 123-24. Garrett calls Southern Baptists modified Calvinists but acknowledges that they retain only one of the "five points," perseverance.

[8]W. Morgan Patterson, *Baptist Succession: A Critical View* (Valley Forge: Judson Press, 1969) 22-29.

[9]William Warren Sweet, *Religion in the Development of American Culture* (New York: Charles Scribner's Sons, 1952) 158.

[10]H. Richard Niebuhr, *The Kingdom of God in America* (New York: Harper Torchbooks, 1937) 179-80.

[11]Leonard, 120-21.

[12]Norman Jameson, "We're Being Born Again . . . and Again," *The Baptist Messenger*, 18 September 1986, 4-9.

[13]L. R. Scarborough, *With Christ After the Lost* (Nashville: Broadman Press, 1952) 158.

[14]Ibid.

[15]P. E. Burroughs, *How to Win to Christ* (Nashville: Convention Press, 1934) 70.

[16]Melvin Douglas Clark, "The Evangelism of Children: A Study in Southern Baptist Practice," (Unpublished Th.D. Thesis, 1969); and Samuel S. Hill, Jr., "The Shape and Shapes of Popular Southern Piety," in *Varieties of Southern Evangelicalism*, ed. David Harrell (Macon GA: Mercer University Press, 1981) 89-114. Hill discusses the nature of conversion and his own experience of nurture within the SBC.

[17]James Fowler, *Stages of Faith* (New York: Harper & Row, 1981).

[18]Garrett, Hinson, and Tull, 88-104; and Walter B. Shurden, *Not a Silent People* (Nashville: Broadman Press, 1972) 83-101.

[19]Garrett, Hinson, and Tull, 98.

[20]C. E. Autrey, *You Can Win Souls* (Nashville: Broadman Press, 1961) 33-34.

[21]Adrian Rogers, "The Virgin Birth," tape recorded sermon, Pastor's Conference of the SBC, 8 June 1986.

[22]Ibid.

Toward a Conversionist Spirituality

James Wm. McClendon, Jr.

The earliest witness to Christian existence consists in lives turned around by a startling new fact: Jesus Christ, once condemned and executed, is alive, and for these witnesses there is here and now a new world.[1] This newness, of their Master's resurrection and of their own lives in resurrection light, becomes the axis on which their world will now turn; it entails a revolution in their understanding of Jesus, and of one another, and of the world itself.

Sponsoring Transformation

If we should call this radically changed state of affairs simply "the new that comes in Christ," that choice of words would designate a gap in ordinary speech: How is the truly extraordinary even to be named? This linguistic gap corresponds to the primitive disciples' dilemma: How can converted folk ever talk with the inexperienced, or even with one another, about the unprecedented, the unique? If it is new, old terms will not do, while new ones may convey nothing.

New Testament language typically met this difficulty with what rhetoricians call *catachresis*—the so-called 'misuse' of language drawn from other spheres of life in order to indicate the new thing at which existing talk necessarily balks. Thus the language of law ("justify"), holy rite ("sanctify"), medical healing and military rescue ("heal" or "save"), family change ("adopt" or "wed"), life process ("reborn"), commercial practice ("reconcile"), and so on[2]—all these terms drawn from the old ordered world are pressed into "inappropriate" or catachretical use to afford glimpses of the one new state of affairs they share, thanks to Christ Jesus.

Yet time goes by; the new world does not simply pass over into the expected age to come but hovers, waiting for an end that in one sense is present but in another is not. Consequently, terms newly minted to express faith's new possession grow old, and they and the practices that witnessed to the new awareness ossify into a tradition as much in want of redemption as the old had ever been. Thus a perennial problem of Christian teaching arises: How can this religion of salvation remain salvific? How can religious communities that have shaped themselves to maintain and preserve Christian life be open to the hot breath of the Spirit that creates them, open to the onset of the new that comes in Christ?

Catholic theologian Rosemary Houghton frames the question another way: How can communities of formation sponsor—not formation, but—*transformation?*[3] Formation is indispensable, both the formation that can issue in conversion and the further formation that genuine conversion must entail. Transformation has meaning only against a formationist ground. On the other hand, only if transformation comes is the gospel good news; without it, as Haughton points out, formation becomes a lifetime of preparation for an event the community could not accommodate if it were ever to occur.[4]

The Perennial Tension

I propose a pattern for the life of faith, an *ordo salutis,* that correlates formative church practices (namely, catachesis, baptism, eucharist, congregational discernment) with fundamental transformative moments in Christian life. This proposal will be revisionary from the standpoint of churches that practice infant baptism and will also require reinterpretation of another practice, congregational discernment. Yet I will defend this "reformation of formation" here only by urging that it coheres with the transformative pattern Christian faith demands.

The problem of relating Christian practice to faith is perennial. Sixteenth-century developments are a case in point; Martin Luther's new awareness of conversion (from law to grace, from guilt to forgiveness) dominated his early teaching. Salvation was not to be based upon merit accumulated, as his Catholic heritage had taught him, nor was it only at the Last Day, or only at death, or only beyond purgatory. In Luther's new teaching, based on Galatians and Romans, justification was keyed to faith alone and faith was a present possibility, God's gift awaiting acceptance.

The [ana] baptists such as Conrad Grebel, Michael Sattler, and Balthasar Hubmaier (to name three radicals among Luther's contemporaries) believed that despite Luther's advances he had nevertheless failed to provide a solid account of the life of faith. They agreed that conversion was essential, gracious, and salvific, but they went on to insist, in ways Luther thought unevangelical, that faith and conversion were worthless if these did not initiate a new life-course of faithfulness. Significantly, all three rejected infant baptism[5] and taught a conversion-baptism (believers baptism) as the appointed sign of the onset of the transformed spiritual life.

Both of these revisionary models of the Christian journey, the Lutheran and the baptist, were themselves vulnerable to ossification. For Lutherans, the brave new phrase "justification by faith alone" would eventually harden into doctrinal affirmations that evoked fresh appeals for renewal in the new vocabularies of Spener and Franke, Zinzendorf and Wesley.[6] For baptists, too, hardening of more than one sort would occur; some turned toward the predestinarian quietism that opposed mission and evangelism so that it in its turn required correction in the new practices and new vocabularies of the revivals.[7]

A historical pattern emerges: Transformation evokes a new language and calls forth new practices; these are required both to prepare the ground for transformation and to conserve it when it does occur. With the passage of time, however, the patterns of language and practice no longer signify and may even inhibit transformation. Hence, the gospel is said to be a new law, the second blessing turns into a *pro forma* tradition, and speaking in tongues becomes a ritual practice.

The Four Elements of Transformation

To acknowledge that forms can thus be diverted from their original roles need not evoke cynicism or drive us into spiritualist indifference to all forms. In biblical perspective, body and spirit, inner life and outer form, sign and matter signified do indeed belong together. A prime example is New Testament baptism itself, a conversion baptism that both witnessed to and performatively constituted faith's appeal for a new life.[8]

What follows is that the search for the normative Christian journey cannot neglect the search for a form of the church that will nurture both formation and transformation. One cannot ask about spirituality without also asking about the social and structural shape of the church.[9] More neutrally, we can distinguish "spiritualist" spiritualities that bypass structure from "ecclesial" spiritualities that affirm it.[10] To choose the latter is to require both formative structure and formational instruction.

The long experience of Puritans preoccupied with "preparation," as of Keswick and the Pentecostals in quest of a higher Christian life, shows that no outward form of church life meets this need apart from teaching that directs journeyers to the inwardness of spiritual life. In a motto, without "the hour I first believed," baptism is *empty* ceremony, but without "I baptize thee in the name of the Father and of the Son and of the Holy Ghost," conversion is *blind* affect. To be themselves, faith's transformative moment (conversion) and the church's structural form (baptism) require one another.

What must be the shape of a doctrine of the Christian life that consents to this principle and is conversionist or transformationist as well as formationist? First, it must be a travel account, a journey—one with a beginning, continuance, and an end. Unlike Luther in his argument against the baptists, it must not presume the norm of Christian life to be an indefinite series of fresh starts, followed each by a lapse and a return to the beginning.[11] Second, the journey of each must be indexed to the common life of the church; it must have an individual and also a corporate dimension. These guidelines should yield a model of the Christian life that is neither idiosyncratically individualist[12] nor merely the application of psychological truisms to "stages" of Christian development.[13]

Accordingly, the present proposal for a transformationist *ordo salutis* picks out four transformative phases or elements, to each of which corresponds a formative feature of community life. The four are (1) *preparation* (in the Puritan sense[14]), which corresponds to the church's catechesis or religious training, issuing as the Spirit wills in (2) *conversion*, to which corresponds (believers) baptism, leading to the phase of (3) ongoing *discipleship and ministry*, to which corresponds the recurrent eucharist or Lord's supper, and last, (4) a unique or *unpredictable* element, to which we may relate the pastoral and prophetic congregational action commended in Matthew 18 and elsewhere, best known by such misnames as "penance" or "the ban," but which we may construe structurally as prophetic discernment.

Individual and Community in Tension

Since three of these elements are more familiar,[15] I will refer here only to the fourth, the unique or distinctive or *unpredictable* element in each Christian's life, and its relation to the congregational task mandated in Matthew 18 and parallels.[16] In speaking of the unpredictable, I mean to honor the insights of the Wesleys, of Keswick, of classic and neopentecostalism, and of a still broader range of Christian witness that has held forth as norm a higher Christian life, a more intense or deeper or fuller awareness coupled with an expanded capacity for Christian service and marked (in many cases) by distinctive signs.[17] I mean to honor these, but find myself unable to make any one of them definitive to the exclusion of the others. Rather, this fourth element contemplates a stretch of journey that cannot be confined or bounded: In this phase once again the Spirit blows where the Spirit wills (cf. John 3:8). Yet, if this element is not to dissolve into anarchic individualism, it must be met, like each preceding phase, by a church structure designed to recognize it and relate it to the common life.

Acts depicts Barnabas and Paul as co-workers drawn together in a unique convergence of ministries, in their distinct personalities and vocations we find an instance of the unpredictable element in Christian existence.[18] Only then does Acts 13 report the Antioch congregation's role. From within a setting of numinous (eucharistic?) worship, fasting, and prayer, came a word from the divine Spirit: "Set Barnabas and Saul apart for me, to do the work to which I have called them," and so they did (13:2f REB). Here the link between distinctive life story and congregational action is explicit; Acts 13 thus supplements Matthew 18 as a paradigm case of formative congregational discernment engaging Spirit-gifted vocation.

Finally, we must ask about the risks this fourfold pattern faces. Can it, too, be regulated and regularized until no room is left for the transformative Spirit to work? The answer is yes. No more here than elsewhere have we an infallible or foolproof pattern of Christian life.

If there is any advantage, it lies in the pattern's openness to correlation with the patterns of scripture and in its explicit flexibility. At each community or structural checkpoint (gospel catechesis, conversion baptism, the covenant meal, the congregation met to discern) is a fresh opening for the formative mind of the Spirit.[19] Nothing can go well without the anticipated yet unmanipulated entry of the Spirit into the life of the Christian pilgrim, illuminating the seeker, achieving conversion, opening a life of witness, and—in still further, unpredictable ways—introjecting God's presence into each pilgrimage. On the other hand, nothing can avail without the church's ordered life of teaching, baptism, eucharist, and common discernment, guiding the learner, shaping conversion baptismally, forming vocation along eucharistic—cross-shadowed—lines, and withal discerning the distinctive work of the Spirit in each disciple's life. If this is so, we have a pattern for Christian life that is as well a pattern by which the church can be the church.

Notes

[1]Reading the *ei tis en Christō, kainē ktisis* of 2 Cor. 5:17, with REB (and other versions) thus: "For anyone united to Christ, there is a new creation: the old order has gone; a new order has already begun."

[2]Here, I follow the line of thought suggested by my teacher W. T. Conner in *The Gospel of Redemption* (Nashville: Broadman, 1945) 178, 193ff. I regard these varied terms not as the names of separate acts of God or as steps or stages in an *ordo salutis*, but as synonymous though varied windows through which light is shed upon the one forgiving, healing, renewing gift, the new that comes in Christ.

[3]Rosemary Haughton, *The Transformation of Man: A Study of Conversion and Community* (Springfield IL: Templegate, 1980) part two.

[4]Ibid., chap. 7.

[5]On Conrad Grebel, see Leland Harder, ed., *The Sources of Swiss Anabaptism; The Grebel Letters and Related Documents* (Scottdale PA and Kitchener, Ontario: Herald Press, 1985), and Harold S. Bender, *Conrad Grebel, c. 1498-1526* (Scottdale PA: Herald Press, 1950). Grebel's conversion is discussed in Bender, chap. 6, esp. 76f., and in Harder, 193. I believe Harder's negative remarks reflect his classical Mennonite anti-revivalism rather than a denial of what is here called conversion. Grebel apparently never found the leisure to write the baptism of the radical reformation (21 January 1525); on the documents, see Harder, item 68F.

On Michael Sattler, see John H. Yoder, ed., *The Legacy of Michael Sattler*, trans. and ed. John H. Yoder (Scottdale PA: Herald Press, 1973) and C. Arnold Snyder, *The Life and Thought of Michael Sattler*. Sattler's view of baptism and its relation to faith and conversion is discussed in Snyder, 112ff., 122ff., and passim; the documents (esp. the Letter to Bucer and Capito and the Schleitheim documents: the 7 Articles and the congregational order, and Letter to Horb) are found in Yoder, chaps. 1-3.

On Balthasar Hubmaier, see H. Wayne Pipkin and John H. Yoder, trans. and eds., *Balthasar Hubmaier: Theologian of Anabaptism* (Scottdale PA and Kitchener, Ontario: Herald Press, 1989, and the literature cited there. Hubmaier's view of baptism is best represented in "On the Christian Baptism of Believers" (Pipkin and Yoder, item 11); the same document makes his view of repentance and faith and their relation to baptism and good works.

In the sixteenth century the argument for believer's baptism, besides invoking the norm of primitive practice, turned especially on the contest between state-church and believers-church ecclesiologies. (See Rollin Stely Armour, *Anabaptist Baptism: A Representative Study*. Scottdale PA: Herald Press, 1966). If every child born in Zurich was a presumptive Christian and so to be baptized in infancy, the church's members and the state's citizenry were coextensive in principle and the league between church and state seemed inevitable; to think otherwise required not only a new view of baptism but also a new view of the church—and of the state. In our time, with state-church and societal-church widely questioned, the debate over baptism can better examine the question, how the forms of a given church practice make each Christian pilgrim sensitive to the winds of the Spirit. (Answering that question will not terminate the debate, but may set it on new and fruitful structural, i.e., ecclesial, ground).

[6]On pietism, see F. Ernest Stoeffler, *The Rise of Evangelical Pietism* (Lieden: E. J. Brill, 1965); for a valuable brief account see Dale W. Brown, *Understanding Pietism* (Grand Rapids MI: Eerdmans, 1978).

[7]There is a vast literature on revivals and revivalism, beginning with the unmatched contemporary histories by Jonathan Edwards. See The Works of Jonathan Edwards, vol. 4, C. C. Goen, ed., *The Great Awakening*, and vol. 2, John E. Smith, ed., *A Treatise Concerning Religious Affections* (New Haven CT: Yale University Press, 1972 and 1959). A convenient reference to the secondary literature is Richard F. Lovelace, *Dynamics of Spiritual Life: An Evangelical Theology of Renewal* (Downers Grove IL: Inter-Varsity Press, 1979) chap. 1. See also Lovelace, "Evangelical Spirituality: A Church Historian's Perspective" in *Journal of the Evangelical Theological Society* 31/1 (March 1988): 25-36, which usefully covers ground omitted in this chapter.

[8]A good bibliography on baptism is found in the systematic theology by Geoffrey Wainwright, *Doxology: The Praise of God in Worship. Doctrine, and Life* (New York: Oxford University Press, 1980) 482-84; to which I add my own "Baptism as a Performative Sign," *Theology Today*, 23/3 (October): 403-16, and "Why Baptists Do Not Baptize Infants," in *Concilium* 24 (*The Sacraments: An Ecumenical Dilemma*, New York: Paulist Press, 1967).

[9]On the concept of social structure and its relation to the life of faith, see my *Ethics: Systematic Theology, Volume 1* (Nashville: Abingdon Press, 1986) part two, "The Sphere of the Communal," and especially the discussion of powerful practices, 158-77.

[10]A distinguishing mark of much of the literature on spiritual life that has flooded bookstores in the last two decades is its disconnection from visible congregational life. It is easy to think of pejorative descriptions of this phenomenon; it seems better to recognize that much of the literature has been created by writers whose practice is better than their preaching: they are simply not trained to ask about the connections and relations that theology demands.

[11]Defending the integrity of infant baptism against the enormity of the radicals, Luther wrote: "Were we to follow their reasoning we would have to be baptizing all the time. For I would take the verse, 'Whoever believes' with me, and whenever I find a Christian who has fallen or is without faith, I would say that this man is without faith, so his baptism is fruitless; he must be baptized again. If he falls a second time, I would say, see, he has no faith, there must be something wrong about his first baptism. He will have to be baptized a third time, and so on and on. As often as he falls or there is doubt about his faith, I will say he doesn't believe, his baptism is defective. In short, he will have to be baptized over again so often that he never considers that his baptism is complete?" "Concerning Rebaptism," in *Luther's Works*, American ed., vol. 40 (Philadelphia: Fortress Press 1958) 247f., cited in Eric W. Gritsch, *Born Againism; Perspectives on a Movement* (Philadelphia: Fortress Press, 1982) 95. What Luther (and Gritsch) assume, however, is that the Christian life is typically an on-again

off-again affair. In that case, baptism cannot begin the journey, for there is no continuing journey to be taken—only a series of states of faith or unfaith.

[12]Idiosyncratic individualism makes it so difficult to appropriate the otherwise brilliant psychological musings of Søren Kierkegaard in a discussion of the Christian life. Nevertheless, see his *Stages on Life's Way* (citation to follow).

[13]The allusion, of course, is to the enormously popular and successful work by James W. Fowler and his associates. See *Trajectories in Faith; Five Life Stories* (Nashville: Abingdon Press, 1980). This work has come in for what would seem daunting criticism. See for example Neill Q. Hamilton, *Maturing in the Christian Life: A Pastor's Guide* (Philadelphia: Geneva Press, 1984), a valuable discussion of Christian growth in its own right. What one should consider, though, is that despite the criticism (perhaps partly because of it?) it has been widely imitated and employed as the normative model for Christian growth by religious education experts. I attribute its success in part to its dependence upon Piagetian models of psychological change. For a contrasting, conversionist approach to life stories, see my *Biography as Theology* (Nashville: Abingdon Press, 1975). There is an interesting evaluative comparison of my work and Fowler's in Michael Goldberg, *Theology and Narrative* (Nashville: Abingdon, 1982) chap. 3. However, I think that Goldberg is wrong to complain of the analysis of lives in *Biography as Theology* that "there is virtually no methodological structure to it." While it is true that Christian life stories find themselves in the biblical story in a variety of ways that are ineluctably distinctive aspects of those individual lives, it is also true that the broad pattern of each of those life stories conforms to the pattern displayed in the present paper. To put the matter crudely (too crudely), Fowler shapes the stories he tells on Piagetian developmental lines that he hopes are universal; I pattern mine on the biblical story, which is 'universal' only by being irreducibly particular.

[14]On Puritan preparation, see Norman Pettit, *The Heart Prepared: Grace and Conversion in Puritan Spiritual Life* (New Haven CT: Yale University Press, 1966); E. Brooks Holifield, *The Covenant Sealed: The Development of Puritan Sacramental Theology in Old and New England, 1570-1720* (New Haven CT: Yale University Press, 1974); Sacvan Bercovitch, *The Puritan Origins of the American Mind* (New Haven: Yale University Press, 1975), and (forthcoming in the dissertation series of the National Association of Baptist Professors of Religion, published by Mercer University Press), Michael Joseph Schuldiner, "The Doctrine of Spiritual Growth and Church Polity in Early America," a Kent State doctoral dissertation accepted in 1979.

[15]I only note concerning communion that a long preoccupation with sin in the Christian life has kept the church from adequate treatment of the Lord's supper as the life-giving and life-guiding covenant meal that in this present perspective it can be. Seeing the discipleship-ministry aspect of Christian existence linked both to the commissioning ceremony of baptism and to the renewal of allegiance in the ancient covenant sign of bread and wine restores integrity to the long Christian journey while powerfully supplementing an exclusive emphasis upon guilt and forgiveness in the Supper itself.

[16]By the parallels to Matthew 18:10-20 I mean to refer here, not only to other passages reflecting corporate forgiveness (such as the insufflation of John 20:19-23) and

judgment (such as 1 Cor 5:3-5), but to all the New Testament instances of community or corporate judgment. This would include the Acts 13 passage discussed below; 1 Cor 14:37-38 (with which compare *Didache* chap.11); the primitive instructions concerning "ordination" in 1 Tim 4:6, 13-16; the instruction "by their fruit you-all shall know them"(Matt 7:20, plural imperative, and again in John 10:38); the instructions to the Corinthian congregation regarding their ecclesial handling of controversies (1 Cor 6:1-6) with the remark in passing about the eschatological judgment role of the saints (cf. Rev 4:4, and Matt 19:28); and recall that in antiquity the roles of ruler and judge were not distinguished—a fact reflected in employment of English "court" to mean court of law as well as king's court. Our supposition that judgment necessarily means destructive criticism and condemnation is contradicted by the role of Christ, who according to John 3:17 came not to condemn the world, but to save it. So Christian judgment, in this spirit, is salvific judgment; it declares the wisdom and justice of God, which is a wisdom and justice perfectly consistent with love. Again, we assume that such judgment must of necessity be authoritarian, but that is contradicted by the word of Christ, who teaches that while the rulers of the Gentiles lord it over them, "it shall not be so among you, but whoever would be great among you must be your servant, and whoever would be first among you must be your slave, even as the Son of man came not to be served but to serve, and to give his life as a ransom for many" (Matt 20:26-8 RSV). A valuable study is Marlin Jeschke, *Discipling in the Church: Recovering a Ministry of the Gospel* (Scottdale PA: Herald Press, 1988).

[17]My own study of these movements is my doctoral dissertation, "The Doctrine of Sin and the First Epistle of John: A comparison of Calvinist, Wesleyan, and Biblical Thought" (Fort Worth, Texas: Southwestern Baptist Theological Seminary, 1953). While the very title suggests some of the naivete of the "biblical theology" movement of that past age, less naivete is present in the work than one might expect. "Calvinist" and "Wesleyan" there reflect two broad trends in the doctrine of the Christian life, the Calvinist "realistic'"in its view of sin's ubiquity and persistence, the Wesleyan (and holiness) "perfectionist" in its sense of the fullness of redemption and the possibilities of holiness. The Keswick teaching is treated as a synthesis of these two broad streams, and all are properly brought under the searchlight of Johannine doctrine especially as that is represented in the First Epistle. The standpoint of the dissertation, like that of the present paper, is nearer to Keswick and "perfectionism" than it is to Reinhold Niebuhr's Calvinist "realism." What the dissertation lacked, and the paper suggests, is the important role of the community in the progress of the Christian life.

[18]According to Acts (4:36f), Barnabas was a Cypriot and a Levite; he appears in the narrative of Acts as a wealthy member of the Jerusalem church who devoted capital to the cause. As a native of Cyprus, he would have shared with Paul a Hellenistic background that fitted him for Gentile missions, yet he may have been Jesus' own convert in Jerusalem and was thus close to (conservative) Jewish Christianity. His preaching in Antioch (Acts 11:19-22) to mixed hearers opened the way for the growth of the church there, and it was he who recruited Paul from Tarsus for further work in Antioch. Thus their paths converged, and when they went missioning in Cyprus with John Mark, Paul gained the ascendancy according to Acts placement of their names. Since Paul's career is well known, it seems appropriate to set the lesser-known alongside it here: the striking matter throughout is Barnabas' gift for self-effacing

greatness. This was recognized in the second century when certain prized Christian writings were attributed to him. See M. J. Shroyer, "Barnabas," in *Interpreter's Dictionary of the Bible* (New York: Abingdon, 1962).

Timothy George discusses a slightly later period in "Early Anabaptist Spirituality in the Low Countries," *Mennonite Quarterly Review* 62/3 (July, 1988): 257-75; George arrives at a two-fold communal structure ("the bath" and "the ban") that compresses under these labels the material I have here unfolded under a four-fold formational scheme. See also the literature he cites there.

[19]See 1 Cor 2:6-16. Paul speaks of the "mind of the Lord" (v. 16) and the "mind of Christ" (ibid.). Yet, the passage makes clear that Paul identifies this with the "mind of the Spirit" (not his phrase)—the mind that "explores everything, even the deep truths of God's own nature" (v. 10 REB).

The Hermeneutics of Conversion

Randy Hatchett

Simon was a Baptist. He had moved often and seen many different expressions of what it meant to be a Baptist. Born in 1900, he had joined our church as a boy and left only to return as a man in his eighties. He spoke with joy of "ending up" in the same church he had "began in."

One night I concluded a sermon series on what it meant to be a Baptist. The sermon included things that I had been taught as a boy, had challenged as a young man, and then reclaimed in my thirties. Simon particularly affirmed my homiletical effort. He recounted a previous pastor he had known as a child. Shaking his head, with tears in his eyes, he said, "Tonight you stood on the rock he stood on." My vision and imagination was transformed that night. I could now see that I was not alone in my convictional struggles; I belonged to a people and a tradition.

Baptist convictions provide illuminating and transforming analogues (or types) for understanding the Christian life in which community and conversion go together. These analogies provide a strategy for reading scripture that pictures people being converted into a community that stands separate from its culture even in the face of persecution. They are Christ's people who find models of conversion for those entering the new messianic community in the Bible. These analogies of community and conversion protect the reader from hermeneutical systems that suggest obedience is impossible or futile. The experience of Christ's transforming power in conversion and Christ's ruling presence in the community enable a hermeneutical imagination necessary for faithful reading.

Biblical Reflection

The Baptist understanding of church and conversion has its roots in the New Testament. The rhetoric of suffering in the Petrine letters provides a rich laboratory for Baptist readers. Its picture of a persecuted church of resident aliens is noteworthy for Baptists whose ancestors were numbered among the poor and oppressed. Early Baptists identified with the Petrine church's independence from the powerful culture and were captured by the vision of the priesthood of believers. The book of Acts narrates dramatic accounts of conversion and missionary advance. Baptists also found numerous "types" there for their own conversions and read of the transforming power and political turmoil that accompanied the gospel around the world.

Recent studies have observed the sociological setting of the New Testament that suggest conversion is best understood as participation in a community. For example, the book of 1 Peter is typically read as encouragement to suffering pilgrims whose hardship was cushioned by the news that our world is transitory, giving way to an eternal heavenly reality. From a sociological viewpoint, however, Peter's distinction is between the establishment people whose identity was rooted in their place in the community and the resident aliens (*paroikoi*). The Greek word for house (*oikos*) brings to mind the most fundamental associations in social life—the place where one dwells and belongs. The alien (*paroikos*) was a displaced person who had no roots—a foreigner. The sociopolitical usage is crucial. Residents without standing (*paroikoi*) ranked below full citizens (*politai*) but above transients. As "by-dwellers," resident aliens never possessed the full complement of rights belonging to citizens but did receive varying degrees of social recognition from the community. It was their place to live and work, but they did not belong.[1] Not all of the community envisioned by Peter may have been, socially speaking, *paroikoi*. Full citizens (*politai*) may have also been persecuted because of their identification with the church.[2]

Christian outsiders are not, however, merely to wait for heavenly bliss. They are to build a house of God here on earth, knowing that an eschatological reversal is to come. The doctrine of election holds an eschatological promise of reversal and a key to understanding their identity.[3] Those that are by social standards outside or beside the house (*paroikoi*) now become God's house. What the church builds will stand judgment. Now they are permitted to see their privileged destiny. The experience of Jesus and his Old Testament people is the pattern for the experience of Christian outsiders. Their rejection and suffering is like that of Israel and Jesus. They see the narratives of Jesus and Israel as their own. They are God's true inheritors.

The book of Acts further defines the Baptist understanding of conversion as accounts are witnessed throughout the book. Although many were converted at Pentecost, such transformation is also illustrated by representative conversions of Cornelius, the Ethiopian eunuch, and most importantly Paul.[4] The accounts of Paul's conversion are particularly paradigmatic.[5] Luke's narration stipulates that the voice that confronted Paul was the voice of the resurrected living one and indicates that Paul, who was blinded by the light, finally became the great light to the Gentiles. Luke's account also describes how the one who had caused God's people to suffer was shown what he would have "to suffer for the sake of the name" (Acts 5:41). The themes of confrontation with a living Jesus, suffering, testimony, and mission are commonalities of the accounts of conversion in Acts.[6] The repetition of Paul's conversion story suggests its importance. Interestingly, the testimony is narrated differently, depending on the audiences to whom Paul wished to give an account of his life.

Conversion is not the invention of modern pietism. The ancient world was filled with talk of conversion. For example, many of the ancient philosophical schools exhibited a kind of missionary zeal and called individual members to moral conversion. The lack of transformation in philosophical conversion, however, is due in part to the absence of social organization for the care of souls.[7]

Sociological analysis regards conversion as a change of communities. According to the sociological account, however, once converted or initiated into the new community, there would be no need for children brought up in the group to convert.[8] The ancient and contemporary reflection upon the importance of community for conversion is important because it demonstrates that conversion is not the self-actualization of modern individualism. One's socialization in a community and the community's standing within broader culture are important for this study, but the practices of believer's baptism and infant baptism imply that entrance into the early Christian community was not simply automatic.[9]

Hermeneutics of Distance

The notion of historical distance is the *mysterium tremendum* of modern historical criticism. The politics that promote the hermeneutics of distance are enormously powerful. For example, modern readers may be so perplexed by the Pauline descriptions of primitive worship at Corinth as to say, "This is not anything like my church." The discomfort could hardly be greater. Worried clerics often respond to such a problem by suggesting that one must address through historical research the question of what the text *meant* when it was written (to either its author and audience or both). Only then can a second question be addressed: What does the text *mean* in our context today?[10]

Liberals and conservatives alike build hermeneutical schemes to alleviate the anxiety evoked by historical distance. Classical dispensationalists, for example, did this by rejecting earlier Christian affirmations of the harmony and continuity of the Bible. Instead, they discerned basically incompatible covenants and economies that were assigned to different ages or epochs. Lewis Sperry Chafer claimed that Jesus' theology differed from Paul's because Jesus spoke primarily to the Jews. Chafer wrote of the Sermon on the Mount that "as a rule of life it is addressed to the Jew before the cross and the Jew in the coming kingdom [millennium], and therefore not in effect."[11] By dividing scripture into separate, disparate compartments, the dispensationalist avoids the admirable but troubling directives of Jesus. The grace of Paul's theology is more to the church's liking. Charles Ryrie, a contemporary dispensationalist, writes in the same vein that "people get sidetracked when they attempt to impose kingdom ethics on the world today without the physical presence of the king [to enforce them]."[12]

A famous German New Testament scholar, Albert Schweitzer, popularized a remarkably similar approach. He believed Jesus' teachings were directed to a future kingdom. He accounted for the theological diversity of the New Testament by holding that some theologians adjusted their teaching when Jesus failed to return.

Whether in the name of liberalism, demythologizing, or dispensationalism, the hermeneutics of distance are apologetic programs addressing the distance between the New Testament world and our own contemporary practice. For Bultmann, Jesus' modern existential challenge is couched in a mythological perspective and language. Schweitzer believed that Jesus' noble example is to be emulated, but his words are intended only for the short interim before his return. Dispensationalists contend that Jesus' commands are largely directed toward a Jewish kingdom demanding works and not to the grace age of the church with its individualistic and cognitive notion of faith. All three perspectives, although quite different in substance, share a discomfort with the immediacy of the biblical text and thus seek to account for this distantiation.

Hermeneutics of Presence

Baptists have not produced many theologians, but the sociology of early Anabaptists and Baptists did not provide a schoolman's stability. They were more nearly "on the run" than "on the payroll."[13] They addressed pastoral problems in the contexts of believing churches who sought concrete obedience to their living and present Lord. Yet we should marvel at the quality (and quantity) of their work, even though they naively read the text as an immediate expression of God's will and failed to account adequately for historical distance between themselves and the text.

In the 1960s, Southern Baptists attempted to show that they had left the textual naivete of their traditions.[14] They wanted to demonstrate that they had joined modernity and learned to apply historical methods to their faith (which presume and illumine distance). Thus they left behind (in Ricoeur's words) the "first naivete." The challenge of post-modernity is whether we can now use faith to critique the methods and canons of modernity.[15]

Interestingly, ancient interpreters were not overcome by the notion of historical distance. Instead, patristic readings were generally audience-oriented.[16] Contemporary post-modern theorists are articulating a similar interest; they call for a sense of "textual immediacy." Such readings demand the discernment of analogy and metaphors with which to make connections with the text. Reading involves a dialogic relationship between experience and text, but historical distance is not the primary barrier to a careful reading. Our moral and theological distance from the faith world of the text inhibits genuine interpretation. The struggle is to read texts with the ancient interest in transformation and community witness. Texts instruct communities as to what to do and who to be. The church learns to read and enact the scriptures by observing paradigmatic reading of previous communities and saints.[17]

We need not claim too much for Baptists. Much in Baptist theology is "first naivete" material rather than "second." Nevertheless, Baptist hermeneutics are marked by a textual immediacy—a sense that Christ is present and speaking to the assembly through the scripture. It is no mere coincidence that the deacon giving a testimony uses typologies drawn from the Bible—of "wrestling with the Lord" and of a "Job experience." The practice seems appropriate with the conclusion that "they [biblical heroes] are people just like us."[18]

The sense that Christ addresses the reader directly is an essential part of Baptist tradition. Keith Clements writes that for Baptists, "scriptural authority has meant not so much the authority of 'the book' per se, as the authority of the living word of God speaking through it."[19] William Carey, for example, believed he was personally addressed by Jesus' Great Commission. He was roundly criticized, suffering the indignity of being called an "enthusiast."[20] Carey could not, however, escape the sense of being personally addressed by Christ, and other Baptists began to share Carey's missionary vision. The commission was for all, not just the primitive audience.

The earliest Baptist, John Smyth, also listened for direct guidance from Christ. As a devout student of scripture, he studied both Hebrew and Greek. Yet he insisted upon a "spiritual worship" and excluded a dependence upon a book. Having the book before the eye would be inappropriate for the one offering prophecy in spiritual worship. The prophet was to translate and relate the scripture depending upon the Spirit's guidance. The entire congregation was entrusted with understanding and applying the scripture.[21] While Smyth was in part reacting to the formality of read prayers from a book of worship, his practice also rested upon the conviction that Christ speaks to his gathered people when scripture is prophetically rendered. The text has an immediate sense for Baptists because Christ is present and speaking in their midst.

The Hermeneutics of Narrative

Current spiritualities face two great opponents in modern individualism and gnosticism, which promise to disclose methods for mastery over the perils of life. While Baptist preaching has been predominantly narrative, our modern age has preferred universalization and generality. With a lingering deism, our age has preferred a deity that is mediated in the "equal access" medium of human reason. For enlightenment, folk stories that were too enmeshed with local customs and contexts had to be translated into timeless truths and principles to have significance. The tendency to reformat narrative into principles and truths sets well with ancient gnosticism (which lusted for spiritual technique)[22] and enlightenment thinking (which in embarrassment discarded husk and searched for the kernel of transcending truths).[23]

Additionally, two enlightenment dichotomies continue to frustrate Christian theology: (1) the tension between human freedom/power and God's power/freedom and (2) the polarity between nature's self- explanatory work and the deity's intervention. Systematic theologies written from those frameworks find it all but impossible to avoid the reductionism that follows. God seems to be responsible for less and less, becoming in time a "God of the gaps" that reigns over only what nature and man forfeit or at least fail to take care of on their own.

If Baptists have (even partially) escaped the harmful intellectual and theological dilemma of this age, it is because they are less inclined toward systematic theology and more comfortable with narrative theology or proclamation. They treat the scripture as a directing story rather than a data book for doctrine. Narrative allows for meaningful human activity and God's control. It resists logical reductions.

Narratives often promote the typological preaching for which Baptists are famous. Again, the narrative does not yield a simple answer. It creates a mysterious world that frustrates readers who strive to remove ambiguity. Narratives have eschatologies because there is an end or goal in sight. Yet there is also an eschatological openness and freedom. For example, Jesus spoke of the certainties of the end. Judgment comes, and those who build lives on his rock solid instruction survive, while all others are on sinking sand. The reader is exhorted to ask, "Where will I stand?"[24] Baptist narrative and eschatological outlooks are related to the Baptist call for conversion. Narrative encourages typological reflection that is destined to provoke the eschatological issue of conversion because narratives are only for those who can hold convictions and make affirmations in the face of mystery.

The Hermeneutics of Community

The decision-evoking nature of gospel narratives and preaching are not merely individualistic. One can hear the story only by sensing that one's own narrative is related to a larger story told by a community. The struggle of Daniel and his friends was part of a larger sociological struggle to maintain the distinctive dietary laws of (and identity with) his people. The call of Moses was not a private affair. It is a call for him to identify with his people. Ruth's affirmation of Israel's God was connected to her loyalty to Naomi and her husband's memory. Her deliverance by Yahweh's invisible sovereignty was inseparable from the preserving of her family line and her role in Israel's destiny.[25]

Baptists frequently include individual testimonies in worship, but such acts are far from individual efforts. These testimonies are offered or submitted to communities that have a formative role that helps to structure and interpret others' experiences. As an analogy, imagine a disorganized sales report that gains little approval from the boss during a company meeting. If it is followed by a well-organized report that shapes the material in a regional or monthly format, it may be well-received by the boss. A further result may be that during lunch break many will amend their report to follow the new form that had proven successful. Personal testimonies function in a similar way to influence others in a church.[26]

What makes a testimony "work" is its correspondence with biblical texts that are themselves heard and read as testimonies. The hermeneutical circle suggests that our reading of Scripture shapes our testimony, and that our testimony shapes our reading of scripture. A typological fittingness can be discerned among those for whom conversion provides an analogy.[27]

Baptists have seen conversion as leading to fellowship and submission to the community's discipline. This gathered community (rather than scholar, cleric, or charismatic) applies Christ's rule. To read the whole canon with discernment, one needs the whole church with all its gifts. Baptists read scripture within this community orientation. Baptism and the Lord's Supper involve a congregational rehearsal of key texts. This analogical (or typological) reading was often as much ecclesiastical as Christological. Baptists saw themselves as the restored people of God. They viewed their gathered community as an eschatological embodiment of an age still to be fully realized.

A community of conversionists share and evaluate one another's spoken and lived testimonies. Only together in such a communal setting can they adequately discern their loyalty to scripture and judge the power-tainted discourses and propaganda of worldly ideologies.[28]

In the work of discipline and disciple-making Baptists have known both the extremes of heavy-handed rule of the body and radical individualism. For example, some Baptist theologians are characterized by the individualism of modernity. E. Y. Mullins and W. T. Conner both attempted to write theologies on the basis of religious experience (understood in the mode of Schleiermacher or the Neo-Kantians). Although Mullins and Conner were "too Baptist" to fall prey to every pitfall of liberalism or the enlightenment, their examples underscore postmodern warnings about projects that are grounded in a generic religious experience that exists prior to language and community.[29]

Experiential individualism that is divorced from the eschatological concepts of conversion and community lead inevitably to the demise of the virtue of hope and its anticipation of transformation.[30] The Baptist vision of communal obedience to Christ's command counteracts the hopelessness of individualism.

This vision resembles William Willimon's story of a conversation among ministers trying to deal with the dilemma of a pregnant thirteen-year-old. Even the anti-abortionists among them confessed they did not know what the girl should do. Finally a black minister told them about elderly couples in his church who took in such girls. His corporate vision demonstrated kingdom ethics that are unimaginable to isolated individuals. Willimon concludes that, "The church is to prophetically create the real world."[31]

The Hermeneutics of Conversion

As a modern Baptist I am sometimes embarrassed by Baptist rhetoric. A hearer may rightly question if we think we are the only ones to have ever followed Christ in obedience. While we are not all Landmarkers, we must humbly say that we participate in an effort to reconstitute the church by simple, radical, and immediate obedience. Early Baptists found continuity with the New Testament church, not with other churches. Simple reform could not produce the church of Jesus. The Baptist vision is a radical form of restorationism.

Similarly, the individual seeking the kingdom could not simply reform or improve. Entrance into the community required an inward conversion marked by submission and obedience. In a standard Baptist ecclesiology, Harvey E. Dana complained that the controversy about the symbolic nature of baptism may eclipse its practical significance.

> Baptism . . . pictures the renouncing of the old life of sin, and the initiation of a new life in Christ. It assumes that the break between the believer and his old life of unbelief is as complete as the transition that occurs in physical death: a complete transformation of one's state.[32]

Thus far this essay has concentrated on the role of community as an alternative to the rampant individualism of our age. Indeed, Baptist conversion was conversion into a community, but, for Baptists, conversion has also meant a personal experience of transformation. It is an "inner change" that is manifested outwardly in conversion. Mullins noted that conversion is a general term but is used more narrowly in theology to refer to the first turning. He recommended that subsequent turnings to Christ be called something else, such as "reconsecration" in order to avoid confusion. This initial or first turning includes repentance (turning from) and faith (turning to). Mullins was careful to note that it is both a human decision and a divine work, but that this spiritual change is most essential. He wrote that "a converted man is one in whom the grace of God has wrought a spiritual change."[33] Mullins, Conner, and Strong all claimed that the Christian life is centered around union with Christ. Mullins observed that

> becoming a Christian a man enters into a new personal relation. Saving faith is not acceptance of a creed nor of a new intellectual belief of any kind. It is not joining the church nor receiving the "sacraments" or ordinances. It is not believing in the Bible in a mere intellectual way. Becoming a Christian is entering a new personal relation to Christ.[34]

Conner similarly insisted upon a spiritual transformation. He claimed that Paul and John most clearly describe union with Christ. He even called them mystics, "in the good sense of the word," and he asserted that "they emphasize this immediate contact of the soul with the living Christ." Sounding like Bultmann, Conner warned that attempting to return to the merely historic Christ will "devitalize Christianity." He called for a union with a Christ who is living, superhistoric, and transcendent.[35]

So also H. E. Dana wrote about the new relationship as foundational to the nature of the church:

> Each redeemed individual must have a direct and personal relation to Christ. Christian experience is based upon faith, and faith is essentially a personal relation. . . . The believer must recognize and submit to the will of Christ in order to maintain a vital experience in his redemptive relationship. This requires a consciousness of intimate personal fellowship with Christ, whereby the believer may know his Master's will.[36]

Dana's argumentation connected the type of conversion and the political practice of the church. What is distinctive in Baptist rhetoric of church and conversion is that the two go together.

These Baptist theologians also talked about growth or devotional life after conversion and drew on other approaches to Christian spirituality, yet maintained humbling distinctives. Baptists, they believed, understand salvation not only as a process (sanctification) but as an establishment of a personal union with Christ. Such a relationship involves communion and communication with a living Christ who directs the believer's way.

A different notion of salvation brings a divergent and perhaps incommensurable notion of spirituality. For example, the modern and ancient foe of gnosticism calls for a different spirituality. Here salvation is seen as the eventual assent of some spiritual dimension over the physical body or the rule of reason over passion. Genuine Christian spiritualities battled with gnosticism on different fronts—Irenaeus affirmed God's stake in the created order[37] and Augustine affirmed God's vision of transformation for the human emotions.[38] Gnosticism still tempts people to trust in some new technique rather than their union with Christ. Although gnosticism can draw a crowd of those who lust after the latest secret, it ultimately destroys genuine corporate relationship. As Nicholas Lash suggests, "all gnosticism is egocentric and egocentricity subverts relationship."[39]

The Hermeneutics of Obedience

Anabaptists wanted to follow Christ directly. They distrusted interpreters who softened the Bible's grave commands by reference to contexts and called them scribes and Pharisees. Instead they ruled on matters of interpretation and discernment by community consensus.[40] Dana similarly instructed Baptists to be directed by unanimity under Christ, with rule by majority seen as a last resort.[41] Matters of dispute could not simply be settled by appealing to the Bible. John Howard Yoder reminds us that at the time of the Reformation "everyone was a biblicist,"[42] but the free church tradition believed that the community of the converted itself was the most fruitful hermeneutical guide. One's individual sense of Christ's leading was checked by the entire congregation's discernment. The true Christian community should never submit to the institutional hierarchy of the church or the state. The church's political independence was rooted in its understanding of Lordship.

For Anabaptists, obedience was inseparable from discernment. One must be willing to obey to understand scripture. Hans Denck claimed that scripture was a dead letter without the personal struggle, testing, and appropriation in real life.[43]

At a crossroad of my life, I lamented having so little personal direction and discernment of God's will. My grandfather, who served as a Baptist pastor for fifty years, cited John 7:17. I recall thinking that this reference was uncritical for such a historically adept reader, but its message left a powerful impression on me. He advised that I go and help someone who was suffering in my neighborhood, and that I should perhaps tell someone the story of Jesus. I have only begun to understand his wisdom. Obedience opens the door to discernment. Obedience in the face of suffering illumines the story and will of Jesus.

The politics of an independent body of believers proved impossible for many. Luther, despite his vision and passion for a confessing church, could not envision or see such church apart from its territory and institutional power. He hoped that gospel preaching and evangelical theology would move the church to much needed reform,[44] but Anabaptists believed that only congregational acting and obedient enacting could provide the call to renewal.[45] The understanding of community makes a great difference in the hope for the Kingdom's work.

Anabaptist churches sought to embody the words of Jesus as the highest and final revelation of God's intention. Their attitude toward the Old Testament was not a matter of disrespect but the consequence of eschatological obedience. They noted that Jesus resisted the temptation to become king. By contrast Zwingli, with the weight of the city fathers bearing upon him, proposed a static unity between the covenants that supported the identification of circumcision and infant baptism.[46]

In America, Roger Williams proposed spiritual typologies for reading the Old Testament inspired by the eschatological conviction that the church is God's final people. Without eschatological and christological imagination, John Cotten maintained that Old Testament offices were equivalent to contemporary ecclesiastical and political offices.[47]

Such controversies recommend the distinctive free church controls for typological reading. Such controls take the form of interrelated analogies that comprise the heart of Baptist spirituality, but conversion is a central analogy. Conversion is a beginning of fellowship. Yet something new has begun. Baptism marks the believer's passing from death to life, and conversion illumines that experience. In conversion the eschatological promise of regeneration is surprisingly realized. This realization strengthens our conviction that final transformation is a realistic hope. Our continued striving and dying to self hold promise because of our present union with Christ. In Christ, sacrificial service to the church yields fellowship. Life-giving ministry to the world yields mission. Through

Spirit and word Christ comforts, corrects, and counsels in personal communion.

Conversion is the experienced connection with the central Christian analogy, Christ. Jesus loves in word and deed. In obedience he pours out his life, but this is not the end. God's power is witnessed in the losing and finding of life through him. Christ continues to work and speak through his Spirit. His people bear witness to him in word and deed. His return will show that his work has finality. All God has done points to him. His image is seen in another analogy, his church. With eschatological confidence, his people seek to practice his word and work—kingdom ethics and mission. In mutual discipline they learn the obedience of Christ. They stand free of the world, resisting its power and direction as Jesus did. They discern his guidance in obedience to the communal reading of scripture.

Baptist spirituality has no enumerated formula. These analogies are part of a hermeneutical circle. By following Jesus in eschatological conversion and community the spiritual disciplines of prayer, fasting, Bible reading, meditation, worship, and service are undertaken with Baptist conviction.

Notes

[1]John H. Elliott, *A Home for the Homeless: A Sociological Exegesis of I Peter; Its Situation and Strategy* (Philadelphia: Fortress Press, 1981) 21-26.

[2]Ibid., 131. Though far from a sociologist, this line seems reasonable in light of Acts 17:6; 18:12-17; 19:28-40; and 1 Thess 2:13-14. See also Peter H. David, *James* (San Francisco: Harper & Row, 1983). Though not addressing this issue, David notes the socioeconomic context of the temptations the church was facing and the interfacing between the "rich" and the poor in the church, 31-36, 45.

[3]Elliot, 120-29.

[4]Beverly Gaventa, "Conversion" in *The Anchor Bible Encyclopedia*, 6 vols. (New York: Doubleday, 1992) 1:1131-33.

[5]Alan F. Segal, *Paul the Convert: The Apostolate and Apostasy of Saul the Pharisee* (New Haven: Yale University Press, 1990) 118.

[6]Luke Timothy Johnson, *The Acts of the Apostles*, Sacra Pagina Series, ed. Daniel J. Harrington (Collegeville MN: Michael Glazier Book, 1992) 16.

[7]Samuel Dill, *Roman Society: From Nero to Marcus Aurelius* (New York: Meridian Books, 1956) Book 3, chap. 2, esp. 335; and Charles Norris Cochrane, *Christianity and Classical Culture: A Study of Thought and Action from Augustus to Augustine* (New York: Oxford, 1940) 501-503.

[8]Segal. See also G. R. Beasley-Murray, *Baptism in the New Testament* (Grand Rapids MI: Eerdmans, 1962) 333.

[9]For Baptist rhetoric on the corporate and individual relationship see Beasley-Murray, Baptism, 314-29, 368-73; and Dale Moody, *Baptism: Foundation for Christian Unity* (Philadelphia: Westminster, 1967) 215-68.

[10]Krister Stendahl, "Biblical Theology, Contemporary," in *Interpreter's Dictionary of the Bible*, ed. George A. Buttrick, 4 vols. (Nashville: Abingdon, 1962) 1:418-32.

[11]Lewis Sperry Chafer, "Dispensationalism," *Bibliotheca Sacra* 93 (October 1936): 416-17; Chafer, *Major Bible Themes* (Philadelphia: Sunday School Times Company, 1926) 97-98; and Chafer, *Systematic Theology* (Dallas: Dallas Seminary Press, 1947-1948) 1:116.

[12]Charles Ryrie, *What You Should Know about Social Responsibility* (Chicago: Moody Press, 1982) 23-24.

[13]John H. Yoder, "The Hermeneutics of the Anabaptists" in *Essays on Biblical Interpretation: Anabaptist-Mennonite Perspectives*, ed. William M. Swartley, (Elkhart IN: Institute of Mennonite Studies, 1984) 1:18; Liberation theologian Gustavo Gutierrez laments the individualism and interiority of many spiritualities. He calls for a "spirituality of the laity" in *We Drink from Our Own Wells: The Spiritual Journey of a People*, trans. Matthew J. O'Connell (New York: Orbis Books, 1984) 13-14.

[14]Brevard S. Childs views the Broadman Commentary as an effort in historical criticism and free church theology, *Old Testament Books for Pastor and Teacher* (Philadelphia: Westminster, 1977) 32.

[15]Walter Wink offers this sort of assessment in, *The Bible in Human Transformation: Toward a New Paradigm for Biblical Study* (Philadelphia: Fortress Press, 1973) 16.

[16]Frances Young, "The Rhetorical Schools and their Influence on Patristic Exegesis," in *The Making of Orthodoxy: Essays in Honor of Henry Chadwick*, ed. Rowan Williams (New York: Cambridge University Press, 1989) 186, 192.

[17]For an excellent model see Stephen E. Foul and L. Gregory Jones, *Reading in Communion: Scripture and Ethics in Christian Life* (Grand Rapids MI: Eerdmans, 1991) 59-61. Their comments are influenced primarily by Nicholas Lash.

[18]Dallas Willard, *In Search of Guidance: Developing a Conversational Relationship with God* (Ventura CA: Regal Books, 1984) 34; and his *The Spirit of the Disciplines: Understanding How God Changes Lives* (San Francisco: Harper and Row, 1988) 258-65. Willard notes the personal reading required in spiritual transformation.

[19]Keith W. Clements, "A Baptist View," in *The Truth in Tradition: A Free Church Symposium*, ed. Rupert E. Davies (London: Epworth Press, 1992) 7.

[20]H. Leon McBeth narrates the story well, *The Baptist Heritage: Four Centuries of Baptist Witness* (Nashville: Broadman Press, 1987) 183-87. It may be significant that Carey is called an enthusiast. In other contexts the word suggests that God had directly spoken to one. This is the substance of John Cotten's charge against Anne Hutchinson. Edwin S. Gaustad, *Liberty of Conscience: Roger Williams in America* (Grand Rapids MI: Eerdmans, 1991) 41, 53-54.

[21]See H. Leon McBeth, *A Sourcebook for Baptist Heritage* (Nashville: Broadman Press, 1990) for Smyth's "Differences of the Churches of the Separation" (1608) 14-17.

[22]Rowan Williams, *The Wound of Knowledge: Christian Spirituality from the New Testament to St. John of the Cross* (Cambridge: Conley Publications, 1979/1990) 26.

[23]Walter Brueggemann, *The Creative Word: Canon as a Model for Biblical Education* (Philadelphia: Fortress Press, 1982) 21-24.

[24]Amos Wilder, *Early Christian Rhetoric: The Language of the Gospel* (Cambridge MA: Harvard University Press, 1971) 60.

[25]Carmel McCarthy and William Riley, *The Old Testament Short Story: Explorations into Narrative Spirituality* (Wilmington DE: Michael Glazier, 1986) 199-205.

[26]Form criticism is based upon the plausibility of such a scenario.

[27]E.g., Yandall Woodfin's conversionist reversal of the principle of analogy in *With All Your Mind: A Christian Philosophy of Religion* (Nashville: Abingdon Press, 1980) 72-73, 77-79.

[28]See Stanley M. Hauerwas, *Christian Existence Today: Essays on Church, World and Living in Between* (Durham NC: Labyrinth Press, 1988) 12, 21, who follows here Walter Brueggemann's call for sectarian hermeneutics. See also George Lindbeck's exhortation to "relearn the language of Zion" with Rowan Williams' notion of the missionary role of the church in Frederic Burnham's collection, *Postmodern Theology: Christian Faith in a Pluralist World* (San Francisco: Harper and Row, 1989) 55 and 104-105 respectively.

[29]George A. Lindbeck, *The Nature of Doctrine: Religion and Theology in a Postliberal Age* (Philadelphia: Westminster, 1984) 30-45. Garrett Green, *Imagining God: Theology and the Religious Imagination* (San Francisco: Harper & Row, 1989) 120-21, voices this concern with clarity.

[30]Herbert McCabe, *The Teaching of the Catholic Church: A New Catechism of Christian Doctrine* (Collegeville MN: Michael Glazier, 1991) 60. Kenneth Surin notes the devastating influence of individualism in *Theology and the Problem of Evil* (Oxford: Blackwell, 1986) 21.

[31]William H. Willimon, *What's Right with the Church* (San Francisco: Harper and Row, 1985) 65-66.

[32]H. E. Dana and L. M. Sipes, *A Manual of Ecclesiology* (Kansas City: Central Seminary Press, 1944) 282. E.g., the Anabaptist call for obedience and walking "in the resurrection of Jesus Christ." See Donald F. Durnbaugh's discussion of the Schleitheim articles in, *The Believer's Church: The History and Character of Radical Protestantism* (New York: Macmillan, 1968) 73.

[33]E. Y. Mullins, *The Christian Religion In Its Doctrinal Expression* (Valley Forge PA: Judson Press, 1917) 378, 409; W. T. Conner, *Christian Doctrine* (Nashville: Broadman, 1937) 218.

[34]Mullins, 409.

[35]Conner, 216, 217.

[36]Dana and Sipes, 201-202, 204.

[37]John D. Zizioulas, "The Early Christian Community," in *Christian Spirituality: Origins to the Twelfth Century*, ed. Bernard McGinn, John Meyendorff, and Jean Leclercq (New York: Crossroad, 1985) 35-36.

[38]Williams, 74-76.

[39]Nicholas Lash, *Easter in Ordinary: Reflections on Human Experience and the Knowledge of God* (Charlottesville VA: University Press of Virginia, 1986) 183.

[40]Ben Ollenburger, "The Hermeneutics of Obedience" in *Essays on Biblical Interpretation*, ed. William M. Swartley (Elkhart ID: Institute of Mennonite Studies, 1984) 49-50; and Yoder, "Hermeneutics," 23.

[41]Dana and Sipes, 226.

[42]Yoder, "The Hermeneutics of the Anabaptists," 15.

[43]Ibid., 18, 19.

[44]Durnbaugh, 4.

[45]Yoder, "The Hermeneutics of the Anabaptists," 16.

[46]Ibid., 26.

[47]Henning Graf Reventlow, *The Authority of the Bible and the Rise of the Modern World*, trans. John Bowden (Philadelphia: Fortress, 1985) 104-105 offers a complete bibliography. See also Gaustad, 84-85.

Horace Bushnell, Spiritual Formation, and Conversion

James E. Reed

The Man Horace Bushnell

Horace Bushnell, sometimes called "the Father of American Liberalism," was born on 14 April 1802, in Bantam, Connecticut. His father was a Methodist of Huguenot descent. His mother, also of Huguenot ancestry, was raised Episcopalian. Both parents rejected the total depravity of man and predestination.[1]

Bushnell characterized his mother as someone whose life was never excessive or inconsiderate. She lived virtuously and was a fine teacher and speaker. Above all, she never sought to coerce her children into religion.[2]

In later years Horace's brother described the Bushnell family as a household where religion was taken seriously. It was less an obligation than an atmosphere. From their father the children experienced fairness and consistency, and from their mother they knew unselfish and untiring devotion and, above all, love. Of Horace, his brother wrote, "If ever there was a child of Christian nurture, he was one—nurtured."[3]

In 1820 Horace professed faith in Jesus Christ and joined the New Preston Congregational Church where his parents had been members since his birth. In 1823 Bushnell entered Yale College and graduated in 1827. At Yale he first expressed doubts about religion based on emotion.

Between 1829 and 1831 Bushnell served as a tutor at Yale and studied law. Near the completion of his law studies, a large number of students at Yale experienced revival. In 1831 Bushnell made a new decision of conversion for Christ. This was expressed as "a simple and profound desire to be and do right, rather than to have a personal relationship with God."[4]

Horace Bushnell, even with his strong religious doubts, was a changed person. His daughter later recounted that despite the irregularity of his conversion from some theological viewpoints, there was no doubt that he was profoundly changed. "It was," she wrote, "a complete turning-about of the life."[5]

1833 was a very busy year in the life of Bushnell. In February he became pastor of the North Congregational Church in Hartford, Connecticut, where he served for twenty-six years (and the only church he served). Bushnell was ordained into the gospel ministry in May, and Mary Apthorp of New Haven became his wife in September.

Horace and Mary became the parents of five children, but in 1837 an infant daughter died, and in 1842 their only son died at the age of four. Concerning the latter event Bushnell said: "I have learned more of experimental religion since my little boy died than in all my life before."[6]

In 1859, due to declining health, Bushnell retired as pastor. From that time until his death on 17 February 1876, he was active in publishing books, pamphlets, and sermons. His life was one with many turning points and crises, yet it also was a life formed with many constants. These constants are evident in his theory of spiritual formation.

The Spirituality of Christian Nurture

In 1979 a distinguished group of sixteen Protestant, Catholic, and Jewish scholars in the field of religious education were asked to identify the three or four most important books ever written in the discipline. The book most often listed was *Christian Nurture.*[7]

The genesis of the book appeared in an 1836 article entitled "Revivals of Religion." Ten years later the first publication of *Christian Nurture* was presented to the public. Various changes were made in the contents of the book until the final edition was printed in 1861.[8] Thus Bushnell followed his own advice as he wrote concerning "The Solving of Doubts" that we should allow doubts their place and time:

> Never be in a hurry to believe, never try to conquer doubts against time. Time is one of the grand elements in thought as truly as in motion. If you cannot open a doubt today, keep it till tomorrow; do not be afraid to keep it for whole years. One of the greatest talents in religious discovery is the finding how to hang up questions and let them hang without being at all anxious about them. Turn a free glance on them now and then as they hang, move freely about them, and see them, first on one side, and then on another, and by and by when you turn some corner of thought, you will be delighted

> and astonished to see how quietly and easily they open their secret and let you in![9]

Bushnell's own experience confirmed that the truth often unfolds before us in the processes of life rather than in dramatic moments. This also held true in his understanding of spiritual development. The first part of *Christian Nurture* concerns the doctrine that "the child is to grow up a Christian, and never know himself as being otherwise."[10] Part two explains the mode or implementation of the doctrine.

The Process of Christian Nurture

Bushnell attempted to clarify what he meant by the child growing up always Christian by distinguishing it from the conversionist idea that a child grows up into sin and has to be converted after he comes to maturity. Rather, the child

> is to open on the world as one that is spiritually renewed, not remembering the time when he went through a technical experience, but seeming rather to have loved what is good from his earliest years.[11]

Bushnell suggested that the primary medium by which the grace of God can be transmitted is through the Christian family. He rejected the conservative theology and sensationalism of revivalism. He especially disliked its teaching of the total depravity of humanity and its disdain for nurture, a concept Bushnell called "ostrich nurture." He proposed instead a Christian family environment, infant or household baptism, and the "organic unity of the family."[12]

Bushnell understood Christian education as radically different from other forms of education. While other forms of education pointed the child toward future conversion, Christian education—namely Christian nurture—constituted "process" or "forming" conversion. Bushnell thus opposed the concept of "instant conversion" but understood conversion as a growth process begun in a Christian environment from infancy and articulated at home and church by example.[13]

Bushnell did not offer his theory of Christian nurture as a mechanical formula for reaching sinless perfection, nor did he not say that parental perfection is required for adequate Christian nurture. He did encourage parents to be living examples and to speak to their children on occasions about personal faults and weak points. Developing these thoughts,

Bushnell explained that growth in Christian virtue is not automatic. It requires that we struggle with evil, a fall, and rescue. We must experience God's help in redemption and learn experientially the bitterness of evil and the value of good. To see nurture as automatic is as mistaken as a hereditary view of sin:

> For it is not sin that he derives from his parents; at least, not sin in any sense that imports blame, but only some prejudice to the perfect harmony of this mould, some kind of pravity or obliquity that inclines him to evil. These suggestions are offered, not as necessary to be received in every particular, but simply to shew that the scheme of education proposed is not to be identified with another, which assumes the radical goodness of human nature, and according to which, if it be true, Christian education is insignificant.[14]

Revivalism as Ostrich Nurture

American revivalism in the 1800s varied in substance and style. It shared little common theology and few common methods among spiritual expressions. Sudden conversion, individualism, adult conversion, and the pioneer spirit in many ways characterized revivalism. To a large degree sensationalism and emotionalism prevailed.[15]

As stated previously, Bushnell professed faith in Christ during the Yale Revival. In the early years of his ministry at North Church he led revival meetings and urged persons of his congregation to profess Jesus Christ as their savior. The church did not have numbers of converts, nor did it experience in a spiritual way any tangible revival of religion. Due to Bushnell's unsuccessful attempts to lead North Church in revival, he confessed that "the most disheartening impediment to the Christian minister . . . is the thought that religion depends only on revivals."[16]

In 1836, calling revivalism an "artificial firework"[17] and "the machinery system,"[18] Bushnell turned to the idea of Christian nurture. Aimed primarily at his Baptist brethren, he criticized revivalism as a cruel abuse, especially as it was perpetrated upon innocent children. It employed pious language and pretexts, which made it all the more deplorable. Instead of achieving the goods that religion should bring, revivalism "looks to campaigns of force that really dispense with holiness," resulting in the loss of all that is best in Christian nurture.[19]

In another criticism of revivals, Bushnell likened the theology of conversion to the ostrich, a symbol of what he called "unmotherhood."

The ostrich, he said, hatches her eggs without warmth, dropping them on the sand, and her young are hatched and go forth only to be tended by nature: "She is both heartless and senseless; too heartless to care for her young, and too senseless to maintain a motherhood as genial even as that of the sand."[20]

Infant Baptism and the Baptists

Baptists have historically, biblically, and theologically rejected the doctrine of infant baptism. Since their origin as a denomination, Baptist leaders have preached that baptism is for believers only. This means that because all persons are sinners, they must repent of their sins and be baptized (Acts 2:38). This individualistic understanding held by Baptist preachers and other conservative theologians of the nineteenth century represented rigid criticism of Bushnell's liberal view of Christian nurture.

In retaliation to the Baptists' quoting the Bible in matters opposing infant baptism, Bushnell also presented biblical support for his position. He cited as examples Paul's baptism of the household of Stephanas (1 Cor.1:16) and of the Philippian jailer's family (Acts 16:31-33). Moreover, he argued that the baptism of infants was a long-standing practice, even during the time of Christ. He also cited Augustine who wrote that infant baptism was not a creation of councils, but "was ever in use."[21]

Bushnell's belief in infant baptism led to infant church membership. He defended both practices by writing that membership in the church is not dependent on what persons can understand or believe, but on the covenant promise and the force of nurture within which they grow up—a force of futurition by which they are to grow up, imperceptibly, into "faithfuls among faithfuls"—in Christ Jesus.[22] If that were not plain enough, he also argued that "in the matter of infant baptism and infant church membership . . . a believing parentage sanctifies the offspring."[23]

The Organic Unity of the Family

This doctrine, more than any other, cohesively bonded Bushnell's expressions of Christian nurture. Infant baptism contributed in large part to Christian nurture, especially from the Christian fellowship of the church. Bushnell found both biblical and historical evidence that supported his theological view about the organic unity of the family.[24]

Bushnell found historical evidence that also suggested that his theological view about the organic unity of the family was not new. He quoted Justin Martyr, who wrote that some "were made disciples to Christ in their childhood," and Ireneus, who wrote of infant baptism that

> Christ came to save all persons through himself; all, I say, who through him are regenerated unto God: infants and little ones, and children and youth, and the aged.[25]

The Moravian Brethren also represent those whose system is distinguished by their emphasis on Christian education. The Moravians, Bushnell said, fully expected through conscientious nurture, that their children would grow up to be Christian. Accordingly it is affirmed that not one in ten of the members of that church recollects any time when he began to be religious.[26]

In organic families one generation is the natural offspring of another. Bushnell's intent was the restoration of the organic family. He believed that "worship is family worship; the god of one is the god of all; the spirit of one, the spirit of all."[27] Bushnell suggested that a "law of connexion" that exerted power over the infant exists from birth.[28]

With no capacity of will, the child forms impressions from his surroundings. As nurture forms character, the child grows in the likeness of his/her parents, especially the mother.[29] The spirit of the house is literally breathed into the child daily. The impressions and moods of that home then become the seeds of the character in the child. The child sees the world through his/her parents' eyes, molded and shaped by them. "He lives and moves and has his being in them."[30] Bushnell concluded his description of the organic unity of the family by comparing parental character to a stream that flows down upon the children hourly.[31]

Modeling In Christian Nurture

The organic unity of the family is the heart of parental modeling. Bushnell's theory of nurture requires Christian parents to provide a living example. As life begins, the child is but "a mere passive lump in the arms, and he opens into conscious life under the soul of the parent streaming into his eyes and ears, through the manners and tone of the nursery."[32] Parental duties in Bushnell's theory build on the premise that like begets like. It is less the parent's inner intention for the child so much as the parent's being that has the greatest effect. In summary, Bushnell's overarching theme is that the life of the parents flows into the life of the child.[33]

Bushnell did not use the term "modeling," but he surely would agree with its meaning in his development of Christian nurture. If the parent is imitating Christ, the child will naturally learn and model his\her life after the parents who model their lives after Christ. The basic proposition of *Christian Nurture* "that the child is to grow up a Christian, and never know himself as being otherwise" *is* modeling.

According to Bushnell, a living example is the best way to teach. Bushnell wrote that "examples are the only sufficient commentaries; living epistles the only fit expounders of written epistles."[34] The prayers of a Christian parent enter into the life of a child, and in this embodiment the parental calling is fulfilled.

Parental Qualifications

While Bushnell magnified the importance of positive parenting, he argued that preparation is necessary. He observed that military officers, school teachers, magistrates, tailors, and other workers usually serve an apprenticeship to qualify for their calling. He lamented the fact that too many parents

> undertake their most sacred office without any sacred qualifications, govern without self-government, discharge the holiest responsibilities irresponsibly, and thrust their children into evil by the evil and bad mind out of which their training proceeds.[35]

For Bushnell, the person who provides the key to salvation for the child is the mother. The impressions given by the godly mother strictly enforces the idea that parents teach religion not by doctrine but by the reality of their lives. Without question in Bushnell's thought and personal life, the love of the mother reveals the love of Christ. He asked, "How often has the profligate son, in the very midst of his dissipation and sin, been led to reflect and repent by a recollection of a mother's prayers and tears!"[36]

Parental Discouragement of Piety

Even though Bushnell stressed parental qualifications, he was painfully aware that not all parents are Christian. He described the parental characteristics that discouraged piety in children. Bushnell warned against a father's injustice and a mother's impatience. He praised the innate God-hunger and impulses to goodness in a child's soul.[37] He warned against the impact of prohibition. When there is too much "thou shalt not do this, nor this, nor this, till, in fact, there is really nothing left to be done."[38] He advised parents to forbid a minimum of things but to soundly enforce the forbidden things.

According to Bushnell, parental fault-finding and being hard to please too often relate to trivial matters. His counter suggestion was for the parent to seek ways to praise children. Also, hard feelings and displeasure should be resolved as soon as possible. Holding resentments and grudges create pain in relationships. Punishment should be dispensed with much thought and gentleness of voice by the parent.[39]

Parents can discourage their children with hasty and false accusations. Therefore, Bushnell encouraged wise parents to be careful of assigning blame, "lest he may discourage fatally all pious or ingenuous aspirations by them . . . harsh justice, exaggerated justice, is injustice."[40] He warned parents not to discipline children by withholding admission to the Lord's table or church membership. His advice was to remember the age appropriateness of children. Parents too often view children as liabilities, limits to their freedom, or obstructions to self-indulgence. Worse, some parents are not fond of their children and do not consider them worth the cost.[41]

Bushnell was equally repelled by "Christian vices." He deplored sanctimony, "a saintly or over-saintly air and manner."[42] Another such vice was bigotry. He judged that "no class of children . . . turn out worse, in general, than the children of Christian bigots."[43] Bushnell viewed Christian fanaticism as disastrous, particularly in its impact on children's characters.

Bushnell termed judging and condemning as censorious habits. These people were "a large class of disciples who think it a kind of duty, and a just acknowledgement of the fact of human depravity, to be seeing always dark things."[44] This kind of behavior negatively influences confidence and esteem in children. Confident parents help to create faith in children, not despair.

Bushnell devoted over one hundred pages to practical matters of the faith process in *Christian Nurture.* Several of these have already been discussed. Four other practices designed by Bushnell to aid the process of Christian nurture are physical nurture, play, family government, and family worship.

Physical Nurture

In the theory of Christian nurture, providing and feeding food to children is an important activity for parents. Caring for physical needs bear fruit in spiritual development and nurture. Citing the story of Daniel and his friends who ate basic foods (Dan 1:8-21), Bushnell advised great care to parents in the feeding of their children. He claimed that improper diet can have adverse effects on children and that "nine-tenths of the intemperate drinking begins, not in grief and destitution, as we so often hear, but in vicious feeding."[45]

Bushnell recommended several other practices about feeding. He discouraged use of the pacifier to stop an infant from crying. He opposed too many sweet and fancy foods. Occasional enjoyment may be permitted but not a "perpetual holiday."[46] He did not consider coffee for children as good physical care. Bushnell favored regulated meal times, and he discouraged snacks.

Good manners, he claimed, promotes self-government. While animals have no manners, a child's positive manners display good religious training. Giving a Christian blessing of thanks at the dining table acknowledges gratitude for God's goodness and promoted spiritual dignity. Bushnell praised personal neatness and dress as another form of physical nurture. Parents should not overdress or "doll up" children simply to satisfy the pride of the parents. Rather, Bushnell said to:

> Dress your child for Christ, if you will have him a Christian; bring everything, in the training even of his body, to this one final aim, and it will be strange if the Christian body you give him does not contain a Christian soul.[47]

Play

One chapter in *Christian Nurture* is entitled "Plays and Pastimes, Holidays and Sundays." Bushnell also wrote a book on *Work and Play,* which deals in detail with theories introduced in *Christian Nurture*. Bushnell conceived the play of children as the symbol and interpreter of Christian liberty. The motive of child's play is more play. Free motion, happiness, and joy of children are some of the first duties of Christian parenting. Parents were to provide playthings and invite the child's friends to play.

Another principle of play in Bushnell's thought involved birthdays and holidays. He encouraged parents to place special emphasis on the birthdays of children, helping to develop a higher self-esteem in children. Bushnell thought state and school holidays should be special pleasures for children. Religious festivals, like Thanksgiving and Christmas, offer parents a chance to educate their children about God's goodness in a spirit of joy and celebration.

Bushnell did not think that children, especially young children, should be on public streets at night. To him, when play is not possible outside, one of the mother's duties is to attract children to cheerful activities in the home. Bushnell suggested reading books, playing games, art, and other activities. Play is natural and approved by God. Bushnell stressed that the children should be creative and invent their own kind of play.[48] Restrictions at church, home, and school are necessary because play is an important aspect of life but not the whole of it. Play on Sunday should be permitted with restriction, and playthings on Sunday should demonstrate religious thought and action. Reading books, drawing pictures, viewing maps, singing hymns, and other religious activities are proper. Bushnell considered music as educational, worshipful, and a form of play, perhaps remembering that his own mother taught him at an early age to play the organ.[49]

Family Government

Bushnell compared family government as productive as preaching in the conversion process. He said that "When a child is brought to do any one thing from a truly right motive, and in a genuinely right spirit, there is implied in that kind of obedience the acceptance of all best and holiest principle."[50] He cited Paul in 1 Timothy 3:4 as support for this position. The authority of a father, however, is from God and genuine only as long as it agrees with God's purposes. Family discipline, rightly administered, contributes to an obedient, pious child.

He warned parents not to oppress a child by means of authority. He believed that discipline is best accomplished in private between parent and child because this spares the child's self-respect. Punishment should never be done out of impatience or passion or without feeling.[51] Nor should a parent convey a spirit of mistrust toward a child:

> Nothing wounds a child more than to see he is not trusted. Under such an impression, he will soon become as unworthy of trust as he has been taken to be. On the other hand, he will naturally want to be worthy of the trust he receives.[52]

Family Worship

Bushnell regarded Bible reading, devotional reading, drill, and repetition as usually positive for children. However, he considered family prayers to be more significant. The context of the prayer is an important consideration. Bushnell upheld the value of prayer principles lived out as an example before children. With this concept of modeling in mind, Bushnell said that "the great difficulty in faith, after all, is to be faithful."[53] Bushnell illustrated this difficulty by saying that God will not honor the prayer of the man who prays for holiness and gets off his knees to defraud his neighbor.

Bushnell proposed that parents remind their children of the positive contributions of their biological and spiritual ancestors. This process demonstrated his concept of faith from generation to generation. Mothers, especially, should lead their children into the practice of prayer. In discussing family prayers, Bushnell noted two contrary types of modeling. The first example is one of inconsistency between a parent's prayers for children at home and the way matters in the household are conducted. Such inconsistency "pulls exactly contrary to the pull of his prayers, and to all their common teaching in religion."[54]

By contrast, he described the impact of a consistent example of parents before their children:

> See that you plan to be, in your undertakings, just what you pray to be in your prayers. Set the general concert of your affairs in God's own order, to accomplish only what is agreeable to His will, so to be always praying with you, and the prophet's rich valley, teeming with all fruits of abundance and luxury, will but feebly represent the unfailing, never blighted, always fruitful, piety of your children.[55]

Bushnell's Christian Nurture in Reflection

The goal of Christian nurture is "that the child is to grow up a Christian, and never know himself as being otherwise." Compared to Baptists and other evangelical ministers of his day, Bushnell was a liberal theologian. This characterization is understandable. Bushnell's critics, according to him, propagated a religion that "men are to grow up in evil, and be dragged into the church of God by conquest."[56] He considered his conservative contemporaries as proponents of "ostrich nurture." This was based on their belief in the total depravity of man that required instant conversion found only in the spirit of revivalism for an individual to meet God, a notion he believed contradicted our usual experience.

Bushnell also rejected the corollary doctrine of an individualistic approach to God. Calling such theology too mechanical, he proposed Christian nurture as conversion by a growth process. The child's organic family nurtures him to God. Bushnell wrote that "a believing parentage sanctifies the offspring."[57] He believed that the child who is guided by nurturing parents will learn to follow God's ways by natural development. Bushnell's critics disagreed completely.

Christian Nurture served as a theological divide with the extreme individualism of old Puritanism. The modeling process by parents has served to place a heavier emphasis on the home. Bushnell was far ahead of his time in advocating a religious relationship that is psychologically positive for the child. Excessive emotionalism is not a contributing factor in a child's development.

Bushnell's educational philosophy was saturated with experimental and naturalistic thought. He believed that proper education can solve the problems of humanity, even its religious problems. This, of course, is less the case than Bushnell had hoped, but education has provided assistance and hope for a large number of people. Bushnell also claimed that morally good parents nearly always produce like children. Although this seems at points extremely idealistic and often not the case, parents would be hard pressed to find a more positive direction to guide their children than Bushnell's proposals.

Bushnell stresses the simultaneous development of the intellectual and experimental dimensions of human personality. Certainly his theory and practice of Christian nurture addresses the biological, cultural, and ethical levels of the foundations of spiritual piety that are implicit in the Baptist educational theory and practice of Sunday School. Baptist educator Temp Sparkman expresses a positive evaluation of Bushnell's theory of nurture for Baptists:

> What Bushnell was teaching is that God can work in a supernatural way through the organic unity of the family so that the child will grow up knowing the Christian way and choosing it over the sinful way. There is no conceivable way that education can be termed Christian education unless it is ordered along this central process; it is, otherwise, to be termed un-Christian education, for it educates the child to the belief that one must grow up in sin and then turn from that sin at a mature age, then, but not before, to be called a Christian.[58]

Bushnell did not propose that the importance of religion in the family become a substitute for the work of the church. Conversely he advocated the necessity of the Christian family to nurture God's goodness and grace as an indwelling of the child. This parental nurturing process provides the appropriate model for the child to grow toward maturity in the nurturing church community.

Some have incorrectly argued that Bushnell did not believe in conversion. Bushnell's own life invalidates this argument. He would, however, dispute the revivalist concept of "ostrich nurture" and its implications for Christian nurture. He dismissed these tactics as serving the needs of the child in negative ways. Bushnell called on Christians both in the home and in the church to consider themselves a most important part of the perpetual Christian nurturing family.

He did not deny the supernatural acts of God in conversion under circumstances that disagreed with his proposition; he simply refused to make them normative. Instead, he seriously recognized the uniqueness of the spiritual development of each child in God's creation. Whereas revivalism stressed conversion, Christian nurture connected and elevated the responsibilities of parents. In considering parents as living examples of Christ to their children, especially during the formative years, Bushnell has reminded the Christian community that neither Christian conversion nor serious parenting is best accomplished within the limitations of individualism.

Notes

[1]See Randolph C. Miller, *Education for Christian Living* (Englewood Cliffs NJ: Prentice-Hall, Inc., 1956) ix; Conrad Cherry, *Horace Bushnell* (New York: Paulist Press, 1985); James O. Duke, *Horace Bushnell on the Vitality of Biblical Language* (Chico CA: Scholars Press, 1984) 1; Barbara M. Cross, *Horace Bushnell: Minister to a Changing America* (Chicago: University of Chicago Press, 1958) 1; William R. Adamson, *Bushnell Rediscovered* (Philadelphia: United Church Press, 1966) 53.

[2]Miller, 9.

[3]Ibid., 7-8

[4]Ibid., 19. John Calvin understood this as the action of the Holy Spirit on us, even if we do not realize it. To him this "instilled a desire for righteousness."

[5]Mary B. Cheney, *Life and Letters of Horace Bushnell* (New York: Charles Scribner's Sons, 1903) 59.

[6]Ibid., 105.

[7]C. F. Melchert, "What Should I Read," *Religious Education* 74 (July-August 1979): 442.

[8]Theodore T. Munger, *Horace Bushnell, Preacher and Theologian* (New York: Houghton Mifflin Co., 1899) 67.

[9]Horace Bushnell, *Sermons on Living Subjects* (London: Gilbert and Rivington Printers, 1872) 182.

[10]Horace Bushnell, *Christian Nurture* (New York: Charles Scribner and Co., 1861) 4. Hereafter, references to *Christian Nurture* will be abbreviated *CN*.

[11]Ibid.

[12]Ibid., 40, 56.

[13]Ibid., 8-10, 142.

[14]Ibid., 12.

[15]David L. Smith, *Symbolism and Growth: The Religious Thought of Horace Bushnell* (Chico CA: Scholars Press, 1981) 66-68.

[16]William A. Johnson, *Nature and the Supernatural in the Theology of Horace Bushnell* (Lund: CWK Gleerup, 1963) 108-109.

[17]Ibid.

[18]Cheney, 81.

[19]*CN*, 49.

[20]Ibid., 40.

[21]Ibid., 24, 96, 102.

[22]Ibid., 106.

[23]Ibid., 127.

[24]Scriptural passages such as Eph 6:4; Lam 4:3; Jer 7:18; Acts 2:39; 1 Cor 1:16; Col 1:2, 3:21; Mal 2:15; 2 Tim 1:5, 3:14; Gen 18:19; Prov 30:8-9; 1 Tim 3:4; Zech 8:5; and Hos 2:21-22 united his family theme.

[25]*CN*, 127.
[26]Ibid., 14.
[27]Ibid., 56.
[28]Ibid.,62.
[29]Cross, 67.
[30]*CN*, 62-67.
[31]Ibid., 74.
[32]Cross, 76.
[33]Perry G. Downs, "Christian Nurture: A Comparative Analysis of the Theories of Horace Bushnell and Lawrence O. Richards" (Ph.D. dissertation, New York University, 1982) 101. See also Horace Bushnell, *Views of Christian Nurture and Subjects Adjacent Thereto* (Hartford CT: E. Hunt, 1849) 6.
[34]*CN*, 241.
[35]Ibid., 164-65.
[36]Cross, 58.
[37]*CN*, 192.
[38]Ibid., 193.
[39]Ibid., 192-96.
[40]Ibid., 196.
[41]Ibid., 167, 198-201.
[42]Ibid., 170.
[43]Ibid., 171.
[44]Ibid., 172.
[45]Ibid., 179.
[46]Ibid. 182.
[47]Ibid., 190.
[48]Ibid., 224-25.
[49]Cheney, 31.
[50]*CN*, 207.
[51]Ibid., 216.
[52]Ibid., 216-17.
[53]Ibid., 252.
[54]Ibid., 259.
[55]Ibid., 264.
[56]Ibid., 21.
[57]Ibid., 127.
[58]G. Temp Sparkman, *The Salvation and Nurture of the Child of God* (Valley Forge PA: Judson Press, 1983) 190.

The Contemplative Tie: The Fellowship of Kindred Minds

On the twenty-fourth Sunday after Pentecost, the pilgrim sat in worship and heard the reading from the New Testament to "pray constantly" (1 Thess 5:17). He began to ask himself the meaning of this admonition. How can one pray constantly? He first sought to find an answer from the preachers in various churches. He heard many sermons on the necessity of prayer and the fruits of prayer, but no one explained the way to succeed in prayer.

One day the pilgrim came upon a devout and wise man, of whom he asked the meaning of praying continuously. The man answered that "prayer itself will reveal this mystery to you," but he added, "it takes time." Later the pilgrim stopped at a monastery and asked the Superior the same question. The Father read from a book that explained that unceasing prayer is contemplative whereby "the mind is constantly fixed on God and communion with Him." Again the pilgrim was told that in prayer itself, God would reveal the mystery to him.

Finally, the pilgrim came upon a monk to whom he turned for spiritual direction. The monk praised the pilgrim's desire to understand ceaseless mental prayer. Then the monk took the pilgrim to his cell, where he opened a book that described the Jesus Prayer as a way to succeed in contemplation. The words of the prayer were simple: "Lord Jesus Christ, have mercy on me!"

After that experience, the pilgrim began to study about this prayer in a book called the *Philokalia* and to practice the prayer every day—first six thousand times, then twelve thousand times. After several months of this exercise, the pilgrim found that his only waking desire was to pray, and even his sleeping thoughts were of prayer. Thus, prayer became for the pilgrim like the beat of his heart and the rhythm of his breath.[1] In the subsequent course of his journey of contemplation and worship, the pilgrim found spiritual communion with other like-minded Christians. To some he became a spiritual director; from others he received spiritual direction.

The anonymous author of *The Way of a Pilgrim* does not just represent a classic example of nineteenth-century Russian spirituality. He draws from the ancient Christian tradition of contemplation. The contemplative way seeks the will of God through "the renewal of the mind" (Rom 12:2) and within "the fellowship of kindred minds." To conceive of the binding tie of the Spirit through contemplative prayer is to understand Christian life and community in terms of loving devotion to God. It is "the way of the heart."[2] William Law, an eighteenth-century English Puritan writer, described the devout Christian as one who

> lives no longer to his own will, or the way and spirit of the world, but to the sole will of God, who considers God in everything, who serves God in everything, who makes all the parts of his common life, parts of piety, by doing everything in the name of God, and under such rules as are conformable to His glory.[3]

Whereas the focus of evangelical piety is *spiritual transformation of the self* through conversion, baptism, and discipleship, the concern of contemplative spirituality is *spiritual formation of the self* through prayer, meditation, and reflection. The contemplative journey is thus normally pursued under the guidance and with the help of a spiritual director. It also is typically accompanied by active participation in communal worship (often daily). The vision of contemplative prayer in Eastern Christianity is enshrined in the *Philokalia*, as the convictions of the Western contemplative tradition are set forth in the *Rule* of St. Benedict.

How have Baptists been influenced by the contemplative tradition, and can they draw from contemporary contemplative spirituality while remaining truly Baptist? The essays of this section attempt to address these questions.

Glenn Hinson displays some of the contemplative roots of Baptist spirituality. He demonstrates a striking concordance between John Bunyan (the Puritan-Baptist tradition) and early monasticism (the Catholic-contemplative tradition). Curtis Freeman attempts to articulate a confession for catholic baptists that provides a theological basis to explore the heights and depths of spirituality within the heritage of the whole church. Tom Turner suggests how Baptists might incorporate the Catholic practice of spiritual direction into the Baptist tradition. Loyd Allen discusses the role of the community in discernment, a particularly relevant question for these highly politicized times. How do we find the will of God, and more importantly, how do we find it *together*? Finally, Gary Furr compares two different Baptist visions of the life of prayer and their concept of how God works in the crisis of faith.

In these days when contemplative spirituality is drawing even secular agnostics to retreat centers to meditate, Baptists would do well to ponder what draws people into silence. What hunger in them is suppressed or ignored by the churches? Are these hungers genuine doorways into the Spirit? How can they help us? What insights do *we* as Baptists bring to the contemplative life?

Notes

[1]*The Way of a Pilgrim,* trans. Helen Bacovcin (New York: Image Books, 1978/1992) 13-25.

[2]This is Henry Nouwen's phrase to describe the spirituality of the Desert Fathers and Mothers, *The Way of the Heart* (New York: Ballantine Books, 1981).

[3]William Law, *A Serious Call to a Devout and Holy Life* (reprint, Grand Rapids MI: William B. Eerdmans, 1966) 1.

The Contemplative Roots of Baptist Spirituality

E. Glenn Hinson

The title of this essay may appear to be a contradiction, for no two religious traditions would seem to stand farther apart than the Baptist and the contemplative or monastic. Baptists are activist Marthas; monks are contemplative Marys. Baptists are in the world (and often *of* it); monks seek nothing more zealously than separation from the world. Baptists do not hesitate to pursue wealth; monks devote themselves to poverty. Baptists beget children; monks are celibate.

I could add other contrasts to make my comparison seem all the more ludicrous. Before you dismiss my idea as an absurdity, however, let me register my chief point. The point I want to make is that Baptists, one of numerous offshoots of English Puritanism, fall into line with the contemplative tradition in their concern for prayer. Like the monks of ages past, they have had an intense concern for "conversion of life and manners" and have regarded prayer as the means to it. They have differed from the monks in the fact that they have made no distinction between religious and secular vocations. Like their Puritan forbears, they have wanted everybody to be a saint.

I have selected John Bunyan to express this idea for several reasons. One reason for this selection is his prominence and early influence as a shaper of the Puritan-Baptist tradition. A second reason is the amount of attention he gave to prayer in the work *I Will Pray with the Spirit*, composed about 1662 or 1663. A third reason is his depth of experience; his treatise on prayer is replete with personal allusions.

Discordances

Before looking at the concordances between Bunyan and the early contemplative tradition, we should take note of some of the discordances. One obvious difference is time and circumstances. Bunyan lived a millennium or more after the desert fathers and mothers, Cassian and Benedict, with whom I wish to compare him. Nevertheless, we must not make too much of this time gap.

Both Bunyan and the monks lived in traumatic times. Bunyan lived during the English Civil War, the beheading of Charles I, the turbulent Commonwealth years, and the Restoration. He spent twelve and a half years in prison for refusal to stop preaching. In the process he had to leave four small children to the care of his eighteen year old second wife and the charity of friends. One of the children was a nine year old blind daughter who, he confessed, "lay nearer my heart than all I had beside."[1] Cassian and Benedict witnessed the collapse of the western Roman Empire and the so-called "barbarian invasions." Like Bunyan, they tasted evil as a mighty force and battled it with holiness of life. In this one respect, at least, widely separated times did not distinguish them greatly from one another.

A second difference has to do with the monastic vocation itself. Bunyan would not have thought he had much in common with monks. The Protestant Reformers had few kind words for monasticism or for monks. In Protestant lands reformers, partly for religious and partly for sociological reasons, slammed monastery doors shut. Henry VIII closed the monasteries in England in 1539. Bunyan would have known them mostly as ruins a century later.

Again, however, it is appropriate to enter a qualifier. The fact that Bunyan was not conscious of any connection with the contemplative tradition does not assure of necessity that he owed no debt to it. Puritanism had much in common with the monastic stream of the Middle Ages. Like the monks, Puritans—Bunyan foremost among them—were zealous for holiness of life, both individual and corporate. The word "sincerity" turns up again and again in both Puritan and monastic sources. In *The Pilgrim's Progress,* Faithful put a finger on the Puritan central concern when he explained to Talkative that one could discover "a work of grace on the soul"

> (1) By an experimental confession of his faith in Christ. (2) By a life answerable to that confession; to wit, a life of holiness, heart-holiness: family-holiness, (if he hath a family,) and by conversation holiness in the world; which in the general teacheth him inwardly to abhor his sin, and himself for that in secret; to suppress it in his family, and to promote holiness in the world: not by talk only, as an hypocrite or talkative person may do, but by a practical subjection in faith and love to the power of the word.[2]

In these words we are not far from the goal of the monks set out by Cassian of Marseilles. "The ultimate goal of our way of life," said Abba Moses, "is . . . the kingdom of God, or kingdom of heaven. The immediate aim is purity of heart. For without purity of heart none can enter into that kingdom."[3] Solitude, watches, manual labor, nakedness, reading, and other disciplines—all are "subordinate means to your chief aim which is purity of heart, or charity, and we ought never to allow them to take precedence over charity."[4]

I will say more about the conjunction of the Puritan and contemplative traditions in prayer later. Presently I note a third difference, namely, in theological foundation. Bunyan drew his theology largely from John Calvin. He owed a lesser debt to Luther, especially for explanation of some of the experiential aspects of faith. Both Reformers would set him some distance from the early monks, for they placed extreme emphasis upon grace and negated monasticism, among other things, on the grounds that it implied salvation by works rather than by faith.

Once more I would enter some qualifying statements. However much Calvin or Luther may have shaped the outlines of Bunyan's theology, Bunyan was not a trained theologian and did not go about the task of theological reflection like the Reformers did. Quite the contrary, like the early monks, he brought experience heavily to bear on his reflections, as his discussion of prayer reveals clearly. As far as theological method is concerned, both of these were nearer the contemplative than the scholastic traditions, a fact that exerted a major impact on what they did.

A fourth difference is the strongly voluntarist character of the Baptist tradition as compared with the more intentionalist character of the contemplative. Bunyan, writing about two years after he first went to prison on refusal to halt unlicensed preaching, directed his treatise on prayer against enforced conformity to the Book of Common Prayer. Christians, he argued, should avoid set forms of prayer. He would not allow use even of the Lord's Prayer or the Our Father as a model. Christ will teach us directly "by his Word and Spirit" and not through repetition of any form. Children should be taught "to know their wretched state and condition." They should hear about "hell fire, and their sins, of damnation, and salvation: the way to escape the one, and to enjoy the other."[5] By way of contrast the monks recited the Psalms, the Lord's Prayer, and several formulas. They counted the Lord's Prayer "the very pattern of a perfect prayer."[6] Abba Isaac, Cassian's chief teacher about prayer among the desert fathers and mothers, prescribed repetition of Psalm 70:1 as a formula for continuous meditation: "O God, make speed to save me. O

Lord, make haste to help me." This same formula appears also in the *Rule* of Benedict.[7]

Concordances

This will be a good place to turn from discordances to concordances, for alongside the formal aspects of monastic prayer stands an affective approach to prayer that comes amazingly close to Bunyan's. One could accurately say that we are dealing in both cases with *prayer of the heart*. In its essence, prayer was viewed by both Bunyan and the monks as an affair of the heart. I will seek to establish this point by comparing Bunyan's definition of prayer, which he elaborated on at some length, with some definitions given by the desert monks, Cassian, and Benedict. In this process, similarities in the method of praying employed by Bunyan and the early monks should become transparent as well. Bunyan defined prayer as

> a sincere, sensible, affectionate pouring out of the heart or soul to God through Christ, in the strength and assistance of the Holy Spirit, for such things as God hath promised, or, according to the Word, for the good of the Church, with submission, in Faith, to the will of God.[8]

He elaborated on this definition in seven points. Only five of these, however, supply direct analogies and merit explicit treatment.

(1) The first quality of prayer, Bunyan contended, must be "sincerity." Sincerity is the sine qua non for prayer, "without which God looks not upon it as prayer in a good sense."[9] It is essential in that it "carries the soul in all simplicity to open its heart to God, and to tell him the case plainly without equivocation; to condemn itself plainly without dissembling; to cry to God heartily without complementing."[10]

The aim of the monks was, in fulfillment of the Apostle Paul's words, to "pray without ceasing" (1 Thess 5:17). The way to achieve it, they thought, is through purity of heart. "No one can offer prayer of a proper intensity and sincerity," Abba Isaac warned, without personal purity. "Therefore, before we begin to pray, we ought to be trying to be the kind of people whom we may wish God to find when we pray." Only if the mind is purified from sin can one "pray without ceasing."[11]

(2) The second quality of prayer, according to Bunyan, is "sensibility." Sensibility does not mean "a few babbling, prating, complementary

expressions, but a sensible feeling there is in the heart." This "feeling" might include "a sense of the want of mercy, by reason of their danger of sin"; "a sweet sense of mercy received; encouraging, comforting, strengthening, enlivening, enlightening mercy"; or "a sense of mercy to be received."[12] Commenting on the first, he added:

> For right Prayer bubbleth out of the heart when it is over-pressed with grief and bitterness, as blood is forced out of the flesh, by reason of some heavy burden that lyeth upon it. (1 Sam 1.10)[13]

Such words sound strikingly similar to monastic insistence on compunction, a concept quite familiar also to the Puritans. Abba Moses explained that the purpose of singing Psalms was "that feelings of repentance may be continually elicited."[14] It is compunction of spirit, said Abba Isaac, "which strikes the spark in the mind and elevates it to prayer of fervent purity."[15] The origins of such compunctions, he admitted, are difficult to trace.

> Sometimes it happens because the soul is filled with an indescribable joy and cannot help breaking out into ejaculations, and even the occupant of the next cell feels the power of the happiness in the heart. Sometimes the mind withdraws into a kind of secret abyss of silence, sudden illumination leaves it speechless, the awestruck spirit locks its feelings within or loses feeling altogether, and pours out its longings to God in groanings that cannot be uttered. Sometimes a compunction of grief overwhelms it, and the only way to express it is by a release of tears.[16]

(3) The third quality of true prayer on which Bunyan insisted is "affection." In his understanding, affection has to do with fervor in prayer. Too many are content, he lamented, "with a little lip-labour and bodily exercise, mumbling over a few imaginary prayers." Affections put to work in prayer claim the whole person "in such sort, that the soul will spend it self to nothing, as it were, rather than it will go without that good desired, even communion and solace with Christ."[17]

The monks obviously struggled to achieve the kind of ardor Bunyan insisted on here. The aim and purpose of solitude, Abba Isaac declared, is "to seek to possess in some measure, even while mortal man, the first bridal gifts from the heavenly country and its glory." The goal of "all true goodness" is "that the mind may every day be lifted beyond the material sphere to the realm of the spirit, until the whole life and every little stirring of the heart becomes one continuous prayer."[18] Bunyan would have applauded. These words are reminiscent of the longer title for his most famous work, *The Pilgrim's Progress.*

A like prescription for prayer appears in the *Rule* of Benedict. Benedict assumed that monks would know how to pray, perhaps from reading Cassian. Twice, however, as he spoke of "affective prayer" or "prayer of simple regard," he emphasized pouring out of the heart to God in much the same way Bunyan did. In chapter 20 he instructed that private prayer should be "not in much talking, but in purity of heart, and compunction of tears." Similarly, in chapter 52 he counseled: "Not in a loud voice but in tears and intentness (*intentio*) of heart."[19]

(4) Bunyan, reacting against the uniformity provisions that put him in prison, devoted the major portion of his treatise to the conviction that prayer is "pouring out of the heart or soul to God through Christ, *by the strength or assistance of the Spirit.*"[20] Prayer not offered "in the strength and assistance of the Spirit," he judged, is "like the Sons of *Aaron,* offering with strange fire,"[21] Prescribed prayers, notably of the Book of Common Prayer but even if apostles had prayed them, are of no effect. Only the Spirit can assure the proper *matter* or *manner* of prayer.

Bunyan cited ten reasons in support of his contention: First "without the Spirit, man is so infirm, that he cannot with all other means whatsoever be enabled to think one right saving thought of God, of Christ, or of his blessed things." Thus, none can pray without the Spirit's intercession. The Book of Common Prayer cannot help, for it is "a mere humane invention and institution, which God is so far from owning of, that he expressly forbids, with any other such like, and that by manyfold sayings in his most holy and blessed Word."[22]

Second, without the Spirit, human beings are so "senseless, so hypocritical, cold, and unseemly in their prayers" that, with their prayers, they "are both rendered abominable to God."[23] Given human infirmity, the Spirit alone can account for "a sincere, sensible, affectionate pouring out of their souls to God."[24]

Third, "nothing but the Spirit can shew a man clearly his misery by nature, and so put a man into a posture of prayer."[25]

Fourth, without the Spirit, human beings who became conscious of their sins would despair of mercy so as not to pray. The Spirit, however, comes and "stayeth the soul, helpeth it to hold up its face to God, by letting into the heart some small sense of mercy, to encourage it to go to God."[26]

Fifth, without the Spirit, "no man can know how he should come to God the right way" nor "what there is in God that makes him desirable."[27]

Sixth, without the Spirit, no one would dare to call God "Father," for that requires knowing and believing. Speaking this one word in faith "is better than a thousand prayers, as men call them written and read, in a formal, cold, luke-warm way."[28] Only when one can say it "knowingly" and "believingly" can one also say with meaning the petitions of the Lord's prayer.

Seventh, only the Spirit "can lift up the soul or heart to God in prayer."[29] Unless prepared by the Spirit of God, the tongue is "apt (of it self) to run without either Fear or Wisdom."[30] "Prayer, without the heart be in it," Bunyan added, "is like a sound without life."[31]

Eighth, "as the heart must be lifted up by the Spirit if it pray aright; so also it must be held up by the Spirit when it is up, if it continue to pray aright."[32] "When the Spirit gets into the heart then there is Prayer indeed, and not till then."[33]

Ninth, without the Spirit, "it is impossible that a man should express himself in Prayer . . . that the heart in a sincere and sensible, affectionate way, should pour out itself before God, with those groans and sighs that come from a truly praying heart."[34] The main thing is not the mouth, "but whether the heart be so full of affection and earnestness in Prayer with God, that it is impossible to express their sense and desire."[35] "The best Prayers have often more groans than words"; Bunyan added, "and those words that it hath, are but a lean and shallow representation of the heart, life, and spirit of that Prayer."[36]

Tenth, without the Spirit, there will be failure not merely in the act itself but "in the prosecution of the work." It is so easy "to fall from the Power to the form" but so difficult "to keep in the Life, Spirit and Power of any one duty, especially Prayer."[37]

This strong emphasis on the Spirit in prayer would indicate that Bunyan was charismatic. That would not be true in the narrower sense of the term, that is, using *glossolalia* as the chief index. As Bunyan proceeded in the next section of his treatise to comment on the other part of his text (1 Cor 14:15), he construed praying "with understanding" as an important accoutrement of praying "with the Spirit." To pray with understanding meant "spiritual enlightenment" rather than tongue- speaking. Thus it would result in edification of the Church, even as Paul enjoined.

Persons who know the writings of or about the desert fathers and mothers will be aware of a similar charismatic thrust. These writings are filled with stories of miraculous healings, visions, raptures, and the like. We should not be surprised, therefore, to find perceptions similar to Bunyan's with reference to the Spirit as the most essential agent in prayer. Accordingly, in Cassian's *Conferences* Abba Isaac declared: "I imagine that no variety of prayer can be apprehended fully without great purity of heart and soul, and the illumination of the Holy Spirit."[38]

Though the monks resorted to set forms with somewhat greater ease than Bunyan did, they coveted most the prayers that "dart up like sparks from a fire."[39] After lauding the *our Father* as "the very pattern of a perfect prayer," Abba Isaac went on to note that it also advances it "to that spark-like and ineffable prayer which very few men know by experience." This prayer

> transcends the senses; is marked by no vocal expression, whether silent or aloud; but the mind, illuminated by an outflowing of light from heaven, does not define it in the narrow limit of human language. With the senses unified, it pours forth prayers, almost with violence as a spring pours forth fresh water, and in a second's time darts up a prayer of such richness that afterwards the mind, returned to normality, cannot easily describe it.[40]

Elsewhere Abba Isaac—emphasizing the value of reciting the formula: "O God, make speed to save me: O Lord, make haste to help me"—spoke directly of the Spirit in this ecstatic form of prayer:

> Perhaps by some joyous rapture I feel that the Holy Spirit has visited me, and I have gained a re-directed purpose, a concentration of mind, a liveliness of spirit, and through these overflowing sensations I discern a sudden disclosure by the Lord of sacred truths hidden from me till now.[41]

Farther on, he alluded to the same words of the Apostle Paul that Bunyan cited so often when he spoke of "the purest of pure prayers." These, he noted, rely on no visual images but "like a spark leaping from a fire, the mind is rapt upward; and, destitute of the aid of the senses or of anything visible or material, pours forth its pray to God with groanings and sighs that cannot be uttered."[42]

(5) One more of the three remaining clauses of Bunyan's definition deserves comment. Prayer is to be "for such things as God hath promised."[43] The other two—"for the good of the Church" and "with submission, in Faith, to the Will of God"—contain no special reflections of contemplative prayer. By "such things as God hath promised" Bunyan meant, as he explained explicitly, in the scriptures. Prayer is prayer only "when it is within the compass of God's word." It is nothing but "blasphemy, or at best vain babbling" when it is "beside the Book."[44] In such statements he was excluding Quaker or Ranter claims of direct revelation that sometimes caused them to diminish the role of the scriptures.

We can see the operation of the Protestant *scriptura sola* principle quite readily in Bunyan's own experience. Like most Puritans, he relied on texts of Scripture, either through zealous study or by sudden inspiration, to offer spiritual guidance, remonstrance, assurance, and so forth. Growing up in the heyday of Puritanism, he learned early the Puritan method of introspection to discover whether one is among the elect. Scriptures would decide. For him this resulted in a near mental breakdown. One text would say yes; another would say no. Texts he laid hold of in sermon or meditation acted only as temporary balms. Little by little, however, the positive side of the biblical message began to prevail. Over seven or eight weeks the text, "My grace is sufficient for thee" (2 Cor 12:9), fixed itself on his mind—first in prayer,[45] then in a worship service. Bunyan tells what force these words carried:

> Oh methought that every word was a mighty word unto me; as "my," and "grace," and "sufficient," and "for thee"; they were then, and sometimes are still, far bigger than others be.[46]

When new doubts assailed him, he prayed that both the passage in Hebrews about Esau selling his birthright, which often came to mind and created a fear that he had committed the unpardonable sin, and the sufficiency passage might wage a contest in his heart and settle once for all which would prevail. "My grace is sufficient for thee" won.[47] Bunyan depicted his experience in *The Pilgrim's Progress* as the battle of Christian with the Giant Despair at Doubting Castle.

Many have doubted the importance of scriptures in early monastic prayer life, but recent scholarly research has put that beyond question.[48] Many monks, being poorly educated, would not have been exposed to scriptures in their entirety, but they at least memorized the Church's prayer book, the Psalms, and much of the Gospels. They used a method very nearly akin to Bunyan's. Abba Isaac, for example, cited several ways in which compunction in spirit might be aroused and thus ignite the spark "to prayer of fervent purity." It might originate from (1) the verse of a psalm, (2) the beauty of a cantor's voice, (3) the clarity and solemnity of the reader of the psalms, (4) the address of a holy person, (5) the death of a brother monk or a friend, or (6) "the memory of my own half-heartedness and carelessness."[49] Abba Isaac counseled that Psalms be recited in "the same attitudes of heart wherein the psalmist wrote or sang his psalms" so as to become like the authors. Thus,

> when we use the words, we remember, by a kind of meditative association, our own circumstances and struggles, the results of our negligence or earnestness, the mercies of God's providence or the temptations of the devil, the subtle and slippery sins of forgetfulness or human frailty or unthinking ignorance.[50]

Bunyan would have nodded knowingly. He would have asked only for a broader use of scriptures.

From Whence the Concordances?

I believe it is appropriate to conclude that there are numerous concordances between Bunyan's understanding of the nature and practice of prayer and those of the early monks. Indeed, concordances are more striking and significant than discordances. Before concluding, we should ask why. What is the source of the agreement?

One would expect Bunyan to have derived his understanding and practice of prayer from John Calvin, the mentor of all the Puritans, and there are affinities. Calvin, for example, defined prayer in language similar to Bunyan's as "properly an emotion of the heart within, which is poured out and laid open before God, the searcher of hearts."[51] He, like both Bunyan and the monks, emphasized the importance of freeing the mind "from carnal cares and thoughts by which it can be called or led away from right and pure contemplation of God."[52] Further, Calvin stressed the necessity of repentance. If "the saints bemoan their sins, chastise themselves, and immediately return to themselves, God pardons them."[53] Calvin also looked upon the Holy Spirit as our teacher in prayer, citing Romans 8:26 and 1 Corinthians 14:15, two of Bunyan's key texts.[54] Such affinities notwithstanding, those moving from Calvin to Bunyan will quickly recognize they have entered a different world. In this case, the concordances are more formal than real. Certainly they do not match the commonalities of Bunyan and the early monks.

In trying to answer the question of sources, it is important to keep in mind that the concordances are with *early* monasticism and not with that of the late Middle Ages. By that time forms of prayer had become much more precisely fixed, even among the noted fourteenth century mystics. The answer to our puzzle would seem to lie in the experiential nature of both Bunyan's and the early monk's theology and practice of prayer and in its common rootage in the Scriptures. Insofar as I can determine,

Bunyan never read the desert fathers and mothers, Cassian, or the *Rule* of Benedict. Had he done so, I suspect, he would have been careful to differentiate some of his own thoughts about prayer from theirs. In this case, however, what he did not know did not divert him. He was carried along by his own experience to a closely similar understanding of prayer. So long as he could find scriptural warrant for experience, Bunyan did not hesitate to follow experience. The early monks did the same.

Since I have commented above on the common use of scriptures, notably the Psalms, I will add here only some documentation about experience. Throughout *I Will Pray with the Spirit*, Bunyan wrote as one inspired by experience in the manner of the "mechanic preacher" he was. On occasion he cited his experience more directly. Arguing the necessity of the Spirit's aid to enable one to continue to pray aright, for example, he added experience to a litany of texts from both Old and New Testaments.

> And verily, may I but speak my own Experience, and from that tell you the difficulty of Praying to God as I ought; it is enough to make your poor, blind, carnal men, to entertain strange thoughts of me. For, as for my heart, when I go to pray, I find it so loth to go to God, and when it is with him, that many times I am forced in my Prayers; *first*, to beg of God that he would take mine heart, and set it on himself in Christ, and when it is there, that he would keep it there (*Psal.* 86.11). Nay, many times I know not what to pray for, I am so blind, nor how to pray I am so ignorant; only (blessed be Grace) *the Spirit helps our infirmities.*[55]

Subsequently, trying to bolster those "oft ready to give up all for lost, upon almost every trick and temptation of Satan," he invoked his own agony of earlier years:

> Much of mine own experience could I here discover; when I have been in my fits of agony of spirit, when I have been persuaded to leave off, and to seek the Lord no longer; but being made to understand, what great sinners the Lord hath had mercy upon; and how large his Promises were still to sinners; and that it was not the whole, but the sick, not the righteous, but the sinner, not the full, but the empty, that he extended his Grace and Mercy unto.
>
> This made me, through the assistance of his holy Spirit, to cleave to him, to hang upon him, and yet to cry, though for the present he made no answer; and the Lord help all his poor tempted and afflicted People to do the like.[56]

Bunyan was not merely invoking experience for the sake of argument in these passages. His spiritual autobiography, *Grace Abounding to the Chief of Sinners*, contains numerous allusions not merely to his reliance on texts of Scripture but also to his battle to pray. The devil, he confessed, would be "continually at me in time of prayer, to have done, break off, make haste, you have prayed enough, and stay no longer; still drawing my mind away."[57] He labored hard to overcome wandering thoughts.[58] Yet great experiences also occurred, "some strong and heart-affecting apprehensions of God, and reality of the truth of his Gospel; but, oh! how would my heart, at such times, put forth itself with inexpressible groanings."[59] Through his own sad experience, briefly described earlier, he professed that through grace his soul was "very apt to drink in this doctrine, and to incline to pray to God, that in nothing that pertained to God's glory, and my own eternal happiness, he would suffer me to be without the confirmation thereof from heaven."[60]

Bunyan was speaking experientially, then, much like the desert fathers and mothers, Cassian, and Benedict when he gave his counsels about prayer. He had learned how to pray not by memorizing prayers—even from the scriptures—but by discovering his wretched condition and the way to escape it. In his agony, he saw the sparks fly upward. So did the early contemplatives.

Having reached this junction, we ought to ask in concluding what it is we would retain for our day from Bunyan and the early monks. Shall we accept their radical emphasis on experience in prayer? Alternatively, shall we disregard them entirely as too extreme and thus find no insights to glean from their experience-authenticated ideas? Or can we accommodate their central concern to our time and circumstances?

I am inclined to go the third route. At the center of this common tradition is a wisdom that we will lose sight of at our peril. Prayer is, after all, as both Bunyan and the early monks taught, essentially an affair of the heart. We, too, need to be concerned in every generation about the substitution of forms and routines for sincere, sensible, and affective engagement with the living God. (A major reason surely for the vigorous re-emergence of a charismatic movement in recent years is that too many Christians have made this substitution.)

Protestantism especially has something to learn here. In closing the monasteries, the Reformers shortchanged their version of Christianity. They retained the intellectual and the institutional expressions, but they undercut the experiential. In a very real sense, Puritanism in its many forms emerged to recover the latter. Unfortunately, they succeeded only in part. Protestantism still lacks the experiential vitality that the contemplative tradition has supplied through the centuries.

The ecumenical era in which we are now living opens some wonderful prospects for the recovery of the contemplative dimension of our

Christian faith. Since the Second Vatican Council we have gained much from one another, but there are more and bigger steps to take as we rediscover our common roots and make all of church history the history of us all.

Notes

[1]John Bunyan, *Grace Abounding to the Chief of Sinners,* 327, ed. W. R. Owens (London: Penguin Books, 1987) 80.

[2]Bunyan, *The Pilgrim's Progress,* in *Doubleday Devotional Classics,* ed. E. Glenn Hinson (Garden City NJ: Doubleday & Co., 1978) 1:387.

[3]John Cassian, *Conferences,* 1:4, in *Western Asceticism,* ed. Owen Chadwick, The Library of Christian Classics, vol. 12 (Philadelphia: Westminster Press, 1958) 197. Hereafter cited as LCC. Scholars debate whether Cassian reproduced his sources or whether he invented most of what he reported. We probably need to assume rather free use of sources.

[4]Ibid, 1.7; LCC, 12:199.

[5]Bunyan, *I Will Pray with the Spirit,* ed. Richard L. Greaves (Oxford: Clarendon Press, 1976) 269.

[6]Cassian, *Conferences,* 9.25, LCC, 12:226.

[7]Ibid., 10.10; LCC, 12:240.

[8]Bunyan, *I Will Pray With the Spirit,* 235.

[9]Ibid., 236.

[10]Ibid., 237.

[11]Cassian, *Conferences,* 9.3; LCC, 12:215.

[12]Bunyan, *I Will Pray With the Spirit,* 237f.

[13]Ibid., 237.

[14]Cassian, *Conferences,* 1.17; LCC, 12:207.

[15]Ibid., 9.26; LCC, 12:227.

[16]Ibid., 9.27; LCC, 12:227.

[17]Bunyan, *I Will Pray With the Spirit,* 239.

[18]Cassian, *Conferences,* 10.7; LCC, 12:237.

[19]Cuthbert Butler has called this "a very simple and downright prayer, in which the operations of the imagination and reasoning are silent, and those of heart and will only, or mainly are active," in *Benedictine Monachism,* 61.

[20]Bunyan, *I Will Pray With the Spirit,* 242.

[21]Ibid., 243.

[22]Ibid., 249.

[23]Ibid., 250.

[24]Ibid., 251f.

[25]Ibid., 251.

[26]Ibid.

[27]Ibid., 251-52.

[28]Ibid., 252.
[29]Ibid., 255.
[30]Ibid.
[31]Ibid., 256.
[32]Ibid.
[33]Ibid., 257.
[34]Ibid.
[35]Ibid.
[36]Ibid., 258.
[37]Ibid., 259.
[38]Cassian, *Conferences*, 9.8; LCC, 12:218.
[39]Ibid., LCC, 12:220.
[40]Ibid., 9.25; LCC, 12:226f.
[41]Ibid., 10.10; LCC, 12:242.
[42]Ibid., 10.11; LCC, 12:244.
[43]Bunyan, *I Will Pray With the Spirit*, 243.
[44]Ibid.
[45]Bunyan, *Grace Abounding to the Chief of Sinners*, 204 (53).
[46]Ibid., 206, (53).
[47]Ibid., 213.
[48]See especially Douglas Burton-Christie, *The Word in the Desert: Scripture and the Quest for Holiness in Early Christian Monasticism* (New York: Oxford University Press, 1993).
[49]Cassian, *Conferences*, 9.26; LCC, 12:227.
[50]Ibid., 10.11; LCC, 12:244.
[51]John Calvin, *Institutes of the Christian Religion*, 3.20.29, ed. John T. McNeill and trans. Ford Lewis Battles (Philadelphia: Westminster Press, 1960); LCC 21:892.
[52]Ibid., 3.20.4; LCC 21:853.
[53]Ibid., 3.20.16; LCC 21:873.
[54]Ibid., 3.20.5; LCC 21:855-56.
[55]Bunyan, *I Will Pray With the Spirit*, 256f.
[56]Ibid., 265f.
[57]Bunyan, *Grace Abounding to the Chief of Sinners*, 107, (29).
[58]Ibid., 108, (30).
[59]Ibid., 109, (30).
[60]Ibid., 118, (32).

A Confession for Catholic Baptists

Curtis W. Freeman

Can Baptists Be Catholic?

A group of students from the Baptist college where I teach recently returned from a trip to Europe. On their journey home they stopped in London for several days and attended worship at Westminster Cathedral. Baptists are accustomed neither to such a majestic setting nor to so formal a liturgy, but to their amazement they found it to be a deeply spiritual occasion. When the time came to recite the Apostles' Creed, however, they displayed a collective puzzlement with the phrase "I believe in . . . the holy catholic church." Thinking to themselves that "Baptists cannot possibly be catholic," they quietly declined to join in the recitation. After the service, they were chagrined to learn from their faculty sponsor that the article in question was a claim about the wholeness of the church. It, thus, affirms the universal reign of God through Word and Spirit that is signified by the unity of Christians in worship. They were at least willing to concede that Baptists should be (little c) catholics.

The reticence of these students is typical of many Baptists. By only rarely championing the cause of Christian unity, Baptists have generally resisted the label of catholic. In 1965 Wayne Dehoney, who was then the president of the Southern Baptist Convention, wrote in *Christianity Today* that a rejection of denominationalism in favor of ecumenism "would be to reverse the Reformation and turn the clock back to a medieval Catholicism."[1] Dehoney's caution about Christian unity, however, was balanced by his presidential address to the SBC in the same year that called for seeking "broader channels of communication and cooperation" with Christians of other confessions and communities.[2]

The relationship between mainline denominations in the United States has been described as a "friendly division with permeable borders";[3]

however, Southern Baptists and fundamentalists maintain ever less friendly and less permeable boundaries with other denominations.

In a recent Gallup poll that indexed attitudes of Americans toward Christian unity (or ecumenism), Southern Baptists and fundamentalists were in the lower range of the spectrum in favorable views toward other denominations. Southern Baptists registered a sixty-five percent favorable and seventeen percent unfavorable rating of other groups. Fundamentalists were the least ecumenical with only a forty-five percent favorable and a twenty-six percent unfavorable attitude toward other denominations. Methodists were the most ecumenical with an eighty percent favorable and only six percent unfavorable view of other denominations. Interestingly, Baptists other than Southern Baptists and fundamentalists expressed a strikingly positive attitude toward Christian unity with a seventy-eight percent favorable view of other denominations.[4] Why do so many Baptists (especially among Southern Baptists and fundamentalists) have an aversion to understanding their place as little c catholics? More importantly, how can the spirituality of Baptists within the universal body of Christ be encouraged and enhanced?

The answer lies partially in the heritage of Baptist beginnings that were marked by conflict with ecclesiastical and political establishments. Baptists inherited an attitude of radical protest from Reformation Anabaptists and a conviction of separatist dissent from English Puritans that combined to alienate them theologically from both Protestants and Catholics. That Baptists were "the odd one out" all too often led Protestant and Catholic majorities to agree that it was a good thing to use their political power to teach the Baptists a lesson. Baptist spiritual identity, thus, was forged in the crucible of theological alienation and political isolation from the dominant cultures of Europe, England, and America.

Baptists have also had a difficult time finding a way to express their spiritual voice within the academic setting as they were routinely excluded from higher education or forced to adhere to the confessions of the controlling religious authorities. The educational struggle of early American Baptists gave rise to the saying that you could get a Baptist into Harvard but could not get one out.[5] Although the academic bias against Baptists is less coercive today than in the past, it is nevertheless deeply entrenched in the literature of religious and theological studies. Generations of theological students have been trained to regard Baptists as belonging to a sect rather than to the church.[6] The sectarian account of Baptist life found its way into the popular religious culture as many Baptists adopted a sect-type posture in relation to other denominations.

The current renaissance of contemplative spirituality offers many exciting new (and old) pathways for Baptists, but the exploration of the contemplative tradition cannot be made without some degree of ecumenism. James William McClendon has suggested that at the very least what is required is "an acknowledgment of the grace of God in places other than our place, in persons other than ourselves, in churches other than our churches."[7]

I suggest that Baptists may more easily explore the vast resources of Christian spirituality and that other Christians may more readily receive the unique contributions of Baptist spirituality if we attempt to think of ourselves (at least experimentally) as (little c) catholic (little b) baptists.[8] Catholic baptists are thus open, not only to be shaped by the spiritual pattern that was decisively present in the life of Jesus of Nazareth, but also to participate in the work of the Spirit that continues to be transformingly active in and through the whole church. Those persons inside and outside the Baptist confession who have learned to see religious bodies in terms of Troeltsch's social types (either by academic training or denominational indoctrination) undoubtedly will find the notion of a catholic baptist to be either curiously confused or seriously misguided. This objection must be challenged.

This challenge must be directed first to baptists as they reconsider the relationship of spirituality and the church. If spirituality may be taken to mean the way each believer makes "his or her own that engagement with the questioning at the heart of faith,"[9] then catholic baptists will understand that spirituality rightly refers, not only to the inward practices that nurture and sustain the relationship with Christ (conversion, prayer, meditation, study, and so on), but also to the outward practices that are shared by a particular community (confession, baptism, worship, discipleship, ministry, etc.). Moreover, if this spirituality is indeed Christian (and not just baptist), there will also be the recognition that our signifying of the universal reign of God through the Spirit calls for our participation with all the people of God.

Within this broader view of Christian unity, a truthful witness to the wholeness of the new creation becomes more visible. It is important to recall that early baptists did not discover the practice of praying in the Spirit any more than they invented a baptist doctrine of the Trinity. Baptists are heirs to the theological discussions and spiritual disciplines that have been transmitted through the church catholic. How can baptists attend to the catholicity of spirituality?

First, they can *listen carefully* to voices within the heritage of the whole church because the most interesting and insightful perspectives may not come from their own community or even the traditions that ultimately prevailed in the centuries of fierce struggles that shaped Catholic and Protestant orthodoxies. Catholic baptists may experience the contemplative secret of learning to "pray without ceasing" (1 Thess 5:17) by reciting the Jesus Prayer of Orthodox hesychast spirituality. They may understand more clearly what it means to "let the word of Christ dwell in you richly" (Col 3:16) through practicing the *lectio divina,* the Benedictine spiritual method of reading Scripture. They may learn to love God more deeply (Mark 12:29-33) and to imitate Christ more faithfully (Mark 8:34) by attending to the meditations of Bernard of Clairvaux and Thomas à Kempis. A wonderful chorus of voices within the church catholic can enrich the spiritual life of baptists if they are open to the movement of the Spirit outside their own limited history and narrow tradition.

Second, baptists can *listen cautiously* to the voices of the past by always referring new insights to shared baptist convictions so as to enhance both the particularity of the baptist vision and the universality of their spiritual life. In the final analysis, by taking seriously their role as a minority consciousness within the whole church, baptists may perform their most faithful spiritual task. As catholic baptists practice the disciplines that nurture and sustain their common convictions, they enact a truthful vision of the new creation.

Through the spirituality of conversion they bear witness to the conviction that God's new creation can most clearly be displayed by people who voluntarily and consciously commit themselves to follow Christ as Lord. In the spirituality of believers' baptism they seek to maintain the corollary conviction that within the church catholic all those who are named by Christ must claim him as Lord. By the spirituality of the separation of church and state they declare the conviction that faithfulness to Christ the Lord demands freedom from the control of nation and empire. If this is baptist spirituality, can the spiritual life of baptists be catholic? If it is to be genuinely Christian, it must be catholic. Exactly how can baptists express their catholicity?

Can Baptists Confess Their Catholicity?

One of the ways that early Christians attempted to understand their identity in Christ and their unity in the Spirit was through creeds. The first such statement of faith to gain universal authority in the Christian church was the Nicene Creed.[10] One of the final articles affirms, "We believe in one holy catholic and apostolic church."[11] Baptists have been rightly suspicious of the ways that creeds (including the Nicene Creed), when linked with a church-state unity of the dominant social order, have been used to impose a uniformity of belief and worship.[12] With reservation we ask whether baptists can confessionally agree with other Christians that we too so believe. Is there a theological basis for an ecumenical baptist spirituality?

Unity

Thesis: We affirm our unity with other Christians as we envision the church to be one in Christ through the Spirit. The conviction that the church is one is foundational in the spirituality of catholic baptists. The clear teaching of scripture is that as God is one, the body of Christ is one (Eph 4:4); and that as Father and Son are united, so Christian unity displays a truthful witness to the Incarnation (John 17:20-21). There is, then, in biblical teaching only one church. Protestants and Catholics are in surprising agreement on the biblical teaching of church unity. Far more divisive have been the political questions of how Christian unity is to be enacted and what ends it should serve.[13]

Some Christians hold that the belief in one church demands an *institutional unity.* Baptists who have been shaped by a landmark theology and a triumphalist denominationalism consider themselves to be the local representatives of the one true body. They find ecclesial unity in the rhetorical act of denouncing other denominations as pretenders. An ecumenical spirituality, however, rejects all vestiges of landmarkism and triumphalism. Others regard the notion of one church to be intelligible in terms of a *signified unity.* According to this view "in the sacrament of the eucharistic bread, the unity of all believers who form one body in Christ (cf. 1 Cor 10:17) is both expressed and brought about."[14] Since within this sacramental ecclesiology the eucharist is understood to be both a sign and a source of unity, it is not likely that many will find sacramental theology to be congruous with baptist identity.

Still others have taken the doctrine of one church to imply an *organic unity*. Even the most ecumenical baptists express concern that their doctrinal distinctives might be lost in such an organic union.[15] It has been suggested that a baptist ecumenism may be guided by the ideal of a *fraternal unity* that attempts to foster the expression of one church in the midst of a divided Christendom by seeking harmony with other Christians.[16] I propose that an ecumenical spirituality for baptists might be furthered if the confession of our belief in one church is understood in terms of an *eschatological unity.*

The eschatological unity of the church is poignantly stated in John Howard Yoder's exegesis of 2 Corinthians 5:17. Yoder argues that the meaning of this text has been obscured and misinterpreted by the pietist and revivalist heritage so that it simply echoes the biblical theme of regeneration: "If anyone is in Christ *he* (or *she*) *is* a new creation." The force of the text (as Yoder contends), however, is not the transformation of the person but rather the radical change that God has brought about through Christ: "If anyone is in Christ, *there is* a new creation."[17] This new creation is embodied in a new humanity that was created by the death and resurrection of Christ (Eph 2:15). This new creation is enacted in baptism as we are united with Christ's resurrection and raised to "walk in the newness of life" (Rom 6:4). To live in this new way of life is to "live by the Spirit" (Gal 5:16).

From an empirical perspective, the body of Christ is disunited. By seeing things eschatologically, however, baptists may begin to view themselves—and, indeed, Christians of all denominations and traditions—as the eschatological people of God. Yet even as the new creation has come to pass in Christ and is experienced through the Spirit, the church must patiently await the final consummation when the old order will at last come to an end. This is precisely why in the midst of denominational Babel the confession of oneness must be prefaced by the words, "We *believe.*" That is, Christian unity and the new creation are convictions rooted in hope. We must learn to distinguish the church *as it now is* (denominationally divided) from the church *as it will be* (one body).[18]

An ecumenical spirituality for baptists, however, must resist the apocalyptic distortions of fundamentalism that engender an other worldliness and are too often invoked as an excuse for continued divisiveness. The new creation of which even the church as it now is participates has been inaugurated in the resurrection of Jesus from the dead. It is *not* something that *God will do*. It is something that *God already has begun*. Consequently, the denominational predicates that continue to divide the eschatological people of God are a part of the old order that is passing away.

Holiness

Thesis: We affirm the holiness of the church not only when we recognize the Holy Spirit as the sanctifying source of our life together but also when we call for the church to be a committed company of disciples acting as reconciling agents of the gospel. In Catholicism the church is regarded to be a sacramental communion (*communio sacramentorum*), and thus the holiness of the Spirit is mediated through the eucharist. Protestantism has understood the church to be a communion of saints (*communio sanctorum*), and thus the holiness of the Spirit is mediated through faith. Different bodies within the Protestant and Free church traditions, though, have emphasized that sanctification is effected and evidenced in a wide range of ways: sacraments and proclamation (Reformed), conversion and accountability (Ana/baptist), signs and wonders (Pentecostal).

Emil Brunner's *Misunderstandings of the Church* represents one of the most trenchant critiques of this denominational and congregational pluralism. Central to his argument is the proposition that the *ecclesia* of the New Testament has nothing to do with historic ecclesiastical models.[19] Brunner opts instead for the church as fellowship over the church as institution. This position, however, collapses as the notion of a fellowship severed from any institutional life ultimately exists for Brunner only as an ideal. Lacking any social expression, it is not a fellowship at all.

Against Brunner's theological idealism, baptists have held to the belief that the church as a fellowship should and, indeed, must exist in concrete ecclesial contexts. Moreover, baptists have maintained that the foundation of genuine spirituality is conversion. That is, the pathway of *spiritual formation* begins with *spiritual transformation*, and the proper context for spiritual formation is the church. The baptist witness of the church as a fellowship is displayed by people who have voluntarily committed themselves to Christ the Lord. The baptist vision of a voluntary church membership is further exhibited in the practice of believers' baptism. Mainstream Protestants and Catholics have largely disregarded baptist ecclesiology as sectarian and intolerant, but these epithets have little served the understanding of our convictions. It is not believers' baptism in itself that we have sought to preserve but rather a living church of confessing and committed Christians. As a social practice, believers' baptism marks the visibly and consciously converted with the aim of engendering the holiness of the church.

Early continental Anabaptists and English Baptists attempted to nourish and sustain the community by discipline. Each member entered into covenant with the congregation and agreed to be accountable to one another.[20] Church discipline, however, is seldom observed among contemporary Baptists. Moreover, the fact that many Baptist congregations in America routinely baptize children under the age of eight stretches the meaning of a voluntary membership to the breaking point.[21] With this struggle to exhibit viable models of the confessing church, Robert Middleton observed that "believers' baptism is a good theology in search of a practice to reflect it."[22]

The case for an ecumenical baptist spirituality faces a formidable challenge in the so-called Lima document of the World Council of Churches (WCC) that is entitled *Baptism, Eucharist and Ministry* (BEM).[23] This declaration is the result of more than fifty years of work by the WCC Faith and Order Commission. In spite of much that is commendable about the intent of this convergence statement on Christian unity, it raises troublesome questions for baptist ecumenism. Perhaps the most striking difficulty for Baptists is the call to acknowledge baptism as an unrepeatable act and to avoid any practice that might be interpreted as rebaptism.[24] The declaration goes on to recommend the mutual recognition of infant and believers' baptism.[25]

This aspect of the document avoids entirely the point that baptism in the believers' church tradition has attempted to address, namely, that it stands to ensure a confessing membership and a committed discipleship. As John Howard Yoder comments, it is important that baptists continue to ask why people that have not been asked publicly to be counted as believers should be called Christians.[26] Moreover, even baptists who are inclined toward an open church membership would do so on the basis of the candidate's faith in Christ and not infant baptism. BEM simply disregards the believer's church issue.

Here John Bunyan speaks an ecumenical word to baptists who are attempting to wrestle with the spirituality of baptism. Bunyan stands within the baptist family as a critic of those who would make believers' baptism the primary issue to the neglect of evangelical faith and discipleship. Although Bunyan himself submitted to believers' baptism and practiced it as the proper model, the Bedford church of which he was pastor required it neither for admission to the Lord's Supper nor for church membership. In a rejoinder to William Kiffin, a Baptist minister who championed the cause of both closed communion and closed church membership, Bunyan replied,

> All I say is, that the church of Christ hath not warrant to keep out of their communion the Christian that is discovered to be a visible saint by the word, the Christian that walketh according to his light with God.[27]

Bunyan's view on communion has, in the main, prevailed among baptists. Thus we are reminded that believers' baptism is not itself the end we serve, but rather it too serves the ends of a more determinative community, namely, the confessing church that walks according to the light and proclaims the reconciling word of the gospel.

The ecumenical implications of Bunyan's example for baptists today are twofold. First, we must move to close off the nominal Christianity in our own ranks by schooling Christians to be a community of baptized believers that have voluntarily committed themselves to the radically transformed life of the new creation. Second, we must attempt to raise the question of how communities that practice infant baptism might "develop initiatory rites and educational practices such that they will turn out genuine disciples who are effective as redeeming agents of Jesus Christ in the world."[28]

Universality

Thesis: We affirm the universality of the church when as an inclusive fellowship under the Lordship of Christ and the leadership of the Spirit we give witness to the one-peopleness of humankind. We confess our belief in the church's universality each time we sing, "Elect from every nation yet one o'er all the earth."[29] That Baptists have struggled to understand how to affirm catholicity is partly due to the congregationalist impulse of our ecclesiology. Baptists generally maintain the dual beliefs that each particular congregation is a genuine expression of the church and that the church is a universal reality.

The Second London Confession of 1677/88 mentions the church that "consists of the whole number of the elect" and the "particular congregations" made up of "visible saints."[30] The New Hampshire Confession of 1833 and the Baptist Faith and Message of 1925 are noticeably silent on the subject of the universality of the church.[31] But as James Leo Garrett has observed, when Southern Baptists "have been freed from their nineteenth-century Landmark heritage, [they] have affirmed the reality of the universal church."[32] The Baptist Faith and Message of 1963 returned to a bipolar ecclesiology by recognizing that the church is both "a local body of baptized believers" and "the redeemed of all the ages."[33]

The baptist emphasis on the independence of the local congregation has been widely misunderstood so as to diminish the notion of catholicity. Winthrop Hudson, however, has correctly noted that baptists do not regard each congregation to be a fraction of the church catholic. Each local church is the church catholic as it teaches scripture, proclaims the word, baptizes Christians, observes the Lord's Supper, disciplines saints, and engages in polity.[34] Since each local church is not *part* of the church but a local realization of the church catholic, the bonds of unity are internal to the local church.[35] Moreover, since every local church is fully the church, each one must strive to maintain its connection with other churches of Christ.

Full affirmation of catholicity is surely threatened by rigorous denominationalism that disregards the eschatological unity of the church. An even deeper cause for concern are the predicates of power that divide the church along the lines of race, class, and gender (Gal 3:28; Col 3:11). An important contribution to the baptist theology of catholicity has been made by a group of African-American Baptists. Their statement contends that the notions of church unity and universality are too often spiritualized. They argue that true unity and catholicity are realized in concrete acts of justice and liberation that challenge the political, economic, and cultural hegemony of white Christianity.[36]

Rather than regarding these social divisions as tragic marks of sin and failure, one major voice within the church growth movement has gone so far as to propose that they simply illustrate the principle of homogeneity. That is, even in the church, "Birds of a feather flock together."[37] That homogeneity is right, the author argues, is convincingly shown in the fact that homogeneity works, whereas catholicity does not. The intentional formation of homogenous churches perpetuates disunity, however, denies catholicity, and ultimately belies the gospel. Truly, the church "is composed of . . . one kind of people,"[38] but this oneness must be understood in eschatological and catholic terms. For Christ the Lord has reconciled "all kinds of people" to form "one kind of people" (Eph 4:13-16). Nicholas Lash has wonderfully stated the universality of the vision in the church:

> What we call "the church" is that particular people that *thus* narrates, announces, dramatizes, the origin, identity and destiny of humankind. What

> we call "the church," in other words, are those who use the language of scripture and the creeds to proclaim the fact and promise, possibility and requirement, of the "one-peopleness" of humankind.[39]

This is the vision of the new humanity and the new creation. This is the catholicity baptists must attempt to display.

Apostolicity

Thesis: We affirm the apostolicity of the church by rejecting mythic successionism, naive restorationism, and narrow historicism, and by reclaiming our heritage in a truly apostolic faith. The successionist interpretation states that "the church is apostolic because [it] teaches what the apostles taught and can trace [its] existence historically directly back to the apostles."[40] This claim of historical continuity with the apostolic faith is commonly made by Orthodox, Catholic, and Anglican churches. In each case the claim is measurably credible. The myth of "the trail of blood," however, is but a pathetic parody of traditional successionist theories. The sentiment of Baptist successionism is captured in the following verse:

> Not at the River Jordan, but in the flowing stream
> Stood John the Baptist preacher when he baptized Him.
> John was a Baptist preacher when he baptized the Lamb;
> Then Jesus was a Baptist, and thus the Baptists came.[41]

The successionist theory of Baptist origins now exists merely as a curious antique of our history, as well it should.[42]

Protestants have tended to reject successionist interpretations of apostolicity in favor of restorationism that seeks to return to the apostolic teaching of scripture. Calvin held that the truly apostolic church exists "wherever we see the Word of God purely preached and heard and the sacraments administered according to Christ's institution."[43] Extreme biblicism has occasionally led baptists into the distortion of naive restorationism in an effort to cleanse churches of human traditions and return to the pristine pattern of primitive Christianity.[44] Primitive Christianity, however, was neither uniform nor pristine. The faith and worship of the earliest communities was diverse despite the unity of their shared attention to the story of a crucified and risen Lord.[45]

Furthermore, baptists will not discover the apostolic dimension of our faith in identifying ourselves by means of a narrow historicism. Our apostolic heritage cannot be reclaimed merely by returning to its origins in the English Separatism of Smyth and Helwys or the Continental Anabaptism of Menno and the Brethren. The key to appropriating our heritage in a truly apostolic faith is learning to locate ourselves within the full history of the church—past and present—with all its richness and diversity. Through the display of this story over the centuries we find continuity with the apostolic. In this story we meet a host of faithful witnesses: martyrs and confessors, desert mothers and church fathers, scholastics and mystics, reformers and radicals, puritans and pietists. These and more are our spiritual heritage, too. They are the fount through which the apostolic spring flows. When baptists become ecumenical enough to reclaim the whole Christian story as our heritage, we shall surely stand in the waters of that glad river (Ps 46:4) where John and Jesus stood until that day when we shall gather with the saints before that river glorious whose crystal tide flows by the throne of God and the Lamb (Rev 22:1).

Notes

[1]Wayne Dehoney, "Southern Baptists and Ecumenical Concerns," *Christianity Today* (29 January 1965): 15.

[2]Dehoney, "Issues and Imperatives," in *Annual of the Southern Baptist Convention* (1965) 95.

[3]Michael Root, "The Unity of the Church and the Reality of the Denominations," *Modern Theology* 9 (October 1993): 386-87.

[4]George Gallup Jr., and Jim Castelli, "Americans Endorse Quest for Christian Unity," *Houston Post*, 24 January 1987, 20(A). Robert Wuthnow summarizes the survey data that demonstrates that negative attitudes across denominational lines in the United States have significantly declined since 1945, in *The Restructuring of American Religion* (Princeton NJ: Princeton University Press, 1988) 91ff.

[5]H. Leon McBeth, *The Baptist Heritage* (Nashville: Broadman Press, 1987) 235.

[6]Ernst Troeltsch, *The Social Teaching of the Christian Churches*,. 2 vols., trans. Olive Wyon (New York: Harper and Row, 1960). Troeltsch argued that a sect was socially identifiable as "a voluntary society, composed of strict and definite Christian believers bound to each other by the fact that all have experienced 'the new birth.' These 'believers' live apart from the world, are limited to small groups, emphasize the law instead of grace, and in varying degrees within their own circle set up the Christian order, based on love; all this is done in preparation for and expectation of the coming Kingdom of God." *The Social Teaching of the Christian Churches*, 2:993; see also 1:331-43. Baptists are pigeonholed as sectarian in Troeltsch's typology, in *The Social Teaching of the Christian Churches*, 2:694-729. It is now clear that Troeltsch's typology is not merely

a descriptive social analysis as he claimed but rather a normative theological account that privileges the church-type. For a criticism of Troeltsch see Duane Friesen, "Normative Factors in Troeltsch's Typology of Religious Association," *Journal of Religious Ethics* 3 (Fall 1975): 271-83; Stanley M. Hauerwas, *Christian Existence Today* (Durham NC: Labyrinth Press, 1988) 3-8; and Philip LeMasters, *Discipleship for All Believers* (Scottdale PA: Herald Press, 1989) 103-26.

[7]James William McClendon, "What is a Southern Baptist Ecumenism?" *Southwestern Journal of Theology* 10 (Spring 1968): 73.

[8]I make a distinction between Baptist denominations (big B) and baptists who broadly share a believers' church vision (little b), which in this essay refers to catholic baptists.

[9]Rowan Williams, *The Wound of Knowledge: Christian Spirituality from the New Testament to St. John of the Cross*, 2d ed. (Boston: Cowley Publications, 1990) 1.

[10]The Nicene Creed in the basic form that it now exists was adopted at the ecumenical council of Constantinople in A.D. 381. See Philip Schaff and Henry Wace, ed., *A Select Library of Nicene and Post-Nicene Fathers*, second series (Grand Rapids MI: Wm. B. Eerdmans, reprint 1977) vol. 14, *The Seven Ecumenical Councils*, ed. Henry R. Percival, 163. Hereafter cited as NPNF.

[11] Philip Schaff, ed., *The Creeds of Christendom* (New York: Harper and Brothers, 1877) vol. 2, *The Greek and Latin Creeds*, 58; and NPNF 14:163.

[12]E. Glenn Hinson suggests that baptists might read the Nicene Creed more sympathetically by recontextualizing the fourth century and its confessions from the standpoint of evangelization, in "The Nicene Creed Viewed from the Standpoint of the Evangelization of the Roman Empire," in *Faith to Creed*, ed. S. Mark Heim (Grand Rapids MI: William B. Eerdmans, 1991) 117-28.

[13]James Leo Garrett makes this observation in "Understanding the Church: A Southern Baptist Perspective," *The Theological Educator* 39 (Spring 1989): 62.

[14]*De Ecclesia: The Constitution on the Church of Vatican Council II* (Glen Rock NJ: Paulist Press, 1965) 65.

[15]For example, the Constitution of the World Council of Churches calls for "the goal of visible unity in one faith and in one eucharistic fellowship" (Article 3). Concern about the implications of "visible unity" is a major reason that the SBC did not participate in the modern ecumenical movement.

[16]One of the most thoughtful baptist reflections on this subject is C. Brownlow Hastings, *Harmony Among Christians: A Model Other Than Structural Union* (Louisville KY: Glad River Publications, 1992).

[17]John Howard Yoder, *The Politics of Jesus* (Grand Rapids MI: William B. Eerdmans, 1972) 226-28. Emphasis added. Interestingly, the New Revised Standard Version agrees with Yoder's translation. See also James William McClendon, Jr., *Systematic Theology: Ethics* (Nashville: Abingdon Press, 1986) 249.

[18]Augustine, *The City of God*, 20.9, trans. Henry Bettenson (New York: Penguin Books, 1984) 915.

[19]Emil Brunner, *Misunderstandings of the Church*, trans. Harold Knight (Philadelphia: Westminster Press, 1953) 10.

[20]For example, Balthasar Hubmaier's theology of baptism was not predicated on either a subjective conversion experience or the affirmation of doctrine but rather upon

the candidate's readiness to enter into a covenant of mutual accountability (Matt 18:15). Yoder, "Another 'Free Church' Perspective on Baptist Ecumenism," in *Baptists and Ecumenism*, eds. William J. Boney and Glenn A. Igleheart (Valley Forge PA: Judson Press, 1980) 150. See William L. Lumpkin, *Baptist Confessions of Faith* (Philadelphia: Judson Press, 1959) 33.

[21]For example, in 1976 churches affiliated with the SBC baptized 35,562 children under eight years of age. See Thorwald Lorenzen, "Baptists and Ecumenicity with Special Reference to Baptism," *Review and Expositer* 72 (Winter 1980): 42, note 2. In 1989 out of a total of 351,107 recorded baptisms, SBC congregations baptized 45,224 children eight years of age or younger. See *The Quarterly Review* 50 (July-September 1990): 21.

[22]R. G. Middleton, " 'Believers' Baptism and the Sacrament of Confirmation," *Foundations* 11 (1968): 143. Cited by Lorenzen in "Baptists and Ecumenicity," 30.

[23]*Baptism, Eucharist and Ministry*, Faith and Order Paper No. 111 (Geneva: World Council of Churches, 1982). Hereafter referred to as BEM. Significant reflection about the theological implications of BEM for baptists are contained in *Review and Expositor* 77 (Winter 1980); *Baptist Quarterly* 4 (December 1985); and C. B. Hastings, "The Lima Document: A Southern Baptist View," *Ecumenical Trends* 12 (February 1983): 24-27.

[24]BEM, IV.A.13, (p. 4). For example, in 1987 out of 338,495 total recorded baptisms, Southern Baptists rebaptized 56,918 people from other denominations, and 26,898 were rebaptized Southern Baptists. Ron Johnson, "Where Are Southern Baptists With Evangelism?" *The Quarterly Review* 51 (October-December): 19.

[25]BEM, IV.C.15-16, (p. 6).

[26]Yoder, "Another 'Free Church' Perspective on Baptist Ecumenism," in *Baptists and Ecumenism*, 153.

[27]John Bunyan, *Differences in Judgment About Water Baptism No Bar to Communion*, in *The Complete Works of John Bunyan*, ed. John P. Gulliver (Philadelphia: Bradley, Garretson and Co., 1872) 841.

[28]Hastings, *Harmony Among Christians*, 20.

[29]Samuel J. Stone, "The Church's One Foundation."

[30]First London Confession, art. 26, in Lumpkin, *Baptist Confessions of Faith*, 285.

[31]The New Hampshire Confession, art. 13, in Lumpkin, *Baptist Confessions of Faith*, 365-66; and *The Baptist Faith and Message*, art. 12, in McBeth, *Sourcebook For Baptist Heritage* (Nashville: Broadman Press, 1990) 511.

[32]James Leo Garrett, Jr., "Understanding the Church: A Southern Baptist Perspective," *The Theological Educator* 39 (Spring 1989): 60.

[33]The Baptist Faith and Message, art. 6, in McBeth, *A Sourcebook For Baptist Heritage*, 511.

[34]Winthrop Hudson, "The Associational Principle Among Baptists," *Foundations* (January 1958): 12. Cited by W. Hubert Porter in "Ecumenical Concerns Among American Baptists," in *Baptists and Ecumenism*, 27.

[35]Michael Root, "The Unity of the Church," 390-91.

[36]"Toward a Common Expression of Faith: A Black North American Perspective," *American Baptist Quarterly* 4 (December 1985): 390-91.

[37]C. Peter Wagner, *Your Church Can Grow* (Glendale CA: Regal Books, 1976) 110-23.

[38]Ibid., 110.

[39]Nicholas Lash, *Believing Three Ways in One God* (Notre Dame IN: University of Notre Dame Press, 1993) 86.

[40]Anthony M. Coniaris, *Introducing the Orthodox Church: Its Faith and Life* (Minneapolis: Light and Life Publishing Company, 1982) 3.

[41]Cited by Donald F. Durnbaugh in "Free Churches, Baptists, and Ecumenism: Origins and Implications," in *Baptists and Ecumenism*, 9.

[42]That Baptists once took successionism seriously is evidenced by the dismissal of William Whitsitt from his post as professor and president of the Southern Baptist Theological Seminary. Whitsitt's book, *A Question in Baptist History* (1896), rejected "the trail of blood" and thus was judged to imperil foundational Baptist principles. See McBeth, *A Sourcebook For Baptist Heritage*, 315-16.

[43]John Calvin, *The Institutes of the Christian Religion*, 4.1.9, ed. John T. McNeill and trans. Ford Lewis Battles (Philadelphia: Westminster Press, 1960) 1023.

[44]For example, the "primitive" Baptist movement of the early nineteenth century condemned mission societies, Sunday schools, seminaries, and revival meetings on the basis that the New Testament was silent on these matters. McBeth, *The Baptist Heritage*, 373.

[45]James D. G. Dunn, *Unity and Diversity in the New Testament*, 2d ed. (Philadelphia: Trinity Press, 1990) 1-7, 235-366; and Rowan Williams, "Does it make sense to speak of pre-Nicene orthodoxy?" in *The Making of Orthodoxy*, ed. Rowan Williams (Cambridge: Cambridge Press, 1989) 1-23.

Spiritual Direction and the Baptist Tradition

Thomas B. Turner

Spiritual direction offers guidance in the practice of prayer for people who are drawn to communion with God and want to grow in the grace and knowledge of God. It enables them to discern the presence of God and respond with trust to the movement of God's Spirit in their lives. It is a distinctive form of pastoral care, theological education, supervision, and Christian friendship that brings them together in a unique and powerful way by focusing on prayer.

The historical fact that spiritual direction originated and developed as part of the Catholic tradition may seem an impediment to its introduction in the congregational life of Baptist churches.[1] Spiritual direction can be extricated from an exclusively Catholic context, however, by conceiving of it broadly as a Christian practice through which "the whole body" of Christ "upbuilds itself in love" (Eph 4:16). The evidence that spiritual direction belongs to the whole church will be its capacity to adapt to different church traditions. In support of this claim I want to offer an understanding of spiritual direction that will root it firmly in a Baptist view of the church.

The Need for Spiritual Direction

What need for direction is indicated by the view of church that animates the Baptist tradition? At the heart of our tradition is the conviction that the church stands in need of reform—*radical* reform that involves an ongoing, ever-renewed, and unending process of guiding the church to be the church.

Reformation usually begins with the shocking discovery that the church—one's own church—may not be what it claims to be. This discovery may occur when we hear the critical statements outsiders say about the church, which can be, as H. Richard Niebuhr indicates, a highly charged moral event: "To see ourselves as others see us or to have others communicate to us what they see when they regard our lives from the outside is to have a moral experience."[2] The criticism may also come from within the church from reformers who dare to protest what they see as wrong.

We typically respond to such information in a variety of ways, and much of the time our initial response will be defensive. If we tend toward self-deception, we will deny the truth of what is said because we are blind to what appears obvious to others. If we perceive the critic as a threat to our well being, then we may viciously counterattack, or we may recognize the gap between who we are and what we claim to be but choose none-theless to portray ourselves in public as something we know in private we are not. Such hypocrisy commits us to a strategy of fooling others and brings with it a heavy burden of guilt that must be carried alone in secrecy and thereby fosters a sense of alienation and isolation. We may see the gap but choose cynicism about the possibility of change, sighing with despair about the way things are and how nothing can be done about them, or, while we refuse to become cynical, our sense of integrity may tempt us to quit and run away.

In contrast to these defensive and negative responses, however, we may also have the courage to engage in authentic self-criticism and sub-mit ourselves to the kind of examination that brings freedom and power to change. This is the beginning of reformation.

When we see ourselves in a new and disturbing light and face the reality of being different than we have claimed to be, we will experience a sense of shame that will confuse our identity and frustrate our mission. We do not know who we are or what to do. In order to resolve the crisis, we must discover what changes of conviction and behavior are necessary to justify our self-understanding. That is what reformation does; it sets things right. It is a process of justification in which we make the changes necessary for us to understand correctly who we truly are and become what we rightly claim to be. It frees the church from shame, moves us in the direction of joyful self-discovery, and empowers us to fulfill our mission.

The need for justification, which calls for reform and makes it radical, constitutes the need for spiritual direction in the Baptist tradition. The need is, at one and the same time, both personal and communal.

The Goal of Spiritual Direction

Given the need for justification, the next question to ask is: Where does reformation come from, and what keeps it going with the right spirit in the right direction? The dominant answer in the Baptist tradition has been "the Bible." Reformation occurs when the church sees itself in the transforming light of scripture. Accordingly, the main forms of guidance in the Baptist tradition have been the sermon, Bible discussion groups, and revivalism.

The sermon has provided guidance to the Christian congregation by means of an authoritative interpretation of a biblical text by a theological scholar.

Bible discussion groups, begun by the Anabaptists and continued today in the form of Sunday School classes, have been oriented more toward the laity and have fostered mutual guidance in the context of small groups.

Revivalism, with its fiery preaching and emotional expression—all of it designed to bring about conversion—may be the primary experience of reformation in the history of American Christianity. When churches have members who vaguely believe in God, who admire Jesus and call their admiration "faith," and who consider themselves "saved" but fail to follow the narrow and hard way pioneered by Jesus, then revivals function to disrupt their complacency and guide them to authentic Christian discipleship.

Through the sermon, Bible discussion groups, and revivals, scripture has functioned as a major source and sure guide of reformation in the Baptist tradition. But is this all? Has not prayer, along with scripture, also played an important role? Undoubtedly so, and yet its significance in this regard has not often been appreciated. One Protestant theologian who has tried to give prayer its due is Karl Barth. For example, in the introductory remarks to an interpretation of the Lord's Prayer, he wrote:

> The Reformation appears to us as a great whole: a labor of research, thinking, preaching, discussion, polemic, and organization. But it was more than all that. From what we know, it was also an act of continuous prayer, an invocation, and, let us add, an act of human beings, of certain persons, and at the same time a response on the part of God.[3]

Reformation occurs when the church sees itself through the transforming images of scripture. But this self-perception requires more than good reading and sound interpretation. Reformation occurs when the church, seeing itself in scripture light, invokes the kingdom of God, and God answers its prayer. If we think of prayer in connection with reformation, then the prayer of the church is a powerful practice that inspires reformation and guides it in the right direction—toward the coming kingdom of God. Prayer purifies the spirit of reform by confronting us with our self-deceptions, by calling us away from hypocrisy, by protecting us from cynicism, by leading us away from the temptation to quit, and by creating freedom to change.

The connection of prayer and reformation sets the goal of spiritual direction in the Baptist tradition. Its purpose is to guide the church to invoke faithfully the gracious realm of God's rule.

The Task of Spiritual Direction

So far I have indicated the need for spiritual direction, which is the need for justification that calls for radical reform, and defined its goal—that is, to guide the church to invoke the kingdom of God. The next question concerns the task of spiritual direction. How does it fulfill its purpose?

In guiding the church to invoke God's kingdom, spiritual direction helps form a community of prayer. This may suggest the idea of a group of people always engaged in the activity of praying. But I have something different in mind. The church as a community of prayer means the Christian practice of prayer is so basic that we can identify the church by reference to it.

An outsider may look at the church and see an association of people with a set of common religious convictions. While this is true and illuminating, it hardly touches on the insider's view of what it means to be the church. James William McClendon, Jr., articulates the insider's experience when he says God is companion and partner: "God is a *member* of the community—not of course a member just like other members, but in his own way."[4] Belonging to the church means participation in a convictional community in which God also participates. God dwells among us, as one of us and yet as God, as a powerful and sometimes strange presence who gathers us and holds us together in love and leads us in the narrow and hard way of adventure opened before us by Jesus Christ. This divine and human partnership constitutes the church as a distinctive kind of community.

Here is the crucial point: The existence of such a community requires that it have a special form of speech. Its language cannot be merely the forms of speech by which human beings address one another. There has to be a way for dialogue with God to take place, a form of language that allows God to talk to the other members of the community and hear what they have to say and that allows them to speak to God and hear what God has to say. Prayer is that form of language. It is the charismatic tongue of the church, our peculiar way of talking and listening. Without it we could not know God or make ourselves known to God. That is how basic prayer is to the life of the church and why the church, in order to be the church, must be a community of prayer.

Karl Barth says that prayer is "the first and basic act of theological work."[5] This means that theological work cannot begin until one learns the distinctive language in which that work must be done and becomes gifted in its use. The first step is learning how to pray as the church must pray in order to be the church. The knowledge of God means knowing what we can know only by learning how to praise God, give thanks, confess our sins and seek forgiveness, ask for what we need, complain, interpret the needs of others and speak on their behalf (especially when they have no voice of their own), make wishes, make promises, meditate, and listen. Knowing how to do these things and how to do them skillfully is the first and basic act of theological work. Theology starts with the knowledge of God internal to the church's practice of prayer, and it seeks to interpret what the church knows by virtue of being a community of prayer.

How do people learn to pray? We learn first of all from our participation in worship. From the perspective of spiritual direction, worship should be evaluated in terms of whether it teaches us how to invoke faithfully the gracious realm of God's rule. Thus, spiritual direction in the Baptist tradition should include a liturgical concern to help the church at worship become "a house of prayer for all peoples" (Isa 56:7; Mark 11:15-17), the true home of Christian fellowship where the word of God can be proclaimed and heard and where thankful communion can celebrate the presence of the crucified and risen Christ among us as the Lord of God's creation.

To help guide the church to be the church, spiritual direction should start with a liturgical concern, but it goes on to teach people how to pray by means of formal conversations, sustained over a series of structured meetings and focused on prayer. The conversations are intensely personal, usually but not necessarily one-to-one, and they often become a remarkable source of learning, healing, and spiritual growth. While the focus of these conversations is on prayer, their scope will be as wide ranging as all the things people pray about. They will concern whatever one's prayer is about or should be about—that is, what one's life is about, what God is about, and how the two are related and may become one. Spiritual direction involves a person's most basic convictions about God, self, and others and the need for those convictions to be discovered, evaluated, and—if necessary—changed. Spiritual direction can be that intense, that specific, that broad, that deep, that powerful, that transforming.

A person who serves as a spiritual director will listen, ask questions, make observations, give encouragement, and offer instruction. Sometimes a director will use the skills and techniques of counseling. At other times he or she will serve as a teacher. At its best, spiritual direction becomes a partnership of friends engaged in the theological work of learning how to pray.

While people seek spiritual direction because they are drawn to communion with God, what often motivates them to seek the help of a spiritual director is suffering connected to their spiritual lives. They may have a sense of inner pain or emptiness they can no longer ignore, or they may struggle with a crisis. Perhaps there has been a loss of faith, or God may seem absent or not real or abstract. Prayer may be impossible, problematic, frustrating, or shameful. Religious language may have come to lack concrete meaning. Persons may have had a bad experience with abusive or oppressive religion. There may be sin that needs to be confessed, but fear and distrust block the way to forgiveness. Persons may struggle with a difficult decision concerning the direction of life and its meaning, perhaps related to work, family, or church. The stresses of ministry may have become overwhelming. Perhaps sickness, disability, or tragedy may have brought confusion and doubt about God's care. A sense of hypocrisy may trouble them, or conflict with others and anger may prevent spiritual growth. They simply may desire a more suitable spirituality and a more authentic form of Christian community.

In one way or another, something has gone wrong that affects the spiritual life. Thus, spiritual direction often begins with complaints about God, church, family, friends, work, self. In spiritual direction these complaints are regarded as implicit prayer. At the beginning of the process, the primary responsibility of a spiritual director is to listen attentively to troubled individuals, hallowing the need to be heard and the need for God to hear. Patiently and gently, a director allows what needs to be said (especially to God) to disclose itself. Spiritual direction offers the safety and freedom for telling the truth, a necessary skill in prayer, which addresses God "to whom all hearts are open, all desires known, and from whom no secrets are hid."

Again, learning to pray is the primary purpose of spiritual direction, and such learning begins to take place with the experience of being listened to by the loving presence of a caring person and by learning to reflect theologically in search of the right story to tell about one's life in relation to God. Prayer requires trust that God listens and cares; a person needs courage and skill to say truthfully what his/her life is like and to interpret what is happening through the image of God's grace. One also needs imagination to anticipate what may come next. Spiritual direction provides a nurturing environment where the trust, courage, skill, hope, and vision necessary for prayer can be cultivated.

Furthermore, as spiritual direction guides people in the practice of prayer, it will help them develop a contemplative spirituality. Contemplation itself is not a distinctively religious experience. It is the kind of experience (usually joyful and empowering) in which attention becomes so sharply focused that people forget momentarily about themselves. Contemplative prayer is simply paying attention to God. In order to help people develop a contemplative attitude toward God, a spiritual director may ask them to start with ordinary contemplative experiences they already enjoy, which may seem to have little or nothing to do with prayer, and to think of them as places to encounter God. Contemplative ways of reading scripture or enjoying nature may also be suggested. These experiences become the subject of conversation in spiritual direction as people describe what happens, what they feel, and any interaction with God that occurs. An important shift occurs when the focus becomes what they are learning from these contemplative experiences about how they recognize and respond to God's presence and the movement of God's Spirit in their lives.

Spiritual direction does not focus on analyzing or solving problems, which may only encourage self-preoccupation. Rather, it centers on the awareness of God, and its goal is a healthy practice of prayer that draws on the full resources of Christian faith, hope, and love to form in people the maturity of Christ.

The art of spiritual direction is knowing how to engage people in conversation about prayer, something we do not normally feel comfortable talking about in any manner other than abstract generalizations. Training and practice are required to develop the skill necessary to guide people gently and helpfully in the kind of conversation spiritual direction intends to engage. Given the distinctive emphasis that the Baptist tradition places on the priesthood of all believers, however, it would be unfortunate for spiritual direction to become the responsibility of a special class of religious experts. The congregational life of the church would be greatly enhanced if more Christians knew better how to engage one another in conversation about prayer, what questions to ask, how to respond, when to be silent and wait, and what not to say—in short, how to serve as priests to one another. The church needs gifted pastors, teachers, writers, counselors, and friends to show us how to do this, but they will not be specialists in some obscure area of theological work far removed from the common life of the church. Rather, their task will be to guide the church to learn a basic part of what we need to know how to do in order to fulfill God's purpose for the church in our worship, discipleship, mission, and fellowship. Their work will help us learn how to pray and how to talk to one another about prayer in order that we may grow in the grace of the knowledge of God.

The Ways of Spiritual Direction

One may understand spiritual direction in many ways. One obvious approach would be to describe the process in detail and give examples or case studies. We could survey the literature and discuss the best books written about it. We might also study guidance as it occurs in scripture with special attention to the wisdom tradition, especially how Jesus and Paul made use of it, and attempt to apply wisdom as a source of guidance in Christian community. We could take the historical perspective and contrast the modern practice of spiritual direction as a form of companionship with its more authoritarian role in earlier periods. Perhaps we should examine our society in terms of sociology and talk about the religious hunger generated by the secularism of western Europe and the materialism and superficiality of American culture. This would lead us to see spiritual direction as a way for us to obey the command Jesus gave Peter to "feed my sheep" (John 21:15-17). We might focus on the therapeutic dimension and discuss the healing that often occurs in spiritual direction, comparing it to pastoral counseling and psychotherapy. We could also narrate and reflect on personal experiences of spiritual direction.

Each perspective is important. The phenomenological, the bibliographical, the biblical, the historical, the sociological, the psychological, the biographical—all will contribute to a full account that does justice to the complexity of spiritual direction (which requires interdisciplinary study).[6] The ecclesiological approach I have taken provides only a partial view, yet it shows how spiritual direction can be rooted firmly in what is central to the Baptist vision. I have approached it from a theological perspective centered on the church and commented on *the need* for spiritual direction (to call for radical reform based on the need for justification), the *goal* (to guide the church to invoke the kingdom of God), and the *task* (to help Christian disciples learn how to pray). This kind of conceptual groundwork is necessary for spiritual direction to function as an authentic part of Baptist church life.

In closing, let me emphasize that spiritual direction belongs to the whole church. The most compelling evidence for the truth of this claim will be the increasing number of church leaders and congregations in the Baptist tradition who make spiritual direction part of their education for ministry and their practice of pastoral care. As they learn how to use it fruitfully as a resource for spiritual formation, I believe they will find that it is an exciting possibility for church work in the future development of the Baptist tradition and the continuing reformation of the church.

Notes

[1]For a brief survey of the history of spiritual direction in the Catholic tradition, see Janet Ruffing, *Uncovering Stories of Faith: Spiritual Direction and Narrative* (New York: Paulist Press, 1989). She provides a useful description of several types of direction. Other historical surveys are offered by Tilden Edwards, *Spiritual Friend: Reclaiming the Gift of Spiritual Direction* (New York: Paulist Press, 1980) and Timothy Leech, *Soul Friend: The Practice of Christian Spirituality* (San Francisco: Harper and Row, 1977).

[2]H. Richard Niebuhr, *The Meaning of Revelation* (New York: The Macmillan Company, 1941; paperback edition, 1960, sixth printing, 1970) 62.

[3]Karl Barth, *Prayer*, ed. Don Saliers and trans. Sara F. Terrien, 2d ed. (Philadelphia: Westminster Press, 1985) 23.

[4]James Wm. McClendon, Jr., *Ethics: Systematic Theology, Volume One* (Nashville: Abingdon Press, 1986) 182-83.

[5]Karl Barth, *Evangelical Theology: An Introduction*, trans. Grover Foley (Grand Rapids MI: William B. Eerdmans, 1963) 160.

[6]For more information about spiritual direction, see William A Barry and William

J. Connolly, *The Practice of Spiritual Direction* (New York: The Seabury Press, 1983); Kevin G. Culligan, ed., *Spiritual Direction: Contemporary Readings* (Locust Valley NY: Living Flame Press, 1983); Tad Dunne, *Spiritual Mentoring: Guiding People Through Spiritual Exercises to Life Decision* (San Francisco: Harper Collins Publishers, 1991); Katherine Marie Dyckman and L. Patrick Carroll, *Inviting the Mystic and Supporting the Prophet: An Introduction to Spiritual Direction* (New York: Paulist Press, 1981); Tilden Edwards, *Spiritual Friend: Reclaiming the Gift of Spiritual Direction* (New York: Paulist Press, 1980); Kathleen Fischer, *Women at the Well: Feminist Perspectives on Spiritual Direction* (New York: Paulist Press, 1988); Alan Jones, *Exploring Spiritual Direction: An Essay on Christian Friendship* (New York: Seabury Press, 1982); Jean Laplace, *Preparing for Spiritual Direction*, trans. by John C. Guinness (Chicago: Franciscan Herald Press, 1975); Kenneth Leech, *Soul Friend: the Practice of Christian Spirituality* (San Francisco: Harper and Row, 1977); Gerald May, *Care of Mind, Care of Spirit: The Psychiatric Dimensions of Spiritual Direction* (San Francisco: Harper and Row, 1982); Thomas Merton, *Spiritual Direction and Meditation* (Collegeville MN: Liturgical Press, 1960); Jerome M. Neufelder and Mary C. Coelho, eds., *Writings on Spiritual Direction by Great Christian Masters* (New York: The Seabury Press, 1982); Janet Ruffing, *Uncovering Stories of Faith: Spiritual Direction and Narrative* (New York: Paulist Press, 1989); Martin Thornton, *Spiritual Direction: A Practical Introduction* (London: SPCK, 1984); Francis W. Vanderwall, *Spiritual Direction: An Invitation to Abundant Life* (New York: Paulist Press, 1981); John R. Yungblut, *The Gentle Art of Spiritual Guidance* (Rockport MA: Element, Inc., 1988).

Spiritual Discernment, the Community, and Baptists

Wm. Loyd Allen

This writing is a modest attempt to begin recollection of a "lost" dimension of spirituality in my own Baptist tradition. Baptists in the American South once practiced spiritual discernment for individual believers by community process. Gradually that aspect of the Baptist heritage of spirituality receded in importance, as can be demonstrated from Baptist autobiographies. I trace this change within one element of the Baptist tradition because I agree with Carolyn Gratton that "guidance in recalling communities and families to their deepest heritage turns out to be a form of group direction much needed by today's Christians."[1] Baptists in the American South are my community, my spiritual family. Recovery of their spiritual heritage may provide direction for an extended family of seeking sisters and brothers.

Spirituality, Guidance, and Discernment

Christian spirituality is the process, contents, and results of humanity's personal encounter with God. Throughout Christian history persons have served as channels of disclosure, as a means of grace in divine-human encounter. Having individual experience interpreted, clarified, and validated by the help of fellow travelers may occur one on one or in group settings. Formal or informal actions by the community to nurture spirituality are one kind of spiritual direction or spiritual guidance.[2]

Community guidance is the norm in Christian experience. Among Protestants its forms, broadly defined, are corporate worship (especially preaching), Bible study, teaching, singing, and prayer.[3] A more specific form of spiritual direction, the one addressed in this essay, occurs when a believing community or a group within that community focuses on helping persons discern and respond to the invitations of grace in their lives.

Discernment is one of the gifts of the Holy Spirit (1 Cor 12:10). *The Westminster Dictionary of Christian Spirituality* defines this gift as the skill to know the "orientation or direction according to the gospel principle" of the inner spirits urging a person toward one choice or another.[4] To discern means to separate one thing from another. To orient means to turn in the right direction. The noun orient originally meant the direction of the rising sun. Early Christians at baptism turned toward the east to symbolize their orientation to Christ.[5] The Christian life is a repeated turning toward Christ for direction.[6] A community of believers acting from a common vision to help a disoriented pilgrim separate true paths from false ones serves as a spiritual guide.

Community guidance for spiritual discernment is scarce in present day Western Christianity. To declare the erosion of a common vision within Christian traditions, even among local congregations, is to state the obvious. Another truism is the individualized and privatized nature of the search for religious experience among many persons in the current generation.[7] Today's spiritual literature abounds with references to this problem. A mobile, mechanized, computerized culture has given rise to an alienated, isolated, anxious class of searchers. Gratton correctly observes they have lost their "original sense of 'we'."[8] With few exceptions, the larger body of Christ has met this challenge with what Richard Foster terms a "profound silence" (not to be confused with the fertile, creative silence historically associated with his Quaker heritage).[9]

The failure of communities of faith to listen as a body for the leadings of the Spirit has produced direction by legalistic and denominational decree.[10] Disoriented, many turn to subjective, private guidance, playing solitaire with the hand they have been dealt. Others place themselves under demagogues in institutions where the sheer number of followers and an intolerance for diversity provide a false sense of belonging. They let someone else play their hand for them. Lacking is a balanced community guidance that respects both individual freedom (required for authentic personal relationship with Christ) and commitment to Christian community (necessary for the diversity of gifts that brings that relationship to mature fruition).

The Baptist heritage harbors a spirituality that combines positive regard for both individual autonomy and community guidance. We may glimpse this spirituality, rooted in the Reformation, in the autobiographies of Baptist clergy in the early American South, gradually fading from the tradition over time.

Reformation Roots

The Reformation emphasis on the doctrine of the priesthood of the believers led to a recovery of group discernment practiced by and among the whole community of faith. John T. McNeill noted the role of Baptists in this renewal:

> The favorite reform doctrine of the priesthood of all Christians encouraged mutual or group procedures in guidance. They have not always been given recognizable organized form, but the principle has found notable expression in Pietism, Methodism, and Quakerism, and in the Reformed, Presbyterian, and *Baptist churches*.[11]

Individual believers seeking discernment assistance in pre-Reformation Catholicism looked primarily to a spiritual director for guidance. The director's standard of reference was liturgical spirituality, inner conformity to the shape of official worship structures.[12] The means came by the director, the Church's formal representative, usually a priest or other religious professional. His or her training ground was most often the intense group guidance experience of monastic community. One aspect of the Protestant stress on the priesthood of all believers was to shift responsibility for discernment from trained spiritual directors to the larger body of believers. (Unfortunately the proven wisdom of the monastic community's spirituality was usually left behind in this transition.)

The Protestant stress upon community guidance was more pronounced in some movements than in others. The Baptist heritage lies with those segments of the Protestant expression best known for insisting upon informal mutual guidance and community decision-making. This was a corollary of the voluntarist emphasis on the Holy Spirit effecting obedience more through the individual will than through the corporatist structures of the hierarchal church.[13] Mutual guidance affirmed the activity of the Spirit in each member of the Body, leaving unhindered the full array of spiritual gifts.

Baptist beginnings are associated most closely with the Puritan tradition and to a lesser extent with the Anabaptists. The spirituality of both of these groups is identified with the community-centered ascetical and contemplative traditions of the middle ages.[14] Baptists and their close spiritual cousins, the Quakers, exhibit modified remnants of the contemplative spirituality of middle ages monasticism, a spirituality tempered in communal living.[15]

Early Baptists distinguished themselves from other traditions by the intensity of their emphasis on protecting the freedom and ultimate responsibility of the individual believer to relate to God without interference, what Kenneth Leech calls their "sturdy independence, a 'do-it-yourself' spirituality."[16] The direct encounter of the individual will with the Holy Spirit is the primary element of Baptist spirituality. The Baptist expression of Christianity took as its point of origin the direct encounter between the human and the divine; it unfolded from assumptions about the unmediated and free personal relationship between the individual believer and Jesus Christ. Baptist spirituality sought to clear the way for an unhindered encounter of the individual with God.

Early Baptists realized the place community guidance could play in nurturing this ideal as well as the threats spiritual direction posed to the undelegated sovereignty of Christ.[17] They kept some influence of community guidance in an informal form, rejecting the more coercive external mediating aspects of other Protestants just as those counterparts had jettisoned that of the medieval monastic institutions. They took one step closer to voluntarism than the Puritans or the Anabaptists. For example, they discarded the Puritan dependence upon magistrate-enforced piety, and they did not take up the more severe forms of the Anabaptist excommunication by congregational ban. On the other hand, they did not embrace community guidance as much as the Quakers, whose mutual admonition and mutual direction Leech calls their distinctive feature.[18]

Such distinctions do not take early Baptists outside the camp of those who looked to the community of believers as a central source for guidance in individual discernment. Early Baptist spiritual guidance tended to be group oriented without displacing the centerpiece of their Christian experience: the believer's personal encounter with God and its accompanying freedoms and responsibilities. This tradition of balance (tension?) between individual liberty and community guidance is visible in the autobiographies of Baptist clergy in early America.

Community Guidance and Baptist Clergy in the American South before 1845

Community guidance in the spirituality of Baptists in the American South before 1845 can be demonstrated to a certain degree by way of autobiographies of clergy. Religious autobiography addresses the question of grace remembered and interpreted in a way that opens a window into the inner consciousness of the writer.

These autobiographies also have some serious shortcomings. Only a narrow portion of the believing community is represented. Baptist women, minorities, laypersons, and the illiterate are generally excluded. Some might plead—weakly—to be excused from these omissions by appealing to writers on spiritual direction: for example, Morton Kelsey's note that the "quality and nature" of group guidance is determined by its leadership; or the discovery of Gerald May and Tilden Edward of the necessity of strong leadership in creating the conditions for spiritual growth; or John Gunstone's opinion that even mutual direction that denies human leadership really depends heavily upon the charisma of presidency.[19] I do not. The weight of final conclusions about spiritual direction in the early Baptist heritage cannot be borne by these autobiographies, even conceding the considerable contributions of their authors. A great deal of further construction lies ahead before any reliable bridge to the spirituality of the early Baptist heritage can be crossed. Perhaps this study can serve as a narrow plank in the framework.

Spiritual guidance among Baptists has tended to be informal. Baptists in the South did not assume primary responsibility for formally training persons in the ways of encounter as more liturgical and hierarchal traditions have done. They did act as congregations to inform persons about encounter with God as discerned within the Baptist tradition. They communicated to the individual the tradition's instrumental images, the inward and outward means found useful within a particular community for opening life to encounter with God.[20] This mutual responsibility among members for one another's welfare, body and soul, was excercised by the local congregation without that group assuming the major burden for the spiritual formation of the individual.

Guidance Inward: Conversion

Conversion was a central issue for discernment among these Baptists. Through the Great Awakening, specifically the Separate Baptists, pietistic spirituality added its distinctive flavor to the Puritan-based spirituality of Baptists in America. A major component of this pietistic influence was an evangelistic zeal for introducing individuals to the opportunity for an authentic encounter with the divine: a zeal for conversion.[21]

Admission to membership in a local Baptist church was a time of vigorous community guidance in relation to this key process of conversion. The congregation, usually chaired by an ordained minister, would sit to hear testimonies. William Hickman (1747–1834), a Virginian who was one of the first Baptist ministers in Kentucky, wrote of one such meeting:

> Knowing the church was to set and hear experiences, I insisted on brother Tanner to take the seat, as he was the oldest man, but he utterly refused; I was compelled to take it myself. The first man that came up was a raw Irishman of the name of Watson. He came trembling; and if I am any judge, he related a good work; I asked him all the questions necessary, and when we were to receive him brother Tanner rose up and said he did not believe he was a Christian; I desired him to ask him questions; there was another old man who backed Tanner; however he asked him some deep questions on eternal decrees; I replied I did not think they were proper questions to put to a child.[22]

This description reveals something about what one early and influential Baptist in the American South believed should occur at the community guidance event of an admissions hearing. Hickman related this particular event because it was an exception to the rule, an example of the abuse of corporate guidance. Testimonies were not to be tests of an applicant's cognitive assent to certain objective truths. They were to be opportunities for improving new believers' understandings by comparison with the combined experience of the community. Individuals brought their raw religious experience and the community labored to help them understand it.

The testifier was not petitioning for acceptance from a standpoint of certainty. He or she was seeking to discern individual status before God. More often than not in these autobiographies the congregation recognized the genuineness of the encounter before the petitioner did. Hickman's own conversion was an example of this, as was the conversion of fellow Virginian and Kentucky pastor, John Taylor (1752–1835).[23] James Ireland (1748–1806), Separate Baptist remembered for suffering for freedom's sake in Virginia, was part of a Christian community that said, "if ever a work of grace was wrought in the heart of any it was in [him]," yet at the time he would not give them credit for what they said.[24]

The community of believers was not a jury passing final sentence on those who did not meet objective criteria composed of prearranged answers. They were spiritual travelers sharing their experiences with beginners on the way. The inner life of the new believer was thereby lifted from a primarily subjective context to be viewed within the more wholistic one of the full tradition. This added dimension was accomplished without diminishing the personal quality of the original encounter. Guidance was communal; spiritual discernment was ultimately personal and individual.

Guidance Outward: The Life of Action

Once an individual became a part of the community of believers, the direction of corporate guidance turned toward the outer life of action. The Christian believer on pilgrimage was guided by a firm and redemptive discipline. The society in which this discipline occurred was a rough and violent one in much of the antebellum South. The issues included in ecclesiastical disciplinary actions were numerous.[25] For Baptists, the aim of discipline was not to oust erring members but to guide them in understanding the forms that creative action in the world often took after divine-human encounter. Habitual offenders were confronted repeatedly. Hickman complained of a member who, though often dealt with, "was one of the best men to repent and promise [Hickman] ever saw, but as bad to perform."[26] To be examined for misbehavior was not difficult, to be expelled from the congregation was. Taylor believed a unanimous vote should be required for expulsion.[27]

Testimony hearings for admission to membership served to place the new believer's inner life alongside the community of believers' experience. Church discipline guided the believer's continuing journey by comparing the individual's outer life to the full tradition's actions in the world.

Vocational Calling

The relative influence of community discernment among the leaders of early Baptists is revealed by the congregation's part in vocational decisions by pastors. The recognition of a call to preach was the responsibility of the gathered congregation. John Taylor wrote:

> My own belief is that none properly understands the gospel or voice of the shepherd, but his sheep, or the true Christian. Therefore the voice of the church is very essential; in the call of the ministry, the bridegroom is out of the way; what the bride does in his absence should be valid.[28]

A minister was unlikely to change pulpits without permission from the congregation that he served.[29] An exception was John Gano's (1727–1804) departure from his New York congregation. A Philadelphia Association missionary and minister in several states including Kentucky and North and South Carolina, Gano left against the advice of his congregation who had "with all possible coolness, left [him] to determine for [himself]."[30] He cited the event as an action he lived to regret.

Marks of Community Guidance

Baptist congregations were small and intimate during the years under consideration. Corporate guidance depended on mutual familiarity and frank honesty for effectiveness. Taylor lamented a busy year on the frontier that left his congregation "such strangers to each other, that confidence was lacking for want of more acquaintance, and our common calls were such that we had not time to become acquainted."[31] As to honesty and frankness, Taylor is again chief witness. He commented on a congregational meeting that concerned a decision about himself:

> I was a little amused when some of them proposed for me to walk out, while they counseled on that subject—to which I replied, if they could not look me in the face and speak what they thought on that occasion, they did not deserve a name in the house of God—and if I could not bear with patience whatever they might say, I did not deserve the name of gospel minister.[32]

While corporate guidance was an important means of grace in the spirituality of early Baptists in the South, it was only that—guidance, never directive. Soul freedom was preserved and the relationship between God and the individual was held inviolable. Final decisions were always left, as Gano put it, to "God and one's own conscience."[33] In some circumstances, according to Taylor, the lone objector might have the "mind of Christ" though a majority vote prevailed.[34]

Guidance by Individuals

Spiritual guidance among Baptists of this era was not exclusively the domain of the community. The informal spiritual guidance by individuals revealed in these autobiographies had a democratic quality. It was not an exercise by clergy alone. Baptist soul friends might be male or female, clergy or laity, slave or free.[35]

The influence of these persons was great. James Ireland wrote of the layman who eventually led him to Christ: "I could not go on with my wickedness in his presence, as well as if he had been absent."[36] John Taylor followed Joseph Reding, a friend and fellow preacher, to South Carolina and Kentucky. He wrote of Reding: "My conclusions were that I could live nowhere but where Joseph Reding lived."[37]

The authority of the Baptists' soul friend was substantial but never ultimate. The will of the individual was left free for direct personal encounter unencumbered by outside authority. John Gano, writing about a Mr. Tennant who was an influential guide for him, articulated this voluntaristic impulse: "Let Mr. Tennant be ever so good a man, his belief is not a divine warrant for me to act upon." Tennant himself may have aided Gano in reaching this conclusion. He advised Gano: "Do not be always doubting. . . . If you cannot think as I do, think for yourself."[38] Spiritual guidance in the lives of Southern Baptists was a means of enhancing direct divine-human encounter, not a substitute for personal engagement with the divine.

Baptists informally gave and received discerning personal counsel as they sought to fully participate in unmediated encounter with God. No antebellum Baptists in this literature, however, relinquished their direct relationship with God to the mediation of a spiritual director. All participated in community guidance in one form or another. Community guidance for discernment was the norm for early Baptists in the American South.

Bigger and Better Organized: 1845–1891

Beginning in 1845 the self-identity of most Baptists South of the Mason-Dixon line became attached to a distinct organizational form: the Southern Baptist Convention. This process reached maturity and independence in 1891 with the creation of the Southern Baptist Sunday School Board. Thereafter Baptists in the Southern Baptist Convention (SBC) were no longer dependent on any other group for missions, education, or literature.[39]

Along with closer affiliation with extra-congregational organizational structures, these decades also saw the rise of the evangelist-led, efficiently structured, goal-oriented revival model. This occurred in three stages: The first revivals happened in local churches during the normal cycle of activities; next came Baptist involvement in camp meetings; and as these were institutionalized, they were gradually replaced with protracted meetings led by professional evangelists. Baptists in the region became bigger and better organized. Community spiritual guidance declined.

Guidance Inward: Conversion

Revivalism is the key to diminished community guidance in the introductory encounter of the believer with God among these Baptists. Revivalism introduced abbreviation of the conversion process.[40] The journey from conviction of sin to conversion event of the earlier Baptist tradition had normally taken months and had included community guidance for discernment. By 1891 conversion was routinely accomplished within the span of one meeting without any communication with the congregation.

The success of camp meetings altered Baptist practice. Early in the Second Great Awakening, Baptists held in derision the relatively brief, emotional conversions of the Methodist camp meetings. Quoting the sarcastic remarks of Elder William Davis, Jeremiah Bell Jeter (1802–1880) of Virginia wrote:

> The Baptists . . . are the greatest bunglers that I have ever known. I have been attending their Associations for many years, but I have never known a soul convicted, converted, and finished off at a single meeting; but the Methodists can convict, convert, and finish off from 50 to 100 souls at a single camp-meeting.[41]

Hesitantly, in 1831 Jeter helped organize the first ever Baptist camp meeting in the Northern Neck of Virginia. He reported this method of evangelism was so "much at variance with the views and tastes that had long prevailed among the brethren that they could scarcely look one another in the face without laughing."[42] They stopped laughing when the number of Baptist confessions of faith skyrocketed. According to Jeter, the success of the venture "slew all the prejudices" against revival meetings among Northern Neck Baptists.[43] They quickly built permanent grounds and organized camp meetings on an annual basis. This adoption of revival methods, including briefer conversions, is a miniature lesson of what happened throughout Baptist communities in the American South between 1845 and 1891.

Community guidance, anchored among Baptists in conversion—the introductory event of the divine-human encounter—faded in the light of successfully organized revivals. The heart of the conversion process had heretofore been the unique personal testimony given before a community of believers. Pastors who were approached by inquirers would refer them to Saturday conferences of local congregations.[44] The experiences related were usually after the conversion event, clarifying and giving perspective for individual and personal discernment. Most testifiers were known to the congregation and the hearers had a common vision of spiritual tradition.

With camp meeting conversions, a rift developed between the inquirer and the congregation. The most obvious reason is that the conversion event often occurred at an interdenominational revival meeting outside a local fellowship. The people who heard the public confessions often did not know the confessors well. As time passed, the testimony was normally given after the inquirer was certain of salvation. An uncertain inquirer relating his or her experience before an empathetic congregation was uncommon in meetings held by professional evangelists such as Thomas Teasdale (1808–1891), Mississippi pastor become full-time revivalist.[45] He and other foremost Baptist revivalists such as Elder Jacob Knapp provided arguments for sudden conversion.[46] Illustration after illustration in their sermons stressed the possibility and importance of conversion "right here and now." Those who did not respond were in danger of losing through procrastination their only chance for salvation. No time to wait for a careful hearing of testimony before the gathered community. The role of the believing community in spiritual guidance at conversion began to decrease among these Baptists.

Guidance Outward: The Life of Action

Community guidance after conversion also declined. Very little mention of church discipline is found in the autobiographies of this period, and the spiritual guidance that was given fits the category of advice more than discernment. Johnson Olive (1816–1885) of North Carolina suffered severe depression for years. His uncle convinced him to submit to the questioning of the "old brethren" in the community of believers. Instead of lifting his lot into the larger context of the spiritual experience of the community, Olive's guides, he wrote, "would ask questions, and without waiting for me to answer them, would try to help me by answering themselves, as they would have it to be."[47] He complained: "Every neighbor and friend became a preacher to me."[48] He did not need "thus sayeth the Lord," he wanted guidance through shared experience, something he did not find in his community of believers.

This loss of community guidance was related to an overall loss of shared personal experience among Baptist believers. A sharing of inner conflicts and victories by mature Christians was a staple of the religious diet found in abundance in the pre-1845 autobiographies of these Baptists.

Not so in the writings of a later era. Toward the end of his life, J. B. Jeter noted this decline with sorrow:

> In nothing has there been so striking a change among Baptists, within the range of my observation, as in religious conversation. We have now much talk on topics more or less closely connected with religion. We hear much of plans for usefulness, the doings of conventions, the merit of preachers, the qualities of books, the progress of churches, and the like, but we rarely hear a conversation on personal piety. That was the almost universal topic among our fathers. Wherever and whenever they met they conversed of their experiences—the dealings of God with their souls.[49]

Jeter was not so discerning about the relationship between the innovations he promoted and the loss of the life's blood of community guidance he grieved. He had come to believe that "passing through a round of experience in order to be prepared to receive Christ" was a "serious defect" in the teaching of his Baptist forebears because this "mistake" led souls to labor longer than they should in conversion.[50] Institutionalized revivalism made the Baptist denomination bigger and better organized. This success changed Baptist minds and coincidentally and unknowingly diminished community guidance for discernment.

Corporate Guidance or Corporation? 1891–1942

With the founding of the Sunday School Board in 1891, Southern Baptist centralization began in earnest. In the fifty years that followed, the corporate business model became the norm among the Baptists under consideration here.[51] Successful business persons were celebrities. Virginia Baptist pastor, educator, denominationalist, and revivalist William E. Hatcher (1834–1912) invited millionaires to speak to his Sunday School classes, and Texas Baptist newspaper editor J. B. Cranfill (1858–1942) gave a chapter in his first autobiography to R. W. Sears without once mentioning God or religion.[52] Clergy were encouraged to instill these models into religious life. George W. Gardner (1851–1926), Baptist editor in Mississippi and South Carolina, wrote: "I am sure that a man is a success or failure just in proportion to his business sense."[53]

Affiliating with California Southern Baptists in 1942, the Southern Baptist Convention became an ecclesiastical bureaucracy of nationwide scope. The identity of the Baptist segment under consideration became more and more bound to the apparatus and goals of the convention. The adoption of the efficient mangement model came slowly to the majority of Baptist laity in the rural south, but reigned supreme among the ministerial leadership of the convention—the clergy who wrote autobiographies and planned for the future of their heirs.

Guidance Inward: Conversion

This "upsizing" of Baptist relationships to a corporate level further eliminated the traditional impact of local community guidance for discernment. The conversion process became part of a mass production campaign. Revival methods were streamlined and put in the service of producing significant statistics to establish the success of congregational efforts and investments. Professional Baptist evangelists such as W. E. "Major" Penn (1832–1895), Texas lawyer turned lay evangelist, carefully recorded and reported decisions. Penn would announce the name and number of each convert as he or she walked the religious assembly aisle.[54]

Whether the name or the number was of greater interest to Penn and his employers is open to question. That the link between personal conversion event and community guidance was absent is not. One of Major Penn's new measures was the requirement that no one speak to convicted sinners in a gathered congregation except the pastor or evangelist.[55] Hatcher argued that the first confession should be made as easy as possible and the pastor should do most of the talking.[56] "I have long ceased to expect an extended and connected story from those seeking membership in the churches," wrote Alabama state missions director W. B. Crumpton (1842–1926). "The process by which they were led to this confession would be interesting, but is not at all necessary."[57]

Guidance Outward: The Life of Action

Community guidance for the continuing pilgrimage of new Christians among these Baptists was rare. George W. Gardner admitted late in his life that "the churches no longer practice discipline."[58] One cause for the lack of ongoing community guidance was the changing image of the pastor as professional. Under the corporate business model, leading pastors were often viewed as paid professionals hired by a congregation who supported these specialists mainly by their presence and contributions.[59]

Mass evangelism produced another factor in the decline of community guidance: the lack of a common vision. Church members with no prior knowledge of one another and without a common means of sharing religious experience were incapable of providing the guidance necessary for discernment. An extreme example of this existed at the "Nickel Church" in Palestine, Texas. Built by nickel contributions gathered in the revivals of Major Penn, this church's pastor, W. T. Tardy (1870–1919), complained that "the congregation had been gathered by evangelists from the four winds and in consequence the church never had been a substantial, aggressive, and dependable fraternity."[60] To a lesser extent, many Southern Baptist congregations, especially in influential urban areas, were constructed by the same methods.[61]

Southern Baptist churches in the care of denominational leaders in the first half of the twentieth century gradually displaced the congregational guidance of the voluntarist community. It is yet to be revived in any substantial way in this stream of the Baptist tradition.

Reclaiming Community Guidance

Though precipitating factors, revivalism and the corporate model cannot ultimately be held responsible for the loss of community guidance among the Baptists whose descendants populate the American South. The deeper difficulty was the lack of an understanding of their own spiritual heritage. They were heart religionists who needed to love their tradition with their minds as well, analyzing and critiquing cultural shifts. The hope for preserving valuable elements within the rich spiritual tradition of Baptists lies in unearthing that heritage and refurbishing it for contemporary use. This essay is an exercise in the former, but I want to close with a suggestion for the latter.

The community guidance that was part of the experience of early Baptists cannot be resurrected. Too much has changed. Our churches are generally not small enough to have the relational background necessary, to say nothing of setting aside Saturday afternoons (or any other time) for entire congregations to hear testimony, but we can assess the value of those bygone structures and seek ways to retrieve their intimacy. Perhaps small groups devoted to mutual discernment could be designed to meet the need. The writings of Tilden Edwards and Gerald May of the Shalem Institute are a good beginning. For others the work of Morton Kelsey or Richard Foster's Renovaré movement are more appropriate. Among Baptists the work of Glenn Hinson and Edward Thornton has laid a worthy foundation of theory and practice. Baptist Tom Turner, minister of spiritual direction at Pilgrim's Rest Retreat Center (3431 Stokesmont Road, Nashville, Tennessee 37215) is nurturing multiple ministries in Baptist spirituality, including conferences, a journal, and this book.

All efforts at individual discernment in group settings wrestle with the tension between individual freedom and submission to spiritual discipline. Who can better balance discipline with liberty than Baptists?—Baptists, who have glimpsed freedom in their ancestral origins and known attenuation of that freedom in their present circumstances. Surely such a people have a stake in earnestly seeking discernment, together.

Notes

[1]Carolyn Gratton, *The Art of Spiritual Guidance: A Contemporary Approach to Growing in the Spirit* (New York: Crossroad, 1992) 196.

[2]For a brief history of spiritual direction in the Christian tradition see Kenneth Leech, *Soul Friend: A Study of Spirituality* (London: Sheldon Press, 1977) 34-89.

[3]Tilden H. Edwards, *Spiritual Friend: Reclaiming the Gift of Spiritual Direction* (New York: Paulist Press, 1980) 174. See discussion of community guidance, 61-64.

[4]Ernest E. Larkin, "Discernment of Spirits," *The Westminster Dictionary of Christian Spirituality*, Gordon S. Wakefield, ed. (Philadelphia: Westminster Press, 1983) 115.

[5]Josef A. Jungmann, *The Early Liturgy* (Notre Dame IN: University of Notre Dame Press, 1959) 82.

[6]See Wm. Loyd Allen, *Crossroads in Christian Growth: The Bible and Personal Crisis* (Nashville: Broadman, 1989) especially 15-16.

[7]See the findings of the conference "The American Denominational Future: The Southern Baptist Case," (Louisville Institute for the Study of Protestantism and American Culture, Louisville, Kentucky, 12-13 March 1993). A brief summary of the presentations may be found in the *Western Recorder* (23 March 1993) 7. See also Kirk C. Hadaway, "Church Growth in North America: The Character of a Religious Marketplace," in *Church and Denominational Growth*, David A. Roozen and C. Kirk Hadaway, eds. (Nashville: Abingdon Press, 1993) 346-57.

[8]Gratton, 153-54.

[9]Richard J. Foster, *Celebration of Discipline: The Path to Spiritual Growth* (San Francisco: Harper & Row, Publishers, 1978) 151.

[10]Gratton, 152-53; Foster, 150.

[11]John T. McNeill, *A History of the Cure of Souls* (New York: Harper and Row, 1951) ix. Italics mine.

[12]See Louis Bouyer, *Liturgical Piety* (Notre Dame: University of Notre Dame Press, 1955); Richard Kieckhefer, "Major Currents in Late Medieval Devotion," *Christian Spirituality: High Middle Ages and Reformation*, Jill Raitt, ed., World Spirituality: An Encyclopedic History of the Religious Quest, vol. 17 (New York: Crossroad, 1987) 75-108; James F. McCue, "Liturgy and Eucharist: West" *Christian Spirituality: High Middle Ages and Reformation*, Jill Raitt, ed., World Spirituality: An Encyclopedic History of the Religious Quest, vol. 17 (New York: Crossroad, 1987) 427-38; Robert Duggan, "Liturgical Spirituality and Liturgical Reform," *Spiritual Life* 27 (Spring, 1981).

[13]E. Glenn Hinson coined this voluntarist to corporatist scale to interpret Baptist distinctiveness. He places early Baptists alongside the Quakers at the voluntarist pole and away from Roman Catholics at the corporatist extreme. See "Endangered Species: Will the Baptist Tradition Survive?" *Report from the Capital* (September 1993): 5.

[14]See Richard F. Lovelace, "The Anatomy of Puritan Piety: English Puritan Devotional Literature, 1600-1640," *Christian Spirituality: Post-Reformation and Modern*,

Louis Dupré, Don E. Saliers, eds. in collaboration with John Meyendorff, World Spirituality: An Encyclopedic History of the Religious Quest, vol. 17 (New York: Crossroad, 1989) 294-323; Charles E. Hambrick-Stowe, *The Practice of Piety: Puritan Devotional Disciplines in Seventeenth-Century New England* (Chapel Hill NC: University of North Carolina Press, 1982); C. M. Dent, "The Anabaptists," *The Study of Spirituality*, Chesyln Jones, Geoffrey Wainwright, and Edward Yarnold, S.J., eds. (New York, Oxford University Press, 1986) 350-54; and K. R. Davis, *Anabaptism and Asceticism: A Study in Intellectual Origins* (Scottdale PA: Herald, 1974).

[15]E. Glenn Hinson, "Baptist and Quaker Spirituality," *Christian Spirituality: Post-Reformation and Modern*, Louis Dupré, Don E. Saliers, eds. in collaboration with John Meyendorff, in World Spirituality: An Encyclopedic History of the Religious Quest, vol. 17 (New York; Crossroad, 1989) 324-37; also E. Glenn Hinson, "Southern Baptist and Medieval Spirituality: Surprising Similarities," *Cistercian Studies*, 20 (1985): 224-36.

[16]Leech, 87.

[17]This caution they shared to a greater or lesser degree with most Protestants. See Gerald G. May, *Care of Mind, Care of Spirit: Psychiatric Dimensions of Spiritual Direction* (New York: Harper and Row, 1982) 2.

[18]Leech, 87.

[19]Morton T. Kelsey, *Companions on the Inner Way: The Art of Spiritual Guidance* (New York: Crossroad, 1983) 120; Gerald G. May, *Pilgrimage Home: The Conduct of Contemplative Practice in Groups* (New York: Paulist Press, 1979); John Gunstone, "Group Prayer," *The Study of Spirituality*, Cheslyn Jones, Geoffrey Wainwright, Edward Yarnold, S.J., eds. (New York: Oxford University Press, 1986) 570-72.

[20]Urban T. Holmes, *A History of Christian Spirituality* (New York: Seabury Press, 1980) 28. Examples include regular times for prayer, Bible reading, and acts of compassion.

[21]Wm. Loyd Allen, "Spirituality among Southern Baptist Clergy as Reflected in Selected Autobiographies," (Ph.D. diss., The Southern Baptist Theological Seminary, 1984) 25-31.

[22]William Hickman, *A Short Account of My Life and Travels* (Typescript, n.d., Dargin-Carver Library, Southern Baptist Convention Sunday School Board, Nashville TN, rpt. 1928) 13-14.

[23]Hickman, 9; John Taylor, *A History of Ten Baptist Churches* (Frankfort KY: J. H. Holeman, printer, 1823) 73, 106-107.

[24]James Ireland, *The Life of the Reverend James Ireland*, J. Foster, compiler (Winchester VA: J. Foster, printer, 1819) 20.

[25]See William Warren Sweet, "The Churches as Moral Courts on the Frontier," *Church History* 2 (1933): 3-21. Page eleven contains an extensive list.

[26]Hickman, 11.

[27]Taylor, 74-75.

[28]Ibid., 399. Ireland agreed, 161-62.

[29]See Hickman, 14; and Taylor, 49-51.

[30]John Gano, *Biographical Memoirs of the Late Rev. John Gano*, Stephen Gano, ed. (New York: Southwick and Hardcastle, 1806) 118-19.

[31]Taylor, 43.

[32]Ibid., 143.

[33]Gano, 81. See also Gano, 35-38, 118-19; and Hickman, 9.
[34]Taylor, 49.
[35]Ibid., 18, 46, 156.
[36]Ireland, 46.
[37]Taylor, 298.
[38]Gano, 21, 25.
[39]Of course, not all Baptists joined the Southern Baptist Convention. By necessity African-American Baptists remained under its authority until emancipation, but the spirituality of minority Baptist expressions awaits further research.
[40]See Bill J. Leonard, "Getting Saved in America: Conversion Event in a Pluralistic Culture," *Review & Expositor* (Winter 1985): 111-27.
[41]Jeremiah Bell Jeter, *The Recollections of a Long Life* (Richmond: Religious Herald Co., 1891) 92.
[42]Jeter, 154.
[43]Ibid., 156.
[44]See James Madison Pendleton, *Reminiscences of a Long Life* (Louisville: Press Baptist Book Concern, 1891) 28-29; also Jeter, 55.
[45]Thomas C. Teasdale, *Reminiscences and Incidents of a Long Life* (St. Louis: National Baptist Publishing Co., 1887) 122.
[46]Jacob Knapp, *Autobiography of Elder Knapp*, Reuben Jeffery, ed. (New York: Sheldon & Co., 1868) 43-44.
[47]Johnson Olive, *One of the Wonders of the Age* (Raleigh: Edwards, Broughton, 1886) 156-58.
[48]Ibid., 147.
[49]Jeter, 318.
[50]Ibid., 39.
[51]Nancy T. Ammerman discusses characteristics of this model such as mass production, centralized relationships, and specialized organization. See "SBC Moderates and the Making of a Postmodern Denomination," *The Christian Century* (22-29 September 1993): 896-99.
[52]William E. Hatcher, *Along the Trail of the Friendly Years* (New York: Fleming H. Revell, 1910) 164; James Britton Cranfill, *Dr. J. B. Cranfill's Chronicle: A Story of Life in Texas* (New York: Fleming H. Revel, 1916) 491-93.
[53]George William Gardner, *Echoes from the Fleeting Years, 1851-1923*, (unpublished manuscript on microfilm at The Southern Baptist Theological Seminary, Louisville KY, 1922) 130.
[54]W. E. Penn, *The Life and Labors of W. E. Penn the Texas Evangelist* (St. Louis: C. B. Woodward, 1896) 286.
[55]Ibid., 279.
[56]Hatcher, 164.
[57]Washington Bryan Crumpton, *A Book of Memories, 1842–1920* (Montgomery: Baptist Mission Board, 1921) 19-20; italics mine.
[58]Gardner, 116.
[59]Ibid.

"The Road of Ashes": Spirituality and the Prospects for Disillusioned Baptists

Gary Furr

Spirituality and Baptist Conflicts

Robert Bly describes an archetypal aspect of the spiritual quest in mythology as "the road of ashes, descent and grief."[1] His reading of classical mythology, the great religions, and fairy tales find the common thread of humiliation as the way to ascent. In all lives—all those worth living, at least—come times of testing, temporary defeat, and wandering. He cites the poet Antonio Machado:

> Mankind owns four things
> That are no good at sea—
> Rudder, anchor, oars,
> And the fear of going down.[2]

In the institutional dissension that has racked the Southern Baptist Convention since 1979, many Southern Baptists find themselves looking for a rudder, afraid of going down.

This chapter looks at Baptist spirituality in three parts. Part one gives a brief "survey of the scene" in Southern Baptist life today and notes four major options in Baptist spirituality. Part two considers two of those options, the contemplative and the deeper life movement, as exemplified in some of the writings of Glenn Hinson and Henry Blackaby. These two views will be compared by their treatment of three aspects of the life of prayer: (1) what it means to love God, (2) passing through the "road of ashes" (crisis of faith) and, (3) the results of the life of prayer in the lives of believers. Part three summarizes and sets forth a proposal for a contemporary Baptist spirituality.

Four Options in Current Baptist Spirituality

The practical forms and structures of Christian living are not easily analyzed. Baptist spirituality involves the practices of millions of individuals, most of which will never be publicly detailed. Generally, however, Baptist spirituality incorporates an emphasis on personal experience (heart religion rather than head), the centrality of the Bible, and an emphasis on freedom—both in church-state issues and in matters of individual conscience toward structures, forms, and creeds. Baptists also are zealous to lead others to Christ and strongly emphasize the church as a local community of faith. Baptists generally admire simplicity and holiness, emphasizing personal holiness more than social holiness. Consistent with their principles, Baptists favor simplicity, warmth, and enthusiasm in corporate worship.[3]

Four major expressions of devotion are prominent in the current context. While they are not the only options, they are the most obvious, and all can claim to be rooted in Baptist identity.

Bill Leonard contends that diversity has always been a part of Baptist identity. Leonard builds on the original insights of Walter Shurden, John Loftis, and Leon McBeth, in his contention that Baptist identity has always consisted of an uneasy configuration of diverse traditions. Each has its own theological, ecclesiological, political, and cultural assumptions. Baptist denominational identity survived by holding these traditions in creative tension through common causes, shared heritage, broadly interpreted theological distinctives, and cultural uniformity. The tensions between them made consensus-building leadership essential. Since the takeover movement began in 1979, the "Grand Compromise" (Leonard's term) has collapsed.[4]

Two of these traditions are significant to understand the current forms of Baptist devotion. The Charleston Tradition has its roots among the Particular Baptists of England and the Puritans. Represented by figures such as Screven, Hart, and Furman, its affirmations include: (1) the centrality of religious experience and (2) the authority of Holy Scripture.

The Charleston tradition has a passion for *order*, according to Shurden. Theologically this expresses itself in its use of theological statements and confessions. In terms of polity, this tradition believes more strongly in connectionalism and discipline. Liturgically, worship, while warm-hearted and personal, is more ordered and stately, with greater emphasis on the ordinances. Its focus is more toward the praise of God. The Charleston tradition is pro-education, especially where ministers are concerned. (Shurden calls them "semi-Presbyterians.")[5]

The Sandy Creek tradition has its roots in New England revivalism and the English Separatists, with a passion for *freedom*. The driving force, according to Shurden, was *ardor*. The Sandy Creek tradition favors worship that is *horizontal* and focuses on the main value of winning others to Christ. Understanding of the ministry is charismatic, with an internal call ranking above formal education and training. Ecclesiology is more independent; here, we find the roots of Landmarkism. Theologically, persons of the Sandy Creek tradition were biblicists. They used the Bible literalistically and believed in "the doctrine of sovereign grace in the salvation of souls, mixed with a little of what is called Arminianism."[6] (Shurden calls them semi-pentecostals.)

The tension between these two streams is also reflected in the four dominant options in current Southern Baptist spirituality. Of course, until recently, these streams were submerged in the larger synthesis of the convention. What we see in a time when those differences are accentuated is not simply different views of the Bible, but distinctive understandings of the Christian life itself.

The traditional piety of Southern Baptists has been oriented for the last half century or so around personal discipleship, local church life, and denominational piety. Prayer life in Baptist churches once focused around special emphases in missions, revivals, and the denominational calendar, in addition to the usual personal and local concerns. Now that the denomination has shifted, new options have emerged.

Social Activism

The first option is social activism. This tradition was long revered by the more progressive wing of the SBC and the pre-takeover Christian Life Commission, with a long heritage going back to Walter Rauschenbusch and others. It presents a vision of social and moral holiness. There are two forms of this understanding. One is what Doran McCarty has called the the "koinonia movement." The koinonia movement—represented by Clarence Jordan, Millard Fuller, Habitat for Humanity movement, and the

Church of the Savior in Washington, D.C.—fused small-group "covenant" discipleship and concern for public issues and social justice.[7]

Since 1979, a second version of social activism has arisen in the fundamentalist wing of the Baptist denomination. Once disdainful of the political process in favor of "soul-winning," the New Right activists now practice political action as piety. They are particularly focused on issues of family and sexuality. Abortion activism is *the* galvanizing issue for the "traditional family" cluster of concerns.

This form of devotion is rooted in the Sandy Creek tradition of revivalism and its passion for reform. Social activism finds its parallels not so much in the civil rights movement of the 1960s, as its leaders are fond of saying, but in the temperance and anti-slavery crusades of the nineteenth century that aimed not only for justice but national righteousness and spiritual renewal.

The Quest for Personal Spirituality: Charismatic, Deeper Life, and Contemplative Views

Three other options in the quest for personal spirituality are strong among Baptists today. The charismatic movement and what is often known as the deeper life (also victorious life or Keswick) movement share a common heritage. Both of these movements come out of the old Keswick holiness movement that originated in England in the late nineteenth century.[8]

The charismatic movement continues to have a great impact on Baptists worldwide. These individuals and churches emphasize spiritual gifts, personal holiness, and personal renewal through the experience of a dramatic "second blessing." While many of these Christians remain in Baptist circles, they find themselves largely unwelcome in official Baptist life by moderates or fundamentalists.

The deeper life movement is associated with the Sandy Creek tradition, also. Baptist representatives include the late Bertha Smith, Peter Lord, Jack Taylor, and Henry Blackaby. As an alternative to the charismatic movement, it represents a similar appeal for a "deeper" experience of God after conversion and an emphasis on personal holiness. According to Fisher Humphries, the major difference between the deeper life and the charismatic movement is their difference on the necessity of an identifiable second blessing as manifested in *glossolalia*.[9]

Third, among moderates there is a growing interest in the contemplative traditions. More than any other name, this is connected to the life and writings on the subject by Glenn Hinson. During his years at Southern Seminary, he introduced Thomas Merton and the contemplative tradition to thousands of young Baptist seminarians. The fruit of that labor is still evident today in the writings of many moderate Baptists. For moderates in the Charleston tradition, contemplative Christianity presents compatible devotional forms that afford personal emotional fervor as well as structure and transcendent emphases consistent with it.

Because the activist stream represents concerns dealt with in the section three of this volume, and because the Charismatic Movement is still largely marginalized in Baptist life, I will treat the two remaining options. I contend that the Charleston and Sandy Creek traditions are predisposed toward, respectively, the contemplative and the deeper life versions of devotional life.

This is not to say that these two spiritualities are as utterly opposed to one another as current denominational polarization might indicate. In *The Crisis of Piety*, Donald Bloesch categorizes two types of spirituality within the history of the church: mystical and evangelical. While that classification may be too broad, clearly these two options in Baptist life fit comfortably under the evangelical type.[10] I contend that these two spiritualities do not represent alternative religions, but different options for contemporary Baptists within the broader stream of evangelical piety.

The Deeper Life and the Contemplative Compared

These two views of the spiritual life, the contemplative and the deeper life, can be confusing to the casual hearer or reader. They share common vocabulary, such as journey imagery as a metaphor of the Christian life, the importance of surrender to God, the emphasis on quiet and silence and the shift to listening and receptivity rather than action. Both strongly emphasize a work that continues after conversion. Both views advocate forms, disciplines, methodologies, and structures that prepare the seeker for this deeper work. Both describe the spiritual journey as withdrawal from and return to the world.

Beyond the strong resemblances, however, there are many abiding tensions. This chapter will examine and summarize both the deeper life position, represented most recently by Henry Blackaby's *Experiencing God*, and the contemplative view, represented by its most consistent advocate among Baptists in recent years, E. Glenn Hinson. While not a theologically sophisticated program, *Experiencing God* is the most popular current program of Christian devotion among Southern Baptists.

Both views generally agree that there are many stages in the life of prayer. We will examine a three-fold commonality: spiritual awakening as the hunger to love God in relationship, the "road of ashes" as the crisis of faith in the spiritual life, and the resulting transformation that grows out of that crisis. This chapter will compare these two approaches by comparing and contrasting their understandings of these three dimensions.

Loving God: Moving Toward Intimacy

The goal of the deeper life is a love relationship with God, that is, to know God more "deeply" and intimately. Blackaby is struggling with the whole issue of sanctification: the Christian life *after* conversion. He presumes that the average Christian has had an evangelical conversion experience—a personal awareness of sin, a felt need for Christ, a personal statement of repentance and commitment to Jesus Christ as Lord, and some personal assurance of the validity of that experience.

Entry into a love relationship with God is the key to spiritual victory for Blackaby. This relationship rather than methods, accomplishments, or expertise, is the goal of prayer. God desires our love, but it is love as yielding obedience. The initiative in spiritual growth is God's, the goal is the love of God and the results of that growth are entirely the work of God through us:

> Everything depends on this! Everything in your Christian life, everything about knowing him and experiencing him, everything about knowing His will, depends on the quality of your love relationship to God. If that is not right, nothing in your life will be right.[11]

Spiritual disciplines, therefore, are an expression of that love relationship. The desire to love God "will solve most of your problem with your quiet time."[12]

This deeper Christian walk is available to anyone and makes God's guidance and presence available in simple and practical ways. There is no mysterious or complicated journey to spiritual victory and depth, only surrender and openness to the work of God. "Anything significant that happens in your life will be a result of God's activity in your life."[13]

Encounter with God in prayer is purely apart from human initiative. Only God through the Spirit moves us to pray. The role of the Holy Spirit is to persuade us to ask for what, in effect, is already accomplished. Prayer makes us vessels of God's will and increases our faith. The only human tasks in prayer are listening, receiving, adjusting and obeying.[14]

Life for the contemplative, on the other hand, is lived on two levels: One is the outward world of action, activity, and behavior; the other is the interior life "where we commune, communicate, converse with God."[15] Our great need is to move beyond the surface to the depths of life. Contemplation is not seen as a method only, but is best understood by the object of its attention: the love of God. It is responding to the hunger to love God with all that we are. "You can't get the beloved out of your mind. The beloved is present in every thought, shaping and directing every action."[16]

Contemplation means becoming attentive to God. In moving more deeply into our lives, we discover the omnipresent God who meets us in all of life, even in life's struggles. The most basic premise of the contemplative view is that while we search for God, we subsequently discover that God is likewise searching for us.

Here is apparent identity with the deeper life—yet with a crucial difference. In the deeper life, the key is *adapting the self* to what should be, whereas in the contemporary Contemplative view, intimacy with God is learning to *attend to what is.*

Moving past the superficial in the contemplative view means entering the life of prayer.[17] To pray is the center of a life of devotion, and here we truly discover our sense of who we are as human beings. To the charge of the activist that such expenditures of time and energy are a waste in a secular world, Hinson replies that reductionism is actually a waste. The realm of intention and inner reality have great impact on the outer world of action, and contemplation will lead us to renewed energy and vision and action.

Loving God: The Bible and Prayer

How do we experience this "love relationship "in the deeper life view? It is not primarily experiential, if by that we mean visions, feelings, or voices. It is primarily through the Bible. Blackaby reads the Bible with a simple literalism. This does not mean that God never speaks in events, experiences, or the collective voice of the church, but that the Christian must carefully evaluate all other experiences in the light of scripture.

Blackaby utilizes the Bible as trustworthy and its stories as truth in every way. He does not intend to say, however, that a person can simply pick up the Bible and rationally "figure it out." Understanding the Bible requires illumination by the Holy Spirit. At this point, Blackaby parts with hard-line fundamentalism and the Princetonian inerrantists.

He warns against casual claims about "a word from God." Only the Holy Spirit can disclose a word from God for a particular situation, and this word must be tested to see if it comes to pass.[18] Nevertheless, he believes that God leads us specifically and directly. This leadership is available through the Bible, especially in its principles and teachings:

> You cannot depend on traditions, your experience, or the experience of others to be accurate authorities on God's will and ways. Experience and tradition must always be examined against the teaching of Scripture.[19]

Experience, reason, and other external sources are undependable. We are to forsake worldly wisdom and standards:

> It's easy to become so immersed in the world's ways of measuring success that we become increasingly disoriented to what God is saying. We rely on the books of men to figure out how to do our ministry. And that's killing us. I must keep coming back to the Word and ask myself, How does God reveal himself?[20]

Even normal common-sense reasoning does not apply. Logic, practical reason, and self-interest are hindrances to discovering the will of God. In fact, God often works in reverse, leading us to that which confounds our wisdom, contradicts our reason, and leads us to a greater crisis. "Human reasoning will not give you God's perspective."[21]

For Blackaby, experience is untrustworthy, and self-affirmation is the very heart of sin. Therefore, he is suspicious of all psychological and sociological. The self-focused life is one in which "I" is the center of life. This self-centeredness leads to pride in accomplishments, self-confidence in human ability, and self-reliance rather than trust in God. Even "affirming self" is a negative issue. Self-affirmation is an effort to be acceptable to the world and misleads us to look at circumstances from a human perspective. Life then becomes selfish and ordinary.[22]

How, then, do we know that our intuitions in scripture are of God and not our own psychology? Blackaby says that God accommodates

God's self to the uniqueness of every person. The divinity of an experience will be self-evident to the person. He rejects the idea that we must determine from circumstances (for example, closed doors and open doors) or reason, which is misleading. All truth is *revealed* truth, given by the Holy Spirit.

Neither is this encounter with God to be confused with "experience." We are not aiming for some emotional reaction when we seek God. When we understand a spiritual truth or principle in the Bible, it does not *lead* to encounter with God, "it *is* the encounter with God." God's presence is direct, mediated only through scripture.[23]

The contemplative tradition, by contrast, is reluctant to speak as confidently about a single "pathway" to transforming encounter. It may come by an experience of the heart (affective). For others, as in the Orthodox tradition, it is more a pathway of cognitive attention, leading finally to a place "beyond knowing." Thus, contemplation leads us not so much to the vision of God as to the limits of human language to talk meaningfully at all of God. In this "unknowing" we become open to the possibility of encounter with the true God.[24]

Despite this diversity in method among contemplatives, all contemplation is a turning inward. "It is meditation," Hinson writes.[25] For Hinson, though, this is not simply experiential, as in some forms of classical mysticism. Meditation is Baptist when it focuses on scripture. *How* scripture speaks may take many forms: intellectual adjustment, emotional experience, a decision of the will. The scriptures, however, are uncontestably the supreme arena for that disclosure.

Once again, both views share this general conviction that what makes prayer and meditation Christian is their grounding in scripture. Again, the difference is in how it is applied. In the deeper life view, scripture is understood in a direct way with the focus on personal application, not on any ambiguities in understanding. In the contemplative view, on the other hand, scripture functions in a more symbolic, "iconographic" way.

Loving God: The Problem of the Self

If the understanding of scripture in the process of prayer is in question, so is the role of the self in spiritual life. Once again, distinctions are discernible. Both the deeper life and contemplative views talk about the movement away from self and towards God, but there the similarities end.

Despite Blackaby's effort to guard against subjectivity, his "freedom from selfhood" is curiously individualistic. While the church and other people are avenues for encounter with God, ultimately the Bible makes the individual impervious to any doubts. The individual must only be sure that sin is confessed. Thus the influence of community is also suspect. The main role of the Christian community is to guard us against subjectivism by helping ascertain the biblical truthfulness of our "revelations." Blackaby cites George Mueller's three great spiritual mistakes—sin, impatience, and listening to other people—as the temptations that pull us from the vision of God.[26]

Blackaby's primary concern is to guard against an anthropocentric corruption of prayer. Our only spiritual happiness is to be found in the obliteration of what we desire, to be replaced wholly by God's will in us. This will is revealed in the Bible.

The question that inevitably occurs, of course, is, "Whose reading of the Bible?" *Experiencing God* often presents scripture as though its message is immediately obvious. Its simple devotional reading of scripture bypasses complicated and important questions of biblical criticism, social issues, and theological concern.

One might ask, for example, "How do we break through to new understandings of the implications of scripture with such a view?" A modern equivalent of Gentile issue in Acts 15, such as the nineteenth-century question of slavery or (more recently) the question of the rights of women could not be treated by his spiritual reading. In truth, Blackaby's understanding is *not* so much the Bible as literal truth, but the Bible as *personal* truth. He leaves the details of how that "Bible-plus-experiential-interpretation" will work out and leaves the practitioner vulnerable to the subjectivism he wishes to avoid.

Finally, God's "speaking" in the Bible *does* have a purpose, according to Blackaby. It is primarily *moral* and *purposeful* and not simply to provide experiences for us. The answers to our prayers always bring us more deeply into the purposes of God's kingdom. For Blackaby, consistent with his revivalist/Sandy Creek heritage, this means greater empowerment for personal evangelism and the Christian mission. It falls short of helping the individual Christian envision any outcome of prayer beyond the transformation of individuals and groups of individuals.

In the deeper life, the "self" is a problem. The goal of the devotional life is renunciation of the self and selfishness. The predominance of sin justifies a deep mistrust of the capacities of the self to grasp divine truth.

The contemplative tradition, on the other hand, is more ambivalent about the self. While there are many ascetic models of renunciation in the contemplative view, there are also many more concepts of self-actualization, through the "ladder of love," that put more responsibility on the seeker. The very possibility that we can undertake to open our lives up through the practice of spiritual disciplines assumes a human possibility that the deeper life view rejects. At its best, the contemplative view asserts that "fleshly life is not a burden to be borne, nor a prison to be escaped from, but a task to be perfected in grace."[27]

This distinction can be clearly stated: In the contemplative view, the goal is *purification* of the self, and in the deeper life view it is the *total surrender* of the self. The goal of contemplation is not a methodology but a discovery: All along the way, in every place and every experience, God is present to us. Our growth is not a growth in ability but a response to a deepening awareness of Love.

Hence, prayer and disciplines are also at the heart of the contemplative view, but with a difference. Though the spiritual life seems to be such an effort at first, gradually, as Teresa of Avila said, it becomes more effortless as our halting labors yield to a tide of grace.[28]

The Road of Ashes: The Crisis of Faith

For Blackaby, consistent with the Keswick tradition, every Christian seeking the victorious life must come to a place of surrender and crisis. In this encounter the person discovers that all human efforts are doomed to failure and inadequacy, causing people to miss God's best.

This "crisis of faith" sounds similar to the contemplative tradition's concept of "the dark night of the soul." There is a crucial difference, however. For Blackaby, the crisis of faith leads to victory and joy for the believer; crisis is only a prelude to triumph. In the contemplative vision, this is not always so. The goal is mystical union, but it may mean, in some versions, striving faithfully in the darkness until death.

The deeper life view holds that all problems in the spiritual life are traceable to some problem with the person. God is perfect, loving, caring, and available. There is no mystery, no dark night, no psalm of lament—only "adjustment" that we must make to a sovereign God. "If you are having trouble hearing God, you are in trouble at the very heart of your Christian experience."[29]

Three explanations are given for this crisis of faith. (1) Sin is the most common explanation for the hiddenness of God. Blackaby compares it to

Jeremiah's description of the spring of living water. Spiritual dryness, he asserts, means "something is wrong with my relationship to the fountain."[30] (2) Another explanation is that crisis works character development in the individual. (3) Yet another explanation is that crisis is a prelude to God's greater work in us.

The last explanation is demonstrated in Blackaby's account of his daughter Carrie's cancer during her teenage years. It is appropriate, he says, to question God so we might understand what is going on or to know what to do, but never to doubt. "I never said, 'Lord, I guess you don't love me.' "[31] Instead, he meditated on her suffering in the light of the cross of Jesus, that, for Blackaby, is the convincing and final declaration of the love of God for us. Therefore, he asked, "What good is in this?" His answer came from John 11:4: God would be glorified in this sickness. In his meditation on the story of the raising of Lazarus in John 11, he felt that it was as though Jesus were saying to Mary and Martha, "If I had come when you asked me to, I would have healed him. But, you would have never known any more about me than you already know. I knew that you were ready for a greater revelation." Blackaby reflected on that insight:

> When that began to dawn on me, I almost jumped straight out of my chair. I said, "That's what's happening in my life! That's what's happening! The silence of God means that He is ready to bring into my life a greater revelation of Himself than I have ever known."[32]

Blackaby reports that his daughter experienced a spontaneous remission of the cancer. This experience of healing was not only a great personal victory, but "this answer to prayer was what God used to totally renew" the prayer lives of many people who had prayed for her.[33]

Blackaby's view heavily emphasizes God as presence, consigning "absence" or "hiddenness" to a matter of human finitude, rebellion, or immaturity. God is personal, practical, and intimately near us. God is directly available to any of us, if only we meet the conditions of this love relationship.[34]

Who *is* this God that we meet in the night of life and what is the nature of this surrender? He is the perfect and holy God of scripture. Therefore the deeper life calls for *adjustment* of the person to God. We have nothing to contribute. The holy, immutable, all-sufficient God waits for our yielding. God's response is utter and complete grace.

The Road of Ashes: The Dark Night

The goal of the contemplative view is union with God, although this may be only a fleeting experience in this life. The key to this journey is purity of heart and finding the simplicity that gives a center to the soul. This also leads the seeker to "surrender, abandon ourselves, submit, yield, humble ourselves, give ourselves over to God."[35] This is not the same as acquiescence, and neither does Hinson exactly mean "withdrawal from life," although the history of the contemplative view contains many versions of this misunderstanding.

Surrender, in the contemplative view, sounds very close to what the deeper life understanding. This journey may open us to a painful process of purification, suffering, and pain. The growing light from God reveals darkness once unobserved by the person. This brokenness often comes in a time of loneliness, abandonment, or failure called the "dark night of the soul" or the "dark night of the senses."[36]

The dark night is not a self-induced anguish which methodologically leads us to new awareness. It is the anxiety and lament and deepening hurt that we encounter in response to the trials and insecurities of living as a Christian believer in the world.[37] That experience of the hiddenness of God calls forth a trust in the midst of absence and forsakenness. In the dark night, faith comes not as a response to God's answer in the dark, but in the midst of forsakenness itself.

Protestantism, says Hinson, has been troubled by the contemplative tradition because of its tendency toward works-righteousness. But the great guides of the tradition remind us that "contemplation depends on grace. We are respondents."[38] In no experience does this essential dependence upon grace become clearer than the dark night.

In the deeper life, the goal is to replace striving with the power of God in us—all we do is "give up and stop trying." In the contemplative view, on the other hand, the place we come to is *also* a "forsaken place." But it is not to "get the self out of the way" so much as a discovery of the emptiness and inadequacy of our every striving. We learn confidence and trust in God, whether the night ever subsides or not. For the deeper life, this giving up is prelude to victory. For the contemplative, submission *is* victory.

In summary, for the contemplative tradition, God is both mystery and presence on the road of ashes. For the deeper life, God may occasionally be hidden, but ultimately God's presence will be known. The road is not really ashes at all. This time of testing is really a tool for perfection in us.

This difference in the views reflects itself in the different understandings of the outcome of the prayerful life.

The Outcome of Surrender: Adjustment and Victory in the Deeper Life

In the deeper life, our total surrender bears God's fruit in our lives. We are broken, yielded, and available for God's purposes. This is what God has been waiting for; all we must do is to adjust our lives in obedience. This means adjustments in our relationships, in circumstances, in priorities, or whatever God through scripture leads us to change. *We must change* before God will respond to our faith.[39]

This surrender leads to trusting obedience. Our reward is participation in God's own wondrous work. Rewards for God are never merely self-serving but always a part of God's plan. The greatest reward for the believer is to experience God at work in his/her life and thereby gain a strengthened faith.

This yielding brings changed circumstances and the possibility of victory over sin. How do we know the work of God in this "yielded" state? When we pray, we learn to watch for God's response through directives and suggestions. If we use reason or even tell ourselves to "pray about it," we may be evading the promptings of the Spirit. Thus receptivity, passivity, openness, waiting and watching are key words for perceiving God's work. Human initiative has no real role.[40] How this passivity is reconciled with a "how-to" approach to the spiritual life is not clear. All the individual does is to simply pray. God will respond if we believe. "If you do not connect what happens next, you may miss God's answer to your prayer. Always connect what happens next."[41]

For the deeper life, with its radical views of personal holiness and the absolute work of grace in the second blessing, this work is limited primarily to the transforming work of God only within individuals and not in society. It is a personal and subjective work. Here the "disconnectedness" of Blackaby's view becomes evident. In all fairness, his course is a guidebook to prayer and not a systematic theology. Since this course is being taught to millions of Southern Baptists as a normative understanding of Christian living, however, it deserves to be subjected to critical scrutiny and discernment.

As in all of the Keswick spiritualties, the fruit of encounter with God is the enhancement of individuals, the increase of individual soulwinning, the expansion of missions and joyful living. It is disconnected from political, historical, or cultural realms.[42] Though Blackaby does talk about the role of the church in discernment, the main thrust of this work with God is not cultural transformation (except through transformed individuals) nor political revolution; it is primarily *power for witness*. The church is essentially "a world missions strategy center."[43]

The deeper life has, of course, been greatly influential in the lives of Christians whose commitments took them beyond the personal focus and into great mission endeavors. The deeper life probably could find ways to talk about the social, but its negative view toward the world and its strong emphasis on personal purity make this difficult.[44]

In summary, what is the outcome of the prayer of surrender? According to both views, it is participation, in a significant and personal way, with what God is doing in the world. For the deeper life, however, this participation (or more accurately, this *total yielding*) leads to victorious changes in the personal life of an individual, but it is especially manifested in increased personal evangelism and church growth.

The Outcome of Surrender: The New Way of Being

The contemplative view leads instead to a different way of viewing one's life and is less concerned with conforming persons to a mission in the world. We change, though not necessarily in our outward circumstance.

The triumphalism of the deeper life contrasts with the contemplative emphasis on new being. The contemplative understanding of suffering is that it brings about surrender that leads to a new being; however, circumstances may not change. The dark night may continue indefinitely.[45] Victory is not guaranteed, nor are any measurable results necessarily connected with our surrender. Submission and openness to God in trust are ends in themselves.

One frequent criticism of the contemplative view is that it leads to quietism, that is, passive acceptance of the status quo. Both the deeper life and the contemplative views are vulnerable to this criticism: The obsession with personal spirituality leads to the abandonment of society for the sake of saving our own souls. While we cannot defend the entire mystical tradition from such criticisms, it is not necessary in a modern view to divide contemplation and action so radically.

Glenn Hinson does not see quietism as the inevitable outgrowth of contemplation. He cites Thomas Merton's observation that the malaise of our civilization is rooted finally not in lack of action but in the impoverishment of our inner lives.[46] The goal of contemplation is not the enrichment of the individual but empowerment for action. The proper understanding, then, is withdrawal and return, not the hermit's escape from the world.[47]

Thomas Merton presents an attractive model of one who not only demonstrated the power of the contemplative tradition to the world but redirected the tradition itself *toward* the world. The surrender of one's life in the contemplative view means "loving God with all our 'heart, mind, soul, and strength'—with our total personalities. Such submission as this could not allow us to harbor racism in our hearts, to be almost inextricably enmeshed in life-styles that wasted the spaceship earth's limited resources, to drive without feeling through dirty and rat-infested ghettos, to leave ecological concerns to political and legal solutions."[48]

In short, the contemplative view leads to personal transformation and adjustment, though the results do not follow automatically. Much can be learned in the dark night, and sometimes God chooses to leave us there for long periods in order to draw us more deeply into God's own heart.

Toward a Contemporary Spirituality in the Baptist Tradition

Both the deeper life approach and the contemplative perspective have been beneficial to many people and will continue to do so. Both are located within different strands of the Baptist tradition, the deeper life more clearly with the Sandy Creek tradition and the contemplative more compatibly with the Charleston tradition. Both views call people to a more committed life with God. Both center on scripture. Both emphasize our need to surrender to God. Both offer alternatives to rationalistic understandings of faith.

In our best moments, we might concede that different ways of experiencing God have the possibility of enriching the larger body of Christ. In practice, however, there is a tendency to insist on one way as the way for everyone. In this final section, I will offer some reflections and evaluations that any effort to define spirituality normatively for Baptists will take into account. These concerns flow out of an analysis from the previous section.

(1) *A normative Baptist spirituality is incarnational, not other-worldly or life-denying.* One of the most serious questions that any spirituality faces is how to avoid the dualism that has plagued much of Christian devotional history.

At this point, the deeper life has a serious problem. Its central division of Christians into two classes, carnal and spiritual, plunges it straight into this split. The suspicion of physical life and the disdain of any ways of "knowing" that are not spiritually oriented make this an inevitable result.

A second, and equally serious, problem is the matter of the relationship of any spirituality with its world. Both the contemplative and the deeper life views have, by their very inward focus, pushed social, ethical, and church issues to the back burner. There is a danger from the opposite direction as well, that of a lessened interest in evangelism and proclamation of the faith. Incarnation means that every part of a person's life is "spiritual," not simply inwardness or silence.

(2) *A normative Baptist spirituality is personal and communal, lived out within the worshiping community.* For the deeper life, it is hard to see how anything matters more than an individual with his/her Bible, or how gatherings of like-minded deeper life Christians can avoid an essential cynicism toward the church. Despite the statement of McQuilken about the church as one of the four channels of grace—along with prayer, the Bible, and suffering—this is not sufficient to overcome the evaluation of "average" Christians in a given local church as less committed.[49]

If the deeper life view tends toward a biblical gnosticism, the danger of the contemplative view is overemphasis on experience and subjective reality. This is why the tradition warned against the "do-it-yourself" spirituality of which we see so much today. A seeker needs a mentor, a guide, to structure and interpret spiritual experience.

Community is a healing antidote to individualist spirituality. Only when we find the deeper roots of life in the worshiping fellowship can we hope to build the mutual trust so longed-for today. The larger community has a part to play in spiritual growth. Dietrich Bonhoeffer's advice is instructive at this point: "Let him who cannot be alone beware of community. Let him who is not in community beware of being alone."[50]

(3) *A normative Baptist spirituality emphasizes freedom.* The opposite risk of this individualism, of course, is oppression. No sins are as grave to Baptists as authoritarianism and conformity, whether that be in spiritual direction or the victorious life. A Baptist spirituality will always entertain

a certain open-endedness. The reduction of the work of God, however reverent the intent, to a methodology is dangerous.

Freedom also raises the question of how we participate in sanctification. Surrender is only one side of transformation. Christians also discover empowerment. Blackaby's view sounds a note so heavily on the passive side that all striving for virtue is obliterated. If we only give God surrender, how is that "loving"—that is, "willing and uncoerced giving of oneself to another"?

From the contemplative side, there are other issues for a Baptist spirituality. The Baptist emphasis on the freedom of the individual conscience will cause Baptists to struggle with the authoritarian and elitist nature of the contemplative tradition. The very nature of spiritual direction raises questions about specialists and experts. The monastic model offers a vision of the Christian life that is often hierarchical.

Baptists have some positive contributions to offer the contemplative tradition. Baptists and other radical reformers, more than others, have had the privilege to affirm the concept of the "priesthood of the believer." In the realm of the spiritual life Baptists take this to imply that the life of prayer is both *universal* and *mutual*.

Baptists' democratized concept of the church *is* a positive corrective to authoritarianism. Sacerdotalism and special elites have no place in the community of a Baptist fellowship. The authority and submission in some forms of spiritual direction would ill fit the Baptist view of the mutual guidance and humble spirit of fellow Christians in the body of Christ.

A Baptist view, therefore, of the Christian life as a life of prayer would understand the priesthood of believers to mean that this vocation is not a special calling to a few but is one open to all of the people of God. Baptists would probably be at home more with "spiritual friendship" than "spiritual director" for that reason.

(4) *A normative Baptist spirituality is biblically based, but open to "truth."* The danger of the deeper life view is failure to apply its own skepticism about human reason to its own assumptions about scripture. For example, Anthony Hoekema questions whether the deeper life view of two categories of Christians can be justified from scripture. Rather, this view seems instead to be arbitrarily imposed into it.[51]

Both views are correct to insist that prayer, contemplation, and silence are part of the right reading of scripture. The problem of fundamentalism is due to its very effort to exalt scripture. With its emphasis on the historical-objective nature of the Bible and its one-directional understanding of scripture and listener, there is little need for the work of the Holy Spirit as *interpreter* of scripture. Reading the Bible in this way, despite disclaimers to the contrary, is inevitably the same as "rational understanding."

Inerrantists are convinced that critics of scripture only need to use common sense reason properly to see the truth. The problem for many churches today is that our rationalist hermeneutic eliminates the role of God in directing, guiding, speaking and revealing. Both the contemplative and the deeper life views provide positive enrichment of our understanding of how the Bible speaks to us personally.

The danger, of course, is that the "truth" we hear will only be personal and not public, not open to discussion or debate. Blackaby rightly warns against claims of "a word from God." This must be repeated in any "spiritual" approach to scripture.

(5) *Finally, any good spirituality for contemporary Baptists would do well to hear some issues that arise out of pastoral concerns.* First, pessimism and perfectionism are risks, particularly for the deeper life view as it interprets suffering. When the mystery of God is removed as an aspect of human experience of God, we are left with a relentless accounting of all suffering as deserved or beneficial. This goes beyond the Bible's explanations, but does not mean, however, that the deeper life idea of suffering is not partly true.

Suffering *is* often redemptive. Suffering *does* often awaken us to deeper living. Suffering sometimes results from our own disobedience and sin. But no comprehensive explanation of suffering for every situation is given in Scripture. Instead, we are given a variety of partial glimpses into the mystery of life. Further, to call suffering "God's great short-cut to growth"[52] and denounce "self-reliance" in such categorical tones is to invite exercises in denial at best and crushing guilt at worst. To the depressive, the burden of not having sufficient trust to "let go" could be the final straw in a struggle with worthlessness.

This leads to another observation. One can no longer hold to *any* theology or "spirituality" that categorically—and arbitrarily—sweeps aside all of the modern understandings of psychology and the self. The most profound weakness of the deeper life is its tendency to convince people that we can, indeed, leave "self" behind, and that this is a desirable state.

On one hand, this invites all manner of self-deception and self-righteousness. Here, community is so crucial. The direction to "watch what happens next" may or may not be helpful to persons whose impoverished selfhood might lead them to commit what Harry Stack Sullivan called a "parataxic distortion" that incorrectly labels an event with a transcendent causation. Discernment is a tricky business—and with this I am convinced both Hinson and Blackaby would agree. To discern the work of God is no simple matter. It requires maturity, familiarity with the scripture, and often the wisdom of others.

On another hand, this "forsaking the self" also leads to an unhealthy self-deprecation. Many Christians in pastoral counseling and psychology have said that what we often call "self-centeredness" is in actuality a deep impoverishment of the self. Many persons do not need "less self," but a stronger one. The "ego" in most contemporary thinking is not a state of self-exaltation, but is that part of the personality that mediates with reality. The healthier the ego, the less the person is prone to unjustified posturing, self-promoting, and distortion of reality—what the Bible calls sin.

A healthy ego does not lead persons to distort their own self-importance, but enables them to humbly and honestly appraise the self, accept limits, see truthfully and acknowledge needs and shortcomings. No person has less sense of "self" than one who suffers from a personality-disorder. Is this the model for spirituality?

My perception is not that Henry Blackaby or deeper life writers really hold to such a view. Blackaby, in my observations of his programs and preaching, is a deeply caring, sincere Christian who has helped many people. These issues, however, invite some clarification from a program that is apparently influencing many Baptists.

I would like to recommend some further dialogue at this point. Some future amplifications are in order. As with many religious systems, what is often attacked is one *view* within psychology. Some of the differences are due to the same vocabulary being used to mean different things. Some dialogue and deeper understanding of self psychology would be helpful. Also, Henry Blackaby's fundamental building block of the "love-relationship" seems to be a positive and solid corrective to this possible misunderstanding.

To some extent the contemplative tradition is subject to the same critique. Contemplative writers in the last two decades, however, are coming to grip with more realistic appraisals of the self.

In a turbulent and changing scene, Baptists looking for an anchor can find many. In these times, perhaps we can see these various options as less of a threat and more as an opportunity to see new possibilities, explore new forms, and clarify our identity. In identifying these two options as reflective of two different streams of Baptist tradition, I hope that we can engender *respect* and *humility* rather than competition. These strands have much to teach one another. We should also understand that traditions have integrity. We may best recognize that we cannot, with good conscience, teach that what we hold about these views is "all there is" on the subject.

We may rediscover in these fluid times that, as Thomas Green once observed, we are able to float. The water itself will bear us up buoyantly. Spirituality, let us never forget, is not a system or a method. It describes our meeting places with reality, the mysterious and present one who, long before any class or book came along, invited us all to trust in Him. In the midst of our lives, in the church with its imperfections, and in the tumult of human history, Someone is holding us up.[53]

Notes

[1]Robert Bly, *Iron John: A Book About Men* (Reading MA: Addison-Wesley Publishing Company, 1990) 69-84.

[2]Ibid., 75.

[3]See Doran McCarty, "Spirituality: A Southern Baptist Perspective," *Review & Expositor* 79/2 (Spring, 1982): 307-11; Stephen S. Winward, "Baptist Spirituality," in *The Westminster Dictionary of Christian Spirituality*, ed. Gordon Wakefield (Philadelphia: Westminster Press, 1983) 36-38; E. Glenn Hinson, "Baptists and Spirituality: A Community at Worship," *Review & Expositor* 84 (Fall 1987): 649-58.

[4]The six traditions Leonard sees are: (1) The Charleston (Regular Baptist) tradition, (2) the Sandy Creek (revivalist) tradition, (3) the Georgia (denominationalist) tradition, (4) the Landmark (exclusivist) tradition, (5) the evangelical denominational tradition and (6) the Texas Baptist tradition. While these overlap with each other, they represent very diverse directions in Baptist life. See Leonard, *God's Last and Only Hope: The Fragmentation of the Southern Baptist Convention* (Grand Rapids: Eerdmans, 1990) 31-42. See also Walter B. Shurden, "The Southern Baptist Synthesis: Is It Cracking?" in the 1980-1981 Carver-Barnes Lectures, published by Southeastern Baptist Theological Seminary, 1981, 5-6.

[5]Walter B. Shurden, "The Southern Baptist Synthesis: Is It Cracking?" *Baptist History and Heritage* 16/2 (April 1981): 3-4.

[6]Walter B. Shurden, "The Southern Baptist Synthesis," 5-6.

[7]McCarty.

[8]For a summary and an analysis of the theology of the Deeper Life Movement, see Fisher Humphries, *The Way We Were: The Theology of the Southern Baptists* (Waco, Texas: McCracken Press, 1994, forthcoming) 107-116. See also George M. Marsden, *Fundamentalism and American Culture: The Shaping of Twentieth Century Evangelicalism, 1870-1925* (Oxford: Oxford University Press, 1980) 93-101.

[9]Humphries, *The Way We Were*.

[10]Donald G. Bloesch, *The Crisis of Piety*. 2d ed. (Colorado Springs CO: Helmer & Howard, 1988).

[11]Henry Blackaby and Claude V. King, *Experiencing God: Knowing and Doing the Will of God* (Nashville: The Sunday School Board of the Southern Baptist Convention, 1990) 44.

[12]Ibid., 49.

[13]Ibid., 9. Blackaby mentions D. L. Moody approvingly as an exemplar of one who shows us that "[a]nyone who will take the time to enter into an intimate relationship with God can see God do extraordinary things through his or her life," 24.

[14]Ibid., 97.

[15]E. Glenn Hinson, "The Contemplative View," in Donald Alexander, ed. *Christian Spirituality: Five Views of Sanctification* (Downer's Grove IL: InterVarsity Press, 1988) 171.

[16]Ibid., 172.

[17]E. Glenn Hinson, *A Serious Call to a Contemplative Lifestyle* rev.ed. (Macon, GA: Smyth and Helwys Publishing, 1993) 43.

[18]Blackaby and King, 37.

[19]Ibid., 9.

[20]"Diagnosing Your Heart Condition," interview in *Leadership* (Fall 1993): 19.

[21]Blackaby and King, 39.

[22]Ibid., 27.

[23]Ibid., 67-85.

[24]Hinson, "The Contemplative View," 175-76.

[25]Hinson, *A Serious Call*, 49.

[26]Blackaby and King, 33. Psychologically (if only Blackaby allowed its validity), one might wonder if the traditional defense mechanisms might not be peculiarly available to an individual who followed *Experiencing God*.

[27]Rowan Williams, *The Wound of Knowledge* (Boston: Cowley Publications, 1990) 21.

[28]Hinson, "The Contemplative View," 184.

[29]Blackaby and King, 36.

[30]"Diagnosing Your Heart Condition," 23.

[31]Blackaby and King, 42.

[32]Ibid., 94.

[33]Ibid., 97.

[34]Ibid., 54-55.

[35]Hinson, "The Contemplative View," 177.

[36]Ibid., 179.

[37]Rowan Williams, *The Wound of Knowledge*, 11.

[38]Hinson, "The Contemplative View," 174.

[39]Blackaby and King, 130-31.

[40]Ibid., 67.

[41]Ibid., 69.

[42]I would even argue that part of the appeal of *Experiencing God* is precisely as a corrective to the identity crisis that the once apolitical fundamentalists turned social activists are struggling with now that they have entered the ambiguities of the public

arena, especially in the light of political reversals for the Religious Right that call for a "theodicy" of temporary defeat.

[43]Testimonies throughout the book are mostly of the miracles of multiplication that occur when the people of God yield their determination to control and plan the church and instead seek to hear God's vision for the church. Blackaby and King, 162-63. See also Marsden, 167.

[44]McQuilken, "The Keswick View," in *Five Views on Sanctification* (Grand Rapids MI: Zondervan Press, 1987) 155, notes that the fourfold tradition of themes at the Keswick meetings—sin, God's provision, consecration, filling by the Holy Spirit—has been expanded to include "service."

[45]See the discussion of Therese of Lisieux in Simon Tugwell, *Ways of Imperfection: An Exploration of Christian Spirituality* (Springfield IL: Templegate Publishers, 1985) 219-31.

[46]Hinson, "The Contemplative View," 185.

[47]Bloesch, 96. The contemplative tradition is always in danger because of its emphasis on withdrawal, of "Quietism." See Jordan Aumann, *Christian Spirituality in the Catholic Tradition* (San Francisco: Ignatius Press, 1985) 232-42.

[48]Hinson, *A Serious Call*, 50-51.

[49]McQuilcken, 180-81.

[50]Dietrich Bonhoeffer, *Life Together* (San Francisco: Harper & Row, 1954) 77.

[51]Anthony Hoekema, "Response to McQuilkin," *Five Views on Sanctification*, 189.

[52]McQuilken, 181.

[53]Thomas Green, *Drinking from a Dry Well*(South Bend IN: Ave Maria Press, 1991) 142-44.

The Corporate Tie: The Fellowship . . . Is Like to That Above

On 8 April 1945, with the rumble of Allied guns drawing near, Nazi war prisoners watched as Dietrich Bonhoeffer was led from his cell. Implicated in a plot to kill Hitler, this promising young theologian was sentenced by a kangaroo court and hanged. The world lost not only an insightful scholar and teacher but also a wonderful Christian. It is a painful irony that a man whose dissertation was about the church, who wrote about the hunger for authentic community, and who worked tirelessly in the cause of Christian ecumenism would die alone, a forsaken prisoner.

In 1935, Bonhoeffer returned to Germany from abroad to take charge of an underground seminary at Finkenwalde, where students and teachers lived together in hastily-built structures. During this period he wrote his two books most familiar to lay readers, *The Cost of Discipleship* and *Life Together*. In *Life Together*, Bonhoeffer essentially created a daily manual for his Christian community, but it became a manual for the yearnings of all Christians who seek the kingdom of God in the midst of earth's sorrows.

Bonhoeffer warned in *Life Together* (34) that authentic Christian community is a rare and precious gift. We are deluded if we think that we can create it by our own efforts. He saw two distinguishing marks of fellowship created by merely human love. First, it insists on the preservation of fellowship at any price, even the truth. It cannot tolerate dissolution and dissent, even if the purpose of that dissent is to discover genuine kingdom community. Second, human love cannot love an enemy.[1] Truth and depth in our fellowship and social transformation are the acts of God, anticipations of the coming kingdom.

A communion of the Spirit must finally connect not only with its own depths but with the kingdom that transcends it. If the *conversionist* and *contemplative* ties are centered on the formation and transformation of persons, the *corporate* tie is concerned to enlarge spirituality to include the work of God in our midst, both in the church and in the world.

How can the church engage its world without losing its identity in Jesus Christ? How can the believer join meaningfully with other believers in community? How are we properly to worship God together? What does this worship finally have to do with our life in the midst of injustice, brokenness, and suffering? The essays that follow speak to these and other related issues.

Robert Reid begins with an essay on the history of Baptist worship, charting the ambivalent attitudes of Baptists toward the arts in worship. Paul Basden follows with a stimulating typology on the current impasse over worship styles that is frequently a factor in local church conflict.

The final three essays address the struggle to relate the church meaningfully to its world from a Baptist perspective. Philip LeMasters illustrates this by pointing to a Baptist saint, Walter Rauschenbusch, whose life is an example of the integration of prayer and politics.

Samuel Proctor follows with a glimpse into a special tradition, that of African-American Baptists. Proctor was once pastor of the Abyssinian Baptist church in Harlem where Bonhoeffer worshiped while at Union Seminary before returning to Germany. There Bonhoeffer found a quality of life together that many others have noted: the church sustained individuals in the midst of a hostile, racist culture. Proctor reflects on that heritage and raises continuing issues in that struggle for the present.

Finally, Barry Harvey concludes our work with an impressive reflection on the Christian life as a call to both personal spiritual disciplines and involvement in political life. He explores the nature of that involvement and the dangers implied in our efforts to compartmentalize spirituality, dangers well-illustrated in past Baptist sins.

The heavily individualistic emphasis of our tradition means that in times of uncertainty and disintegration we might be tempted to choose forms and structures that are not only in violation of our cherished convictions about liberty but also that lead to questionable forms of corporate life. Hopefully, these essays might present some help from our heritage so that we might choose our corporate forms more wisely.

As Bonhoeffer went to the gallows, he was reported to have said, "For me it is the end—the beginning of life." Christian life is lived out in the conviction that there is a kingdom that draws us forward, the vision of which sustains us in even the meanest and most ambiguous times.

Note

[1]Dietrich Bonhoeffer, *Life Together* trans. John W. Doberstein (New York: Harper & Bros., 1954) 34.

Music in the Spiritual Life of Baptists

Robert A. Reid

More than one observer has noted that Baptists sing their theology more clearly than they preach it. Music is central to any understanding of Baptist spirituality. This "backward glance" is an effort to explore the role of music in Baptist spiritual experience and reflection on some of its contradictions and ironies.

Early Influences

At least two sources from the early period of the Reformation influenced Baptist identity in worship. Baptists inherited the Anabaptist principle that "piety [is] expressed less in acts of worship and devotion than in the whole of life."[1] Anabaptists lived moderately, avoiding ostentation, excesses of behavior, and outbursts of ecstatic utterance. In circumstances of severe testing, however, devout believers openly "sang praises to God while . . . in grievous imprisonment . . . and as they were being led to the place of execution."[2] While certainly not in Luther's camp, the Anabaptists embraced his use of freely-written "hymns" for private devotion and worship.[3]

Baptists are also heirs of Huldreich Zwingli, the Zurich reformer who disallowed any form of musical expression in his congregation's worship so he could avoid any danger of "display." He eliminated choirs and organs and restricted worship to "the exposition of the scriptures."[4] Zwingli contended that Christ had emphasized individual, private prayer to God.[5]

The sixteenth-century English Separatists followed Zwingli's rationale; they "evidently had no music, but eventually began to sing unaccompanied metrical psalms" in the fashion of Calvin's followers.[6] In time, forces within the Separatist movement hammered out several new consensuses. John Smyth "was guided by the principles of simplicity and spontaneity, and he viewed worship as an act of spiritual communion in the presence of God."[7] Richard Pope suggests that this communion was experienced and expressed through a "certain fervency and inwardness" in response to the "mystery [of] regeneration," a reality beyond rationalization.[8]

At this point a dualism in Baptist worship appeared that still exists. On one side, Baptists did not fully trust the mind, because it too easily could be misled into rationalization of divine truth. On the other side, Baptists were also wary of the emotions that could just as easily abuse the spirit of God's truth. Their disdain for artful music, while cultural, was primarily due to this principle. Thus began an ongoing love-hate relationship with music and, for that matter, all of the arts among Baptists.

The seventeenth century followed similar patterns of worship and music. Baptists, Presbyterians, and Congregationalists used a fairly universal order of worship, technically non-liturgical in type but predictably "liturgical" in practice. They all used one version or another of an English psalter, which was popular with many early Baptists. As members of the lowest socio-economic/cultural rung of the ladder in English society, these hearty believers embraced the puritanical program to rid English churches of choirs, organs, and other "aesthetic affections" during Cromwell's tenure. Like other dissenters, they questioned the appropriateness of singing original hymns in devotion or worship.[9]

Many Baptist congregations in England and America sang the psalms exclusively, well into the nineteenth century. Some, however, explored the emerging form of the English hymn. Benjamin Keach was the first to introduce "a hymn of 'human-composing' into the psalm-singing culture of seventeenth-century England."[10] John Bunyan included the lyrical stanzas, "Who would true valor see" (now, "He who would valiant be"), as an epilogue to a chapter in part two of *Pilgrim's Progress* (1684) and spoke in favor of hymns in worship.[11] During the eighteenth century, English Baptists followed Isaac Watts, producing what Eskew and McElrath regard as a "Golden Age of Baptist Hymnody" and generating works that possessed "a quality unsurpassed before or since."[12] John Fawcett (1740–1817) gave Baptists the hymn "Bless Be the Tie that Binds," a parting hymn that shows the importance of Christian fellowship to Baptists of his period.

These new hymnic ventures pulled the reluctant Baptist world into the mainstream of English-speaking Protestantism. This opened to Baptists a wealth of devotional poetry by which their spiritual lives could be nourished. Nevertheless, many still suspected the wider tradition.

The English hymn found no receptive ear among Baptists in America. Even the practice of singing psalms degenerated during the colonial period. Cut off from their cultural roots and sometimes willfully from other Christian groups, Baptist churches were left to their own devices.

It is unclear to what extent they participated, along with Presbyterians and Congregationalists, in the singing schools that proliferated in New England before the Revolutionary War.[13] The music masters of the singing schools sought to upgrade the quality of music in the regional churches. They hoped to enliven the cause of Christ through an appeal to European sensibility.

During that same period, "lining out the tune"[14] facilitated participation where illiteracy or a scarcity of psalters was a problem. It was not uncommon, though, for a family of believers to own a pocket-sized psalter and to use it throughout the week during family devotions and informal gatherings of friends. To a people of modest means, the possession of a Bible, a psalter, and the ability to read them made one wealthy indeed!

Worship on the Frontier

As revival swept the country, Baptists markedly increased in number,[15] especially in the middle colonies where Calvinist influence was the greatest. The revivalist emphasis shifted to the southern states and became increasingly a rural phenomenon. Presbyterians, Baptists, and Methodists came in large numbers to the camp meetings in Kentucky that were characterized by their highly emotional behavior:

> The work of the Holy Spirit was evidenced in the number who "fell"—literally dropped to the ground under the influence of the intense emotion of "conviction of sin." Some also were moved to roll, jerk, dance, and even "bark." Understandably, the music of the camp meetings was highly spontaneous, and as frequently improvised.[16]

Their songs were

> sung and sung and sung. . . . Song filled the camp from morning till night till morning again. The songs helped light revival fires , . . . teach theology, . . . were sung at home in family devotions . . . and at class meetings in answer to personal testimony. . . . [Their texts were] often shallow in their thought, never clever; they [were] seldom poetic, seldom oversentimental, always naive and vigorous.[17]

Many of the texts either included favorite ejaculations ("shouting words" such as "Hallelujah") or were set musically in such a way that such outbursts could be improvised at will by the singer. "Dialogue hymns" were also popular, in which a singer assumed the role of a believer in conversation with his Lord or as a witness to the exchange of ideas between opponents in some simplified doctrinal or moral issue.

The "ballad" was transformed for Christian purposes. The camp-meeting exalted the public testimony, and the balladeer could sing his personal experience to a crowd of encouragers.[18] Use of the ballad in this fashion signaled a peculiarly modern innovation history: the "I"-centered testimony or personal expression song. While subjectivity can be seen clearly in German Pietistic chorales and some hymns of Watts and Wesley, their incorporation of "first-person" does not compare to the increasingly subjective focus of American religious song through the nineteenth and twentieth centuries.

Other popular, even vulgar, lyric forms were brought into use during the camp meetings; such Christianized limericks were shared among campsites.[19] Despite the questionable quality of these camp meeting songs, the revivals did bring "stabilizing and humanitarian elements of religion to the raw wilderness settlements, . . . in spite of occasional fanaticism and excess emotion."[20] Considering the stoic, often rigid, lifestyles of these people, the music at the camp meetings must have provided a powerful and needed catharsis.

Another source of folk song that had a significant, though immeasurable, impact upon the spiritual lives of Baptists in the South was the Negro spiritual. Much of the difficulty in tracing influences is due to the nature of oral tradition through which the music, both black and white, developed.[21] The purpose here is not to look for evidence of musical borrowings, but spiritual connectedness.

Prior to the Civil War, there was little distinction between black and white church music, although whites have carried a persistent ambivalence about this shared heritage.[22] Baptists were largely responsible for Christianizing the slaves:

> Black church members had flocked to the shouting and singing Baptists . . . that is, the one group among whom the religious folk songs were born and bred and still persisted. . . . [The slaves] adopted the revival spirituals which, in those same white religious surroundings, were new at the beginning of the nineteenth century [camp meeting songs] but became, in time, "old slave songs."[23]

The revivalist modality did not appeal to growing numbers of Baptists, however, particularly those in urban centers who objected to black enthusiasm in worship as a disturbance of the peace.[24]

A growing consensus of southern white congregations really did not want blacks in their membership. This feeling reached a crisis after the Civil War, resulting in the exit of 150,000 freed slaves from mixed congregations.[25] The Civil War and its aftermath poisoned spiritual communion between several generations of whites and blacks. This cultural segregation produced two basic church musics, white and black, moving in distinctive directions and purposely avoiding each other for nearly 100 years. Only in recent years has some real merging of sacred music occurred in both content and styling.

Following the War, the singing school movement spread into the southern states.[26] Each singing school provided area enthusiasts with the opportunity to develop basic music proficiencies in an atmosphere of fun and fellowship. Many post-revivalist Baptists had come to appreciate these schools. A series of tunebooks published over a quarter of a century served as the curriculum and source material for the "singings."[27] Merely to be associated with an activity so overtly educational indicated a significant shift in Baptist thinking.

For a people who had spurned an educated clergy and generally shunned hymn singing, this second wave of the singing school suggests a change in attitude. Many Baptists began to value music as an art form. They recognized the need to gain knowledge and develop skills. This was a shift in the Baptist understanding of the connection of spiritual experience through music and the role of disciplined musical study. Now this, too, was an acceptable way to glorify God.[28]

Baptists made little progress in church music during the nineteenth century, particularly in the South. The schism that produced the Southern Baptist Convention did not generate a denominational emphasis on music.

> Southern Baptists . . . have only themselves to blame for the tenacious grip that [singing school] music has on many of their people. While Southern Baptists were debating what to do about the low estate of music in their churches, the teachers from the "paperback" publishers moved in. . . . Perhaps their music was not always the best, but it was more than the denomination was doing.[29]

The establishment of Baptist colleges did not have a serious impact on music education. Even in the seminaries music study had only a token presence during the nineteenth century. Most Baptists saw little need for musical training beyond that of the singing schools or private study. This was partly a result of the musical limitations of the song forms they valued, but, as with every other aspect of regional life, the Civil War most inhibited significant musical advancements in rural Southern Baptist life. Baptist music, however, was about to change.

The Rise of the Gospel Song

The change that most affected Baptist music and perspective was the gospel song. Modeled by Ira Sankey, music leader for the Moody campaigns, the gospel song resembled the popular tunes of Stephen Foster, whose style maintained a strong following through the nineteenth century. The camp meeting style gave way to a more sober and urbanized style. Churches were faced with adaptation or extinction. Protestants exchanged the "personal-emotional gospel" for "the social-ethical-esthetics Gospel."[30] Eric Routley aptly describes the "Sankey" style:

> The basis of the style is an extreme naivety of rhythm, harmony and melody. It is "folk" music in being music which the industrial peasantry of the new age could immediately receive, join in, and take comfort from. There is no kind of sophistication in it; all the tunes are virtually the same tune, and the vocabulary they use is really a small collection of clichés whose repetition gave no kind of offence to its simple constituency. The same is true of the words, and indeed of the preaching that they expressed. Little was demanded, little was given, but that little, often and doggedly. [Still] wherever the "established" church felt that they must make an effort to join in the work, they felt that the music they must use ought to be modeled on the "Sankey" pattern.[31]

Baptists clearly favored the gospel song as they marched into the new century. A glance at hymnals of the period reflects this trend, to the virtual exclusion of earlier sacred folk songs, white and black. Those who wished to continue in the "old ways" had to use the diminishing number of shaped-note songbooks being carried into the twentieth century, such as the ones published by Robert Coleman of Dallas, Texas.

The widespread acceptance of the gospel song further strengthened the role of the piano in Baptist life. Once a people who had denounced the use of any musical instruments in worship, Baptists had opened the door cautiously to the reed organ as early as the 1830s, and it had found general acceptance in urban churches. But Sankey's use of what once had been considered a concert instrument on the one hand and a saloon fixture on the other generated a wave of stylistic exploration that resulted in a distinctive, "evangelistic piano" style.

The lyrics of the gospel songs proved to be a source of spiritual riches for the enthusiasts in the Baptist world. More frequently subjective than objective, they were reminiscent of the "experience" songs of the camp meeting era, but adapted to modern urban realities. In a time of increasing impersonalization and loss of the sense of personal liberty to the regimentation of industry, they were seen as "heart songs".[32] The gospel song dealt with practically every Christian topic imaginable but, unlike the more abstract social-ethical hymn of the Christian intelligentsia and those in the "established" churches, its message was usually direct and personal. This "personal" quality was often expressed as being synonymous with the deeply emotional side of life.[33] Baptists of the period found this personal, often intimate, quality most appealing.

Upon the foundation of the gospel song's popularity, Southwestern Baptist Theological Seminary in Fort Worth, Texas, instituted its new department of gospel music, under the leadership of I. E. Reynolds.[34] One of its earliest "stars," first as a student (1915) and then as a professor (1919), was B. B. McKinney. McKinney developed a widespread reputation as an evangelistic singer and author/composer of gospel songs.[35] If Baptists had not identified before with the gospel song as a medium for spiritual experience and expression, they did in the wake of McKinney's influence. Songs like "The Nail Scarred Hand"/LUBBOCK (1924), "Send a Great Revival in My Soul"/TRAVIS AVENUE (1925), and "Speak to My Heart, Lord Jesus"/HOLCOMB (1927) were among just a few of the McKinney songs familiar to Southern Baptists. So pervasive was his influence that, despite later efforts by the church music department and the seminaries to develop a renewed (or new?) love for classic hymnody (English, Lutheran, and Americana), the rank-and-file of Baptists have continued to prefer the gospel song.

The Rise of "Contemporary" Music

The gospel song shared at least four things in common with its secular sister, the tin pan alley song: Both came upon the American scene at approximately the same time (late nineteenth century); both were based on forms that were flexible enough to bend with the stylistic variants of the lyricists and composers who made use of them, enabling them to remain viable for a long time; both frequently used highly-charged, subjective lyrics; and both eventually gave way to the unrelenting stylistic shifts that burst upon the scene after World War II.

Like the tin pan alley song, the gospel song was targeted at an adult market, as were essentially all art forms to that point in history. But in the 1950s, promoters of rock and roll began to swim against the current of traditional thinking by targeting young adults and older teenagers. It soon became obvious to the industry that there was a receptive market for their products among ever-younger age groups, leading to their movement into practically every area of culture impacting children and teenagers.

The church watched this unfolding with general confusion, alarm, and disdain. Most churches eventually were resigned that nothing could keep young people from having "their music" in the secular world, although some serious attempts were made (such as record "breaking"); but it was naively assumed that the sounds and effects of "their music" would never enter the church. Baptist churches were riding the wave of rapid growth in youth choir programs, a direct result of the expanding provision of published materials (*The Youth Choir*) by the church music department of the Southern Baptist Convention, the youth revivals (traditional in style) of the late fifties, and the consistent growth of high school choral programs. Steadily these choirs were being developed on the "strong foundation" of anthems, gospel song and hymn arrangements, and simple classical works. In informal gatherings (camps, fellowships, etc.) Baptist youth sang simple, tuneful choruses and the newest vein of evangelistic gospel songs. Then came "Good News" and "Tell It Like It Is."

In 1963 Broadman published the first youth musical, Bob Oldenberg's "Good News," a loosely-constructed collection of tunes, lyrics, and script that was enthusiastically received at its premier. Sensing the moment, Word Music, Inc., published "Tell It Like It Is" by Kurt Kaiser and Ralph Carmichael in 1965. Suddenly a distinctively pop religious sound was graced by solid compositional technique, and the church music world was revolutionized. "Tell It Like It Is" became the model for countless works —musicals, cantatas, octavos, solos—by countless composers who wanted to participate in this new art form. Traditionalists "dug in their heels" and gave a wide range of responses, but ultimately the inflexibility of most turned to compromise, then to capitulation. Many declared that "the old songs" no longer spoke to them or helped to express their spiritual feelings. For them, the new "church music," modeled after popular music being targeted at young audiences, solved that problem.

Out of this milieu a number of related expressions emerged. Contemporary gospel music "artists" replaced the music evangelist (revival "sanger") of the previous generation and the evangelistic preacher, effectively rolling both into one new venue: the Christian concert. Publishing/record companies worked feverishly to position themselves as the top publisher, based on marketing-chart proof that their "stable" of artists and published music (in solo, ensemble, choral, and instrumental formats) were "hotter" than those of other publishers. Religious radio stations, once dominated by "preacher programs," gave way to format shifts or were joined on the airwaves by the new generation of "Christian radio station." Professing to play "Christian music," these stations limited air time to playing the "top 20" of Christian "pop" labels. The three together—artist concert, publisher/record producer, and radio (less so, T.V.) programming—formed a triangular marketing system that rewarded a select few aspiring Christian artists.

Unlike the first half of the century, the second half has witnessed style creations, merging, and decay at almost maniacal speed. Though more reserved, the Baptist world has been invaded by the secular music market ("the world's music" to detractors). This has produced a dizzying effect for some and an outcry from others over the "performance syndrome" in Baptist worship. Some operant questions have been raised: "Is the singer truly focusing on the truth conveyed by the lyrics or is he/she more likely just 'getting into' the pop sounds of the musical selection?" "If the music truly is a successful reflection of today's popular music, can it lead the worshiper to godly thoughts, or will it more likely generate carnal associations?" "If the spotlight is so intensely cast on the performer, how effectively can he/she become transparent or invisible so that Christ is seen instead?" The debate continues.

A New Pattern for Worship

Running concurrently with the Baptist world but rarely intersecting it has been the charismatic renewal movement and the resurging pentecostal movement. Over the past twenty-five years, Baptists have begun to explore the music of these two cultures (interchangeable at times). At first many Baptists embraced the simplistic sounds of the "Jesus People," many of whom were participants in the new renewal. Then some tuned in to the incredibly garish sights and sounds of Jim Baker's PTL until its demise. All the while, increasing numbers of churches began to interject the "chorus of the month" into the morning worship service, long a time for hymn and gospel song singing.

Traditional hymn singing gradually assumed a role of secondary prominence, if not importance. In effect, some Baptists were declaring that the gospel song was dead, the hymn was archaic, and there was nothing better (or at least preferable to the chorus) to take its place.[36] Late nineteenth-century Baptists in the south simply ignored social-ethical issues and the hymns that expressed them musically, turning instead to the subjectivity of evangelistic gospel songs. Similarly, Baptists of the 1970s and 1980s in increasing numbers left the hymnal for chorus singing. Creative ways were sought to put together medleys of these choruses (the term "praise and worship" emerged), sometimes wedding them with hymns and gospel songs of similar subject matter.

During the 1980s though, the charismatic praise and worship movement "went public" through the efforts of assorted publishers, and the content and nature of the choruses began to change. No longer simple, tuneful Christian after-thoughts, these new choruses came to focus squarely on one objective—the worship of God.

A new worship pattern emerged, which has become fixed in its basic layout and ideas. In this worship pattern, the congregation engages in a period of singing lively songs of praise and thanksgiving to God, followed by prayer and songs of confession. Worship, comprised of songs and statements addressing God directly or speaking of God's attributes, comes next, followed by the proclamation of the Word. More than just an "order of worship" to its devotees, the new modality is the cutting-edge of a manifesto for worship of a particular sort: a call to combat the humanism of the modern era with a Reformation (reforming) of Christian worship gone stale. Anne Murchison is one of its spokespersons:

> God has given us a pattern, and it is up to God to grow us up. It is not a theological system. He doesn't want us to make a denomination out of it. It is His pattern for the way for the seeking heart to enter into deep communion and fellowship with Him . . . Davidic praise and worship are a mutually great and awesome blessing. . . . Praise and worship are the primary and most likely only activities in Heaven. . . . The Old Testament believers praised this way, so did the Apostles and the early church. . . . It was only after the church fell into darkness in the Middle Ages that the joyful sound stopped, and I believe it is God's great desire and requirement that it be restored before Jesus returns. And it is interesting that He has already begun to restore it all over the world today. . . . I earnestly believe it is the desire of God's heart today that all of His children enter into the ministry of Davidic praise and worship.[37]

The implications are not difficult to discern. Because the movement is pandenominational in scope and its adherents embrace the imminent demise of denominationalism, its eventual effect may be to engender uncertainty and division among Baptists along any number of lines. Its implicit acculturation process may eventually lead to significant doctrinal shifts. For traditionalists, the departure from a structured service and use of the hymnal has been cause for alarm. For more reserved personalities, the renewed focus on display of emotion has not been well received. For the serious musician, the musical repertoire of the praise and worship movement offers little or no lasting musical and spiritual growth. If the trend persists, Baptist church music will continue to undergo massive changes. One can only question if the changes will be for the better.

The "Soul" of Baptist Worship

I contend that there is a distinctive Baptist "soul" of worship. Those who do not share Baptists' musical heritage and do not embrace their biblical world-view see the generally energetic singing in Baptist services as superficial and emotional. I contend that spiritual formation among Baptists takes place through the mind, the emotions, and those aesthetic sensibilities that serve to connect them.

Baptists, being "people of the Book," value song material for the lyrics. Frequently they are reminded to "listen to the words," believing that understanding yields spiritual results. One could almost be led to assume that this scrutinization is done apart from an absorption of the song's musical properties. Of course, this is not the case. The lyrics simply are not as expressive without the music's power to convey lyrical idea.

Southern Baptist music leaders have built on this elemental level of receptivity to music by fostering the development of fully graded music programs in each church, through which an individual can nourish a growing, dynamic understanding of music as a total art form. Unfortunately, not all Baptists value a traditional church music program that challenges the mind and expects of its participants a significant level of musical self-discipline and self-sacrifice.

Don Hustad believes that music should be heard with the mind as well as the affections. A hymn or anthem is a theological concept first of all. Therefore, musical worship

> should involve and transform the mind, as well as the body and the emotions. . . . The worshiper should hear [music] with the expectation of

> "understanding" it. . . . The relationship of emotion to understanding is most important in the totality of worship. Each by itself may constitute an aborted experience. [They are interdependent of each other.] . . . When truth is apprehended, and it is accompanied with strong emotion because the individual realizes its ultimate significance, then there can be an action of the will.[38]

This is not to say that increased musical knowledge will automatically heighten spiritual formation. Furthermore, musical knowledge may tempt the listener to focus on the quality of the sounds while turning a deaf ear to the voice of God. Nevertheless, the "study to show thyself approved" directive applies to all of truth, even the kind expressed in solely musical sound, and it is through musical study that this directive is fulfilled.

As has already been confessed, first and foremost, Baptists are known to process their music through heart-felt emotions. In their best musical moments, they respond to God's claims upon their lives through deep, profound emotion that is directed to God or others in song. At worst, this emphasis risks sentimentality and hyper-emotional display, confusing faith with feelings.

Contemplation should be the headwaters of true emotions. As E. Glenn Hinson observes,

> To be a contemplative Christian will not necessitate becoming a monk. . . . What is necessary is solitude. The question is, how will we find solitude in the . . . city? Is a contemplative style of life possible at all today in the context of a secular style of life. . . . Music . . . has long been thought to be very near to contemplation itself. . . . The lyrics of great hymns obviously present opportunities for God to open insights, but tunes may convey powerful feeling that rises beyond the level of formal speech.[39]

At this point sacred music serves the believer well. While not being a language at all, due to its inability to convey meaning with precision, music provides the receptive ear with an evocative framework on which the listener can construct associative meanings. When text is coupled with music, these associations tend to take direct inspiration from the ideas expressed or implied by the lyrics. The result is a compounding of emotional potential.

The mind has a way of remembering emotive associations and tends to "replay the tape" of emotional experience whenever a "favorite song" is heard. Unfortunately, for the spiritually immature, feeling emotional in religious settings is often confused with having a spiritual experience, and responding to an emotional "trigger" (a song, scene, phrase, or even worship gestures) identified with work of the Holy Spirit. Since aesthetic experience (response to expressive form) is often taken for spiritual experience in religious settings, it is the sacred duty of the church musician (and pastor!) to understand this principle and reject easy emotional manipulation of God's people in favor of a presentation of church music in which the Holy Spirit has full freedom to elicit authentic, emotional response.

The search to understand the nature of beauty dates at least to Greek times.[40] In modern times, entire systems of philosophy have been developed to explain the significance of the aesthetic experience. Church music has always been a functional art form and has generally side-stepped prolonged discussion of aesthetics.

> high culture . . . demands knowledge, experience, sophistication, informed taste, discipline—all of which are likely to be scarce in Baptist colleges, universities, and seminaries. Even if intellectual and cultural qualities were cultivated, the results would be incomprehensible in many of the churches. This leaves the majority of Southern Baptists with nowhere to go but . . . popular culture at its most self-conscious and pretentious. The models are commercial; the folk music of today is the soft drink jingle. . . . The public ceremonies are directed from Los Angeles and New York and beamed at an audience that knows little else but Nashville, rock radio, Saturday Night Live, MTV, and the halftime shows at high school football games. No wonder creativity and authenticity are so scarce. Feeling at home in a comfortable cultural idiom is far more important to group solidarity.[41]

Undaunted, Baptists have rarely concerned themselves with striving to meet the art world's standards in musical quality, although they have frequently sought to apply a self-imposed value system to the music they make. This tendency results from a church music philosophy that holds that God looks on the heart (intent) of the musician and not on the musical quality (content) being produced. For some, this implies total freedom to worship God through whatever creative means; however, carried to its extreme, this can easily become malicious license and abuse of art.

The archives are literally littered with lyrics supposedly written to glorify God but with suspect results. The old country gospel song states with theological accuracy that "There ain't no flies on Jesus 'cause He's risen from the grave," but its effect is so laughable as to make light of the scriptural truth. Such artistic ideas give credence to what Turner sees in American spirituality:

> An emotional response to God had, after all, always been crucial to religion, and from the seventeenth century the aesthetics of the sublime had linked this reaction specifically with art . . . to more and more people, belief in God seemed to express feeling rather than to state knowledge. . . . Belief had slipped into a convenient new category, which helped not only to explain it but to explain it away. . . . This exaltation of religion as feeling made it easier to accept the loss of God as reality.[42]

Musical growth is a joyous process, fulfilling what it means to be made in the image of God but grateful all along that God's grace extends far beyond human limitations to be creative. It suggests that Baptists need not fear the process that objectifies the subjective experience (music, as an example). As long as discernment of beauty does not become an end in itself, the resulting discernment glorifies God. This is good news.

A Plea for True Diversity

The historical record reveals the kinds of music Baptists have made and the stylistic means through which it came alive. What remains to be said, though, is that manner affects response and manner matters.

Baptists constantly demonstrate variety in their expressions of worship and religious life. For a local church to maintain any level of cohesion requires divine love and Christlike tolerance. At times, though, divergence in musical expressions severely strains the "tie that binds." A dual mind-set is partly responsible. On the one hand, Baptists love their heritage, and, as a vital part of that heritage, many cherish their musical culture. On the other hand, Baptists tend to "do church" pragmatically.

For many Baptists, evangelism is the end of the local church; everything else—church music included—comes second. With increasing frequency and predictability, congregations today absorb one mode of musical expression after another for the sake of reaching a specified group of people unreached by "the old music." While each local church should try, it is not the responsibility of each church to reach all who need Christ. Each church should be tolerant of another's worship of God and should be free to explore, experience, and even adopt that worship, if it feels so led. On the other hand, no church (if it is truly Baptist) should succumb to spiritual intimidation by its ministerial staff, denominational agencies, high-pressure "experts," factions within its membership, or even the winds of the larger culture, to modify, adapt, or scrap its worship modality and/or music for fear of becoming out-of-date. There is ample space in the Baptist world for diversity of worship style. If change is to take place, it should be due to the prompting of God's Spirit and not market-driven conformity.

Since the time of the Kentucky revivals, Baptists have been caught in a landslide of subjectivism in their modes of religious expression. Expressed through folk hymnody (white spirituals), Negro spirituals, gospel songs, and contemporary Christian music (CCM), the spirit of this mindset is epitomized in the lyrics: "Jesus is all the world to me, . . . He's my friend" (Will L. Thompson, 1904). The preoccupation with personalized expressions of spiritual realities and relationships is what sets the American Christian experience apart from that of the European consensus. When placed in sacred song, such intense subjectivity tends to focus more on the one testifying than on the object of the testimony. In addition, as stylized performance gestures are used in presenting a "testimony" song, the more likely will be the perception that the singer is "performing" and drawing attention to self. It is precisely this "I" focused performance syndrome that has some Baptists deeply concerned for the future of music in Baptist life.

What the music of worship and devotion will become is unclear. What our mannerisms of musical expression and worship will be is a matter of conjecture, but hopefully Baptists will ever desire to "do them" honestly, artfully, and in good taste. Above all, hopefully Baptists will always seek to search the unfathomable riches of God, to understand fuller what the scripture means:

> Speak to one another in the words of psalms, hymns, and sacred songs; sing hymns and psalms to the Lord, with praise in your hearts. (Eph 5:19)

> Christ's message, in all its richness, must live in your hearts. Teach and instruct one another with all wisdom. Sing psalms, hymns, and sacred songs; sing to God, with thanksgiving in your heart. (Col 3:16, TEV)

Notes

[1]C. M. Dent. "The Protestant Reformation: The Anabaptists," in *The Study of Spirituality*, ed. Cheslyn Jones. Geoffrey Wainwright, and Edward Yarnold, SJ, (New York: Oxford University Press. 1986) 352.

[2]Ibid., 354. From a Hutterite chronicle, cited by J. Horsch in *Mennonite Quarterly Review* 12 (1938): 17.

[3]The Anabaptists produced no body of lasting hymnody, owing to the generally low quality of texts and tunes, as well as the tendencies toward subjectivism and political reaction.

[4]C. M. Dent. "The Protestant Reformation: Zwingli;" in *The Study of Spirituality*, 348. Zwingli viewed music as being irresistible. He could not envision a way for a worshiper to engage in music without being drawn to its powers and, thus, away from spiritual matters.

[5]Charles Garside., Jr., *Zwingli and the Arts* (New Haven CT: Yale University Press, 1966; reprint, New York: Da Capo Press, 1981) 41-49.

[6]Donald P. Hustad, *Jubilate! Church Music in the Evangelical Tradition* (Carol Stream IL: Hope Publishing Company, 1981) 117-18. "They rejected all established liturgical forms; when they met together, . . . their services included only prayer and the exposition of scripture."

[7]William H. Brackney, *et al., Baptist Life and Thought: 1600–1980* (Valley Forge PA: Judson Press, 1980) 51.

[8]Richard M. Pope, *The Church and Its Culture: a History of the Church in Changing Cultures* (St. Louis MO: Bethany Press, 1965).

[9]The Particular Baptist, John Gill, defended singing as a gospel ordinance by citing Paul's urging that the church sing psalms, hymns, and spiritual songs. Yet while he identified hymns as freely-composed expressions of praise and acknowledged that the Church had generated many such creations, he could not "but judge them . . . unnecessary, since we are so well provided with a book of psalms and spiritual songs [certain of the psalms], indited by the Spirit of God and suitable for all occasions." John Gill, *A Discourse on Singing of Psalms as a Part of Divine Worship* (London: n.p., 1734) 18-23, as cited in Brackney, 51.

[10]Hustad, 126.

[11]Harry Eskew and Hugh T. McElrath, *Sing With Understanding.* (Nashville TN: Broadman Press, 1980) 116.

[12]Ibid., 120. Baptist hymn writers included Anne Steele (1716–78), Benjamin Deddome (1717–1793), Samuel Stennett (1727–1795), Robert Robinson (1735–1790), and Samuel Medley (1738–1799).

[13]Jonathan Edwards encouraged vigorous singing as a response to the revivals, suggesting that singing is a command of God to each worshiper. In T. Harwood Pattison, *Public Worship.* (Philadelphia: The American Baptist Publication Society, 1900) 176.

[14]In "lining out the tune," a leader would recite or sing each stanza or first verse before leading the congregation in its singing. Since many psalms had over ten stanzas and it would have been unthinkable to omit a stanza, psalm singing in this fashion must have been arduously slow and often uninspiring.

[15]Robert T. Handy, *A History of the Churches in the United States and Canada* (New York: Oxford University Press, 1976) 96. Baptists accounted for the third largest denominational group in the colonies at the time of the American Revolution, superseded only by Congregationalists and Presbyterians.

[16]Hustad, 149.

[17]Ellen Jane Lorenz, *Glory, Hallelujah! The Story of the Camp meeting Spiritual* (Nashville TN: Abingdon, 1980) 44-45. Her father recalled "a good many grace notes and slurred passing notes in their solos that . . . would be difficult to reproduce on a staff. . . . I remember [hearing] an old local preacher sing . . . with great earnestness over forty years ago in the foothills of the Alleghanies. . . . I remember that it was minor and intensely sad, full of slurrings and quaverings," 57.

[18]"[Baptists] kept the 'experience' songs going. The 'comes' and 'come all ye's' opening such ballads run up to 27 in Dupuy's Kentucky Baptist collection of 1812, and to 34 in Mercer's (Georgia Baptist) Cluster of 1823." Baptists wrote and used in worship ballads making scriptural connection between local tragedies (natural or man-made), human sinfulness, and God's wrath. One such song "was sung 'in the Baptist Meeting House on Wednesday, January 1st, 1812,' less than a week after" a Richmond theater burned, killing 70 people. In George Pullen Jackson, *White and Negro Spirituals: Their Life Span and Kinship* (Jackson MS: 1943; reprint, New York: Da Capo Press, 1975) 60-61.

[19]Ibid., 57.

[20]Bill R. Austin, *Austin's Topical History of Christianity* (Wheaton IL: Tyndale House Publishers, Inc., 1983) 360.

[21]For example, the use of "leader-chorus" patterns in their indigenous work songs directly influenced the use of "tag lines," whether between verses of existing hymns or as integral parts of improvised lyrics, by the revivalists: e.g., "There's not a friend like the lowly Jesus, No, not one! No, not one!"

[22]Ellen M. Rosenberg, *The Southern Baptists: A Subculture in Transition* (Knoxville TN: University of Tennessee Press, 1989) 171.

[23]Jackson, 286.

[24] "On the black side . . . We saw in one [tent] a zealous convert . . . who with violent gesticulations gave vent to his newly-awakened feelings; in [another], women were dancing 'the holy dance' for one of the newly-converted. . . . [Their] hymns (sic) were . . . fervent and beautiful." Quotation by Fredrika Bremer, *Homes of the New World*, I, 306-317, in Dena J. Epstein, *Sinful Tunes and Spirituals: Black Folk Music to the Civil War* (Urbana IL: University of Illinois Press, 1977) 198-99.

[25]Handy, 272.

[26]Leonard Ellinwood, *The History of American Church Music* (New York: Da Capo Press, 1970) 101.

[27]The southern singing school tunebooks included: *Kentucky Harmony* (1816), *Missouri Harmony* (1820), *Southern Harmony* (1835), and *The Sacred Harp* (1844 and later editions to the present time). These tunebooks, so called because they contained both words and music instead of words only, were used only as curriculum material for the singing schools; still, participants continued to used them informally in smaller community and family gatherings as entertainment. Various hymn books were used by Baptists in their regular services: *The Evangelical Harp* (1842), *The Psalmist* (1843), *Revival Hymns* (1845), *The Christian Minstrel* (1846), and *Baptist Hymn and Tune Book* (1857).

[28]To this day, thousands of believers, among them many Baptists, make annual pilgrimages to attend Sacred Harp singings and other shaped-note singing schools.

Although most have mastered traditional notation ("round notes"), they return to experience the singular joy of (as they value it) singing God's praises in the old style and to renew life-long friendships.

[29]Paul McCommon, "Trends in Southern Baptist Church Music Since 1915," in *Baptist History and Heritage* 21/3 (July 1986); feature edition: "Baptist Church Music Heritage."

[30]Jackson, 128-29.

[31]Eric Routley, *Twentieth Century Church Music* (Carol Stream IL: Agape, 1984) 198.

[32]James Turner, *Without God, Without Creed: The Origins of Unbelief in America* (Baltimore MD: Johns Hopkins University Press, 1985) 75-76, writes: "They preached that religion flows from the heart; doctrines mattered, but only if infused with deep personal feeling. . . . The plea to the heart helped Evangelicalism to . . . emerge as the greatest single force in the history of American religion. The movement divided roughly into two wings. One, strongest in the Southern states, typified by . . . Baptists . . . played down doctrine and all matters of intellect. Their preachers became celebrated but not their professors."

[33]Winthrop S. Hudson, ed., *Walter Rauschenbush: Selected Writings* (New York: Westminster Press, 1984) 9, 107-108. Rauschenbush was an enthusiast of Sankey's gospel songs; from 1886–1890, he translated/published *Neue Lieder* in German. He saw a corollary between the gospel song, the hymns of the Welsh revivals (1904–1905), and "speaking in tongues" in 1 Corinthians 14: "Now music is the language of emotion. It awakens emotion. The singing in the Moody and Sankey revivals formerly, and still more in the Welsh revival today, . . . are pent up emotion."

[34]McCommon, 50.

[35]B. B. McKinney was later chosen (1935) to give direction to the new Church Music Department of the SBC Sunday School Board (1941); he remained its head until his death in 1952.

[36]There has been little interest in the new generation of high quality, expressive hymns coming from the renaissance of the English hymn and the Lutheran chorale. While a few hymns of Fred Pratt Green, Brian Jeffrey Leech, and Brian Wren can be found in *The Baptist Hymnal* (1975 and 1991), there is limited indication that they are frequently used. The same can be said for new hymns published by The Hymn Society of American and Canada.

[37]Anne Murchison, *Praise and Worship: In Earth As It Is In Heaven* (Waco TX: Word Books, Pub., 1981) 43, 55, 80, 83-84.

[38]Hustad, 76-77.

[39]E. Glenn Hinson, *A Serious Call to a Contemplative Life-Style* (Philadelphia: Westminster Press, 1974) 64-65, 112.

[40]Hustad , 44, notes that "any argument about the specifics of church music style that is based on biblical authority is extremely tenuous—there is simply no definitive or consistent word."

[41]Rosenberg, 174-75.

[42]Turner, 197-99.

"Something Old, Something New": Worship Styles for Baptists in the Nineties

Paul Basden

Once upon a time, all Baptists worshiped the same way. They attended worship services on Sunday at 11:00 A.M. They listened to the swell of a pipe organ as they quietly awaited the beginning of the worship service. They followed a planned order of worship, written on a bulletin. They sang familiar congregational hymns that they knew and loved. They thrilled to the sound of a choir singing a powerful anthem. They heard a sermon from the Bible on how to love and trust God. Then they dismissed at 12 noon in order to beat the Methodists to the cafeteria!

For all who know the history and heartbeat of Baptists, the above scenario never really occurred, if for no other reason than the fact that a sentence with "all Baptists" could never possibly be true! "All Baptists" have never done anything the same, including the act of offering corporate worship to Almighty God. Only in fairy tales, where "once upon a time" confuses fantasy with fact, have all Baptists shared a common style of worship. In real life, Baptists have always worshiped in a variety of ways, from the revivalism of frontier missions to the formality of big-city congregations to the foot-stomping and hand-clapping of Southern Gospel churches. Baptists have never shared one common worship style.

Baptist worship services in the 1990s give evidence of greater diversity than at any other time in Baptist history. Some welcome this diversity as the work of the Spirit of God, whom they believe continues to guide the church to discover new ways of worship that are still faithful to the Bible. Others resent the diversity, having become convinced that the spectrum of worship has been shattered. Still others try to ignore the diversity, as though their own worship style were the only obvious choice.

Regardless of these reactions, however, Baptists continue to differ greatly in their approach to and practice of worship. Some churches, unaware of this reality, have found themselves in the midst of serious conflict over their style of congregational worship. Previously stable congregations have even split over the issue. This suggests that a new item must be added to the list of potential problems that can cause a church crisis: pastoral authority, women deacons/ministers, denominational controversy, . . . and now worship style.

The New Testament nowhere endorses one specific style of worship for all believers. To the contrary, several embryonic styles of worship appear to have emerged in the early church, all of which were different from one another. For example, there may have been a Jerusalem "style," as described in Acts 2:42, that emphasized apostolic teaching, the Lord's Supper, and prayer. Paul may have provided clues about an Ephesian/Colossian "style" that stressed Christ's teaching and congregational singing (Eph 5:19; Col 3:16). Certainly the Corinthian "style" was well developed by the mid-1950s, incorporating the use of such "sign gifts" in worship as miracles, prophecy, and glossolalia (1 Cor 12-14). One searches the New Testament in vain, however, for a divinely sanctioned style or order of worship that all churches must follow if they are to be true churches. Rather, variety in worship styles emerged during the apostolic era and has been with us ever since.

A word of clarification may be in order here. In claiming that the New Testament never provides an express order of worship, I am not suggesting that there is no biblical guidance for corporate worship. The Bible abundantly reveals the nature and priority of worship for Israel and for the early church. The Old Testament points to the importance of sacred places and altars, animal sacrifices, festivals of commemoration, observance of the Law, singing of psalms, and the use of priests who served as ministers of temple worship. The early church continued the synagogue practices of scripture reading, preaching, singing, and prayer, and added the Lord's Supper and baptism as well. The Bible speaks univocally and unmistakably about the value and privilege of religious worship, pointing the church in every age to constant prayer, vibrant singing, biblical exhortation, sacrificial giving, baptism as initiation, and the Lord's Supper as both sign and mystery. What the New Testament never does is identify one particular patterned emphasis or style of worship that is "more Christian" or "more biblical" or "more holy" than another.

To accept this recognition, even if grudgingly, allows for the possibility of greater objectivity when studying and evaluating worship styles that differ from our own. After all, few things are more sacred to us than the way in which either we learned to worship or we worship most effectively now. The silence of the New Testament suggests that we must be very careful before we hastily dismiss or negatively criticize another's preferred worship style. The aim of this chapter is to clarify the most significant worship styles that Baptists are practicing today, to the end that understanding will replace fear and that unity in diversity will be embraced as a Baptist principle even in the area of worship style.

If one were to visit Baptist worship services around the country for an extended period of time, one would discover, amid all the diversity, several clear patterns of worship. One might be tempted to divide all of these styles into the two simple categories of traditional and non-traditional,[1] or perhaps to use the three designations of traditional, contemporary, and a "blend" of those two.[2] A more nuanced differentiation is necessary for fuller understanding. For the last couple of years, I have identified five unique worship styles that are currently used by large numbers of Baptist churches. These five, from left (most traditional) to right (least traditional) on a worship spectrum, are: liturgical, traditional, revivalistic, praise and worship, and seeker.[3]

The spectrum looks like this:

Liturgical

Traditional

Revivalist

Praise and Worship

Seeker

Liturgical Worship

Liturgical worship is the most formal and traditional style. With roots going deep into patristic and medieval soil, it rightly claims an ancient and noble heritage. Although not very widespread among Southern Baptists, this style continues to be practiced among many American Baptists and most mainline Protestants and Roman Catholics. Its mood reflects a balance of contemplation and majesty, revealing the value it places on reverence. The worship service is well planned and completely structured. Its axiom could well be summarized in the quip attributed to the late John Mackay, former president of Princeton Theological Seminary: "In worship, when the choice comes down to order or ardor, I'll choose order every time."

The purpose of liturgical worship is to lead the church to give corporate recognition to the transcendent glory of God. By comparison, the immanence or closeness of God does not receive much emphasis in worship. The biblical model for this style is found in Isaiah 6:1-9, where Isaiah sees a vision of the holy God, confesses his sin, receives forgiveness, hears the call of God, and obediently answers the call. Liturgical worship seeks to follow this model both in order and in content.

Congregational singing is led by the minister of music or sometimes by the organist/choirmaster. On any given Sunday morning, the congregation will sing three hymns (all verses, not just first and last!) from the hymnal. These hymns generally fall under the classification of traditional hymns, as opposed to gospel hymns. They focus on the adoration of God, the life of the church, and the duties of discipleship.

Some of the favorite hymns of praise and adoration sung in a liturgical service include "Come, Thou Almighty King," "All Creatures of Our God and King," "Praise to the Lord, the Almighty," "Praise the Lord! Ye Heavens, Adore Him," "Come, Thou Fount of Every Blessing," "O Worship the King," "Joyful, Joyful, We Adore Thee," "All Hail the Power of Jesus' Name," and "Crown Him with Many Crowns." These hymns are objective in nature, highlighting the greatness and glory of God, not the worshiper's thoughts or feelings about God.

Hymns concerning the life and ministry of the *ecclesia* likewise focus on the objective identity and mission of the church. Among the most frequently sung hymns about the church are "The Church's One Foundation," "In Christ There Is No East or West," "Brethren, We Have Met to Worship," "Lead On, O King Eternal," and "God of Grace and God of Glory."

Hymns that focus upon the daily demands of Christian discipleship stress service over testimony and social concern over evangelism. Favorite hymns for the Christian life include "Come, All Christians, Be Committed," "Stir Thy Church, O God, Our Father," "Dear Lord and Father of Mankind," "Take My Life and Let It Be," "We Are Called to Be God's People," and "Be Thou My Vision." Charles Wesley, James Montgomery, and Isaac Watts contributed many of the hymns which are frequently used in liturgical services.

The choir provides most of the special music in liturgical services. Its repertoire consists mostly of anthems composed by older classical composers such as Bach, Mozart, or Handel; anthems by modern classical composers such as Ralph Vaughan Williams; and traditional modern anthems such as those by Gordon Young. When soloists or ensembles offer special music, they typically choose classical pieces.

The primary musical instrument for worship in liturgical churches is the pipe organ. Seldom is a piano used, because it is viewed as more of a solo instrument. Taped musical accompaniment is never used.

The reading of Holy Scripture occupies a prominent place in the service. The corporate confession of sin often incorporates scripture passages, while the call to worship and the benediction do the same. At least two public readings from the Bible occur, usually an Old Testament reading and a New Testament reading. If an additional reading is added, it is from the New Testament. More often than not, the Lectionary dictates the choice of scriptures for the day. The Psalms are frequently read at numerous points during the service.

Great fanfare accompanies the collection of the offering. The minister often blesses the offering as the ushers return it to the front of the sanctuary. The congregation may sing the Doxology as a response of gratitude.

When the pastor stands to preach, his or her sermon likely will follow the Christian year, revolving around the great themes of Advent, Lent, Easter, and Pentecost. The Lectionary will guide the pastor to preach "the whole counsel of God" over a three-year period. The sermon tends to have a more intellectual than emotional approach and a more social than evangelistic appeal. Following the sermon is a period of commitment, often tied to a closing hymn of dedication or service. Altar calls are foreign to the liturgical service.

The congregation celebrates the ordinances frequently, the Lord's Supper being served as often as once a month. This pattern differs greatly from the Zwinglian and Anabaptist tendency to offer Communion only quarterly. Baptism is celebrated less frequently.

In some liturgical services, the congregation recites in unison the Lord's Prayer, sings the *Gloria Patri,* and repeats the Apostles' Creed as a common confession of faith.

Liturgical worship contains many strong points. Its form and structure point the congregation to God, who is worthy to be praised for God's majesty and honor. Magnifying God's transcendence evokes in the worshiper a sense of awe, of the numinous, of the *mysterium tremendum.* The prominence of scripture, the centrality of the Lord's Supper, and the pattern of the Christian year reveal a deep reverence for the Word of God.

This style of worship does not appeal to all Baptists, however. For some, the God who is worshiped seems unapproachable, more the "Wholly Other" than "the God and Father of our Lord Jesus Christ." For others, the form and structure of the liturgy do not provide a vehicle for effective worship. Rather the liturgy actually impedes their worship because it prohibits not only spontaneous responses but also any sovereign surprises from the Spirit. For them, the form of the liturgical service quickly becomes dead formalism, nothing more than religion by rote. Finally, the cerebral nature of the service sacrifices the emotional appeal or the evangelistic emphasis that some Baptists want and expect in worship.

Traditional Worship

Traditional worship follows a planned and structured order but is less formal than the liturgical style. In fact, its ministers describe the service as non-liturgical. However, it would be more accurate to identify this style as semi-liturgical. One minister of music has described it as "informal dignity."[4] It originated when liturgical worship met the American frontier, and it earned a permanent place in Baptist worship when the frontier became settled. As such, the traditional style is a hybrid of liturgical worship and frontier revivalism.

The purpose of traditional worship is to lead the congregation to praise and thank God for God's goodness and to hear God speak through The Word. These two aspects—praise and preaching—seem to dominate this style of worship. The biblical model for the traditional style is found in Colossians 3:16, where Paul told his readers: "Let the word of Christ dwell in you richly as you teach and admonish one another with all wisdom, and as you sing psalms, hymns and spiritual songs with gratitude in your hearts to God" (NIV). Not coincidentally, this passage of scripture has adorned the front page of the last three hymnals published by Southern Baptists.

The congregation, led by the minister of music, sings a steady diet of four or five hymns, both traditional and gospel. Although some of the newer contemporary Christian songs like "Worship His Majesty," as well as an occasional praise chorus such as "I Love You, Lord," are beginning to find their way into some traditional services, scripture songs have not yet made a name for themselves. Favorite traditional hymns include "Great Is Thy Faithfulness," "All the Way My Savior Leads Me," "Holy, Holy, Holy," "It Is Well with My Soul," "For the Beauty of the Earth," "Stand Up, Stand Up for Jesus," "This Is My Father's World," "Praise Him! Praise Him!," "To God Be the Glory," "We Have Heard the Joyful

Sound," and "Blessed Be the Name." These hymns, while not specifically revivalistic, manage to give equal emphasis to both the transcendence and the immanence of God. At the same time, they balance both the objectivity of God's nature and the subjectivity of the one who is worshiping.

Traditional worship reflects its revivalistic background in its love for gospel hymns. They are not the brand of gospel hymns, however, that tend toward crass sentimentalism or which might be called maudlin. The best loved hymns of this genre include "Amazing Grace," "What a Friend We Have in Jesus," "Footsteps of Jesus," "Beneath the Cross of Jesus," "Blessed Assurance," "He Leadeth Me! O Blessed Thought," "Standing on the Promises," "The Solid Rock," "At Calvary," "Rock of Ages," "When I Survey the Wondrous Cross," "Wonderful Words of Life," "I Am Thine, O Lord," "I Surrender All," "Wherever He Leads I'll Go," "Faith Is the Victory," "Leaning on the Everlasting Arms," "Love Lifted Me," and "I Love to Tell the Story." Hymn writers who figure prominently in the gospel hymns used in traditional worship are Philip Bliss and Isaac Watts.

A choir and soloists or ensembles provide the special music, usually two pieces per service. The choir regularly sings traditional modern anthems, hymn arrangements by musicians like John Ness Beck, and contemporary anthems such as those by Tom Fettke and Mark Hayes, as well as occasional contemporary popular Christian music arrangements by Sandi Patti, Michael W. Smith, and others. Soloists and ensembles sing primarily contemporary Christian music, gospel music, or hymn arrangements. Classical pieces appear in the music repertoire only occasionally, and then are limited to seasonal holidays.

The organ and the piano join forces as the primary musical instruments in the traditional service. The organ may be pipe or electronic, and the piano is usually a grand or a baby grand. An orchestra of strings, woodwinds, horns, and percussion augments the organ and piano periodically. Interestingly, the electronic synthesizer has started to make an appearance as well, usually to replicate orchestral sounds. The majority of churches that practice traditional worship utilize taped musical accompaniment occasionally, but not regularly.

Usually one scripture reading is used in a worship service. It may be a responsive reading from the hymnal or a solo reading directly from the Bible.

The offering is received prior to the sermon or prior to the special music that precedes the sermon, although a number of churches have moved the offering to the end of the service, after the sermon, indicating its responsive nature.

The pastor's sermon comes from a selected scripture text, chosen according to the Christian year, the denominational and civic calendars, or his/her own preaching plan. The message may be expository or topical, but it will generally appeal to both heart and head. Following the sermon, the pastor issues a public invitation for people in the congregation to make a commitment to Jesus Christ during the singing of the final hymn.

The Lord's Supper is celebrated quarterly. Baptism is observed more frequently.

The strengths of the traditional service are obvious. In many ways, it allows for the best of both worlds in worship: transcendence and immanence, objectivity and subjectivity, intellect and emotions. It is formal enough to maintain dignity, yet informal enough to encourage participation. It is structured enough to point to God, yet more flexible than the liturgical style.

At the same time, the traditional style has some blind spots. The relative silence of scripture in the service, except for the sermon, and the infrequent observance of the Lord's Supper, offend some Baptists. As expected, the structure that is present prevents certain Baptists from making the spontaneous responses that well up within them and which seek unstructured expression.

Revivalist Worship

Today's revivalist worship patterns itself after the frontier tradition, which became prevalent in America in the early nineteenth century. Characterized by informality and exuberance, this style of worship seeks to draw the worshipers closer to God. The upbeat mood of the service directly impacts the emotions, to the point that the worshipers say that they "feel" God's presence during worship. Although revivalist worship prides itself in being anti-liturgical, the order of service is generally planned and structured.

In a revivalist service, the primary purpose is to reach the "lost" with the gospel of Jesus Christ. The biblical model for this style of worship is Peter's preaching at Pentecost, as recorded in Acts 2. When Peter proclaimed the *kerygma* in Jerusalem that day, three thousand Jews believed the Gospel and were baptized. Those who practice revivalist worship look to this passage and others like it for the form and content of their worship services. Secondary purposes of revivalist worship are to encourage

Christians to share their witness with unbelievers and to encourage moral living among Christians.

Congregational singing assumes great importance in this style of worship, for music stirs the emotions and prepares the heart for the sermon. The congregation, under the leadership of a minister of music or "song leader," sings four or five hymns. Although some of these might be classified as contemporary Christian songs or praise choruses, most are gospel hymns. Depending on the church, these hymns might be classic gospel hymns from a standard hymnal or Southern gospel songs from a paperback songbook. Favorite gospel hymns in revivalist services center on several themes, including revival/renewal—"Lord, Send a Revival," "Revive Us Again," "Send a Great Revival," "There Shall Be Showers of Blessing," conversion—"Victory in Jesus," "Heaven Came Down," "Nothing but the Blood," "There Is Power in the Blood," "Saved, Saved!" "Are You Washed in the Blood?" " 'Whosoever' Meaneth Me," "Lord, I'm Coming Home," "Whiter Than Snow," "Just As I Am," "The Nail-Scarred Hand," "Room at the Cross," "The Old Rugged Cross," "Love Lifted Me," prayer—"In the Garden," "Near to the Heart of God," "Tell It to Jesus," and life in heaven—"When We All Get to Heaven," "Shall We Gather at the River," "O That Will Be Glory," and "When the Roll Is Called Up Yonder." Fanny Crosby, B. B. McKinney, and Charles H. Gabriel could be called the patron saints for revivalist music.

Musical accompaniment is by the piano and the organ. The organ may be either an electronic organ or a Hammond organ, but it would almost never be a pipe organ. Pipe organs are too associated with liturgical worship to fit a revivalist service.

Special music by the choir and soloists/ensembles inspires the congregation. Two or three special music pieces are offered at each worship service. The choir never sings classical music, but instead sings gospel music arrangements, such as those by John W. Peterson and Joe Parks, hymn arrangements by Camp Kirkland, and contemporary anthems. Soloists likewise never sing classical music, preferring instead to sing gospel pieces like "Love Grew Where the Blood Fell" and contemporary Christian songs by artists like Steve Green and Sandi Patti. Taped accompaniment is used regularly in the majority of these churches.

Scripture passages are seldom read in these worship services, except at the time of the sermon. The offering is received midway through the service, either before or during the special music, which precedes the sermon.

When the pastor enters the pulpit to preach, everyone in the congregation knows that the sermon is the main event for the day. As important as music is in the revivalist service, the "song service" is often considered to be merely "the preliminaries" that warm the worshipers for the preaching. As one pastor put it, "The music sets 'em up so the sermon can knock 'em out!" The congregation can count on hearing an evangelistic message. Even if the sermon text is not evangelistic, the pastor always moves to a gospel theme and an evangelistic appeal. Following the admonition often attributed to Charles H. Spurgeon, the revivalist preacher "makes a beeline for the cross" in every sermon. By design, the message focuses on an explanation of sin and redemption, with the aim of bringing unbelievers in the worship service to make a personal decision to follow Jesus Christ. The public invitation that follows the sermon is often protracted in order to allow non-Christians to recognize their need of Christ. These altar calls can last up to ten minutes and even longer.

The Lord's Supper is seldom celebrated on Sunday mornings, usually never more than a couple of times a year. Baptism, however, is observed much more frequently, as often as two or three times a month.

The revivalist style of worship has some clear strengths. Its informal attitude and exuberant mood invite the participation of worshipers. The music, both congregational and special, speaks to human emotions and challenges the will. Above all, this type of service places high priority on the new birth, that is, a new relationship to God through Jesus Christ.

In the estimate of some Baptists, however, revivalist services have some glaring deficiencies. Because this style so emphasizes evangelism in worship, the net result is often perceived as an imbalanced worship service, where the congregation's need to worship God is overlooked or not taken seriously. Many Baptists believe that once the purpose of worship is defined in terms of reaching the lost with the gospel, several consequences follow: The church family receives a steady diet of "milk" and not "meat," of evangelism and not instruction, of *kerygma* and not *didache*; the canon for sermons becomes relatively small since the majority of messages are intended to be evangelistic; the canon of hymns becomes equally limited, for the same reason; and the constant preaching about conversion to believers often leads to their re-baptism, inasmuch as young Christians begin to think that the only way to please God is to be saved and baptized, even if they have already done it all before.

For those Baptists who believe that worship has no other end than to glorify God for God's nature and acts, the revivalist style raises additional concerns: The music can tend toward emotionalism; the sermon can stress judgment and condemnation over grace and forgiveness; and the invitation can become manipulative. In short, worship can become a means to an end, which offends those Baptists who identify with the vision of worship as expressed by the late Franklin M. Segler (longtime Professor of Pastoral Ministries at Southwestern Baptist Theological Seminary) who wrote: "Worship is an end in itself; it is not a means to something else. . . . We worship God purely for the sake of worshiping God."[5]

Praise and Worship

Once loosely identified as "pentecostal worship," the style now popularly known as "praise and worship" describes an informal, contemporary service in which the congregation actively engages in outward celebration of the immediate presence of God. Worshipers celebrate their experience of God through expressive, occasionally uninhibited, acts of praise. The praise and worship style can reflect overt charismatic tendencies such as speaking in tongues, interpreting tongues, and exorcising demons, but most Baptists who participate in praise and worship services identify themselves as non-charismatic. They do believe, however, that worship should involve the whole body, so they love to clap their hands, raise their arms, sway to music, and shout out loud. Although the service is decidedly non-liturgical, the ministers carefully plan the service so that it is well structured and orderly.

The purpose of a praise and worship service is to guide the congregation to "offer a sacrifice of praise" to the Lord in a spirit of joyful adoration. The biblical model that inspires this style of worship is Psalm 150, where the people of God are enjoined to praise Him "with the trumpet, . . .with the harp and lyre, . . . with tambourine and dancing, . . . with the strings and flute, . . . with the clash of cymbals." (vv. 3-5, NIV). Music is the element of worship that helps to make this service specifically upbeat. The congregation sings a lot, usually six or seven songs or more in the course of the service. Sometimes they sing a medley of several songs in a row, often repeating the stanzas over and over. Although some congregations still use hymnals, more are printing the words to the songs in the bulletin or displaying the lyrics on the wall by means of overhead projector, thereby allowing worshipers to look up rather than down while they are singing.

Congregational songs are sometimes traditional or gospel hymns, but more often than not they are praise choruses such as "Glorify Thy Name," "I Love You, Lord," and "He Is Lord," contemporary Christian songs like "Majesty" and "Shine, Jesus, Shine," and scripture songs, such as "As the

Deer Pants" and "We Bring a Sacrifice of Praise." The lyrics tend to be more subjective than objective, more devotional than doctrinal, and more affective than cognitive.

For more traditional Baptists, this new music may sound unfamiliar. Its roots are not in the Reformation or the Great Awakening or even the Frontier. It is not the music of Isaac Watts, Charles Wesley, Fanny Crosby, or B. B. McKinney. This music grew out of the Jesus Movement, a spiritual revival among teenagers in America during the late 1960s and early 1970s. Songs that were written, performed, and recorded by young people active in the Jesus Movement began to appear in church worship services across the country by the mid-seventies. Those songs, and their modern-day offspring, provide praise and worship churches with a vast repertoire of congregational music. Songs produced on the *Maranatha* or *Hosanna/ Integrity* labels are among the most popular songs for this style of worship.

The minister of music typically leads congregational singing, although praise teams, of which he or she is often a member, are being utilized more and more for this purpose. Musical accompaniment is usually some combination of piano, electronic organ, and digital synthesizer. Backup bands, with guitars and drums, have become popular for many of these services as well. The sound approaches that of a "light" rock and roll concert, thus appealing to a younger generation of Baptists who do not like classical music and do not identify with revivalism.

The choir or praise team usually sings a couple of pieces of special music. Rather than singing classical or modern anthems, they sing hymn and gospel arrangements such as those by Camp Kirkland, contemporary anthems like those by Mark Hayes, and contemporary popular Christian music arrangements by David Clydesdale and others. Soloists follow the same pattern, singing the contemporary Christian music of Amy Grant, Steve Green, and Babbie Mason. Taped musical accompaniment is a regular feature for these services.

While there is not a steady diet of scripture readings, a passage from the Bible is occasionally read. The offering may be received in the middle of the service or at the very end, but regardless of the time, the congregation perceives the offering as an important act of worship.

The pastor frequently preaches practical sermons from the Bible in which he applies a biblical text to the demands of modern life. The sermons may emphasize daily Christian discipleship, addressing prayer, obedience, spiritual gifts, and spiritual warfare, or they may resemble the Christian self-help approach often identified with Robert Schuller, dealing with such matters as stress, happiness, and addiction. The invitation that follows the message challenges believers to recommit their lives to the lordship of Jesus Christ, expressed in obedient daily living.

In charismatic praise and worship services, the sermon often begins with a passage of scripture and then quickly moves to challenge the congregation to live the "victorious Christian life," which may be apprehended by means of exercising the sign gifts such as healing, exorcism, and speaking in tongues. The public invitation then calls for people to be delivered from demonic oppression and to receive spiritual, emotional, and physical healing.

The Lord's Supper is celebrated quarterly on average. Baptism usually is celebrated more frequently, although the observance may be relegated to Sunday evening worship services.

The praise and worship style is a relative newcomer to Baptist worship. Nevertheless, it has developed quite a following. Its strengths revolve around its celebrational mood and expressive participation. The worshipers acknowledge God's immanence as they sense an awareness of God's presence through the emotional impact of the music. This style allows great freedom to respond to the perceived movement of God's Spirit, whether by singing with raised hands, praying with outstretched arms, clapping as an expression of affirmation, or saying "Amen" during the sermon. Such participation causes the members of the congregation to believe that they themselves are truly worshiping God in the Spirit, a privilege that they do not ever want to give up.

There are some blind spots in the praise and worship style, however. Because experience plays such a prominent role, some Baptists feel that these services can ignore theology. With the obvious emphasis on emotional response, this style is sometimes accused of providing entertainment rather than fostering worship or of degenerating into a religious pep rally. More traditional Baptists often regard the choruses as doctrinally shallow and musically simplistic, not to mention redundant, and fear that the subjectivity and freedom within the service are nothing more than organized chaos.

Seeker Service

A relatively new addition to Sunday mornings is the seeker service, a style that depends more on a specific person than do the other styles considered above. The concept of a seeker service achieved popular recognition in the late 1980s when Bill Hybels, pastor of Willow Creek

Community Church in suburban Chicago, received the attention of the national press in several magazines and newspapers.[6] Having originated and practiced this unique, non-traditional style for a decade, Hybels began to promote it at a "pastors conference" that his church sponsored several times a year. At these conferences, he explained why and how he initiated a seeker service and how any pastor could do the same. Not only have Baptist pastors flocked to these conferences to learn the nuts and bolts of planning and leading a seeker service, but numerous Baptist agencies have invited Hybels to speak to Baptists about this worship style. These factors account for the rising popularity of this style of service, especially among those of a younger generation.

If some of this terminology sounds foreign to the uninitiated, then a simple definition will clarify. A seeker service is a toned-down, upbeat evangelistic service for "seekers," that is, non-Christians who are seeking God but who have not yet made a personal commitment to the Gospel. It is not a service of worship for Christians. Rather, its purpose is to present and explain the Gospel in non-religious terms and in non-traditional ways to unbelievers. Church members are expected to bring their non-Christian friends to these services, which are specifically designed to communicate the Christian message in ways that do not threaten or scare off unbelievers. In other words, the "target audience" of a seeker service is non-Christians. The informal attitude and non-liturgical style may conceal the fact that the service has been carefully planned and structured by the ministers, perhaps more so than any of the other four styles.

The biblical model that guides the seeker style is the story of Paul preaching about an "unknown god" in Athens (Acts 17:16-34). The passage relates how Paul accommodated the presentation of his message to his hearers in order to get its content across to them. Cultural accommodation, without gospel compromise, is the goal of the seeker service.

Believing that seekers do not want to sing many congregational songs, the minister of music or praise team leads the congregation in singing only one praise chorus or scripture song during the service such as "This Is the Day" or "How Majestic Is Your Name." The words to that song are projected onto the wall by means of an overhead projector.

The praise team or soloists perform the special music, singing almost exclusively contemporary Christian music like that recorded by Twila Paris and Stephen Curtis Chapman. A piano, digital synthesizer, and usually a rock or jazz band accompany both congregational and special music. Taped accompaniment also is widely accepted in seeker services as the norm.

When a scripture reading is included in the service, as it often is, the reader carefully, even humorously, explains the background and meaning of the passage in a planned introduction. Behind this practice is the desire and intent to make the biblical message intelligible to those who do not understand religious terminology.

In some seeker services, an offering is collected, while in others it is not. In those churches where the offering is a regular part of the seeker service, it usually takes place at the end. The minister generally explains that guests are not expected to contribute to the offering, other than to drop a visitor's card in the plate if they have chosen to complete one.

Many seeker services have implemented dramatic presentations, which attempt to introduce the topic of the sermon in a form that is readily acceptable to unchurched persons who live in an age of television, cinema, and theater. The actors and actresses in these dramas do not dress in period costumes from Bible times and re-enact a Bible story. They wear clothes just like those worn by people in the congregation that day, and they present humorous and poignant theme interpretations that resemble television sitcoms and dramatic episodes, though obviously abbreviated for the sake of time.

After the drama has raised a pertinent question, the minister preaches a sermon that addresses the "felt needs" of modern life from a biblical/Christian perspective. Rather than expository sermons, the pastor usually preaches topical messages that are pre-evangelistic in nature. They are designed to challenge seekers to give serious and thoughtful consideration to the value and importance of Jesus Christ for their lives. A public invitation is not extended every week, but only occasionally to "draw the net" for those seekers who have decided to become believers.

Baptism or the Lord's Supper are not celebrated in the seeker service.

Since the seeker service, by design, focuses on unbelievers and not on Christians, there is usually another service for believers on either Sunday night or Wednesday night. These services generally reflect the praise and worship style already described.

Many strengths belong to the seeker service. Its aim is to reach unbelievers, who are "without hope and without God in the world" (Eph 2:12, NIV). The sensitivity of the seeker service to the culture in which non-Christians live reveals a deep commitment to build bridges for the Gospel into the world of unbelievers. Also, the Bible is treated as relevant to modern life, not as a relic of antiquity. By devoting an entire service to evangelism, a separate service can be devoted to true worship.

Conversely, the proponents of the seeker service need to consider some dangerous blind spots. Some Baptists conclude that "packaging" the gospel so that unbelievers can understand it may lead to compromising the message. Others fear that the overt use of entertainment features to attract non-Christians may result in the commercialization of the church, the marketing of the gospel, and the manipulation of evangelism. Many Baptists question whether it is wise to change the time of congregational worship from the Lord's Day, a practice that dates back to the apostolic church, to another day—regardless of the justification offered. Other Baptists, who are equally committed to the church's task of evangelism, believe that the seeker style has substituted a "come and hear" approach to evangelism for the "go and tell" approach of the Great Commission.

Observations

Blends

Although many Baptist churches practice one of these five worship models in its pure form, many congregations would identify their worship style as a blend or combination of two or more of the styles treated above. Perhaps the most prevalent blends in Baptist life at the present time are traditional-liturgical, traditional-praise and worship, traditional-revivalist, and seeker-praise and worship. These pairs blend most easily because each style shares several commonalities with the other, thereby allowing the creation of a *tertium quid* that does not seem repulsive to the worshipers who have been used to one specific style. Some styles do not easily blend with others, however. Churches find it most difficult to blend the seeker style with traditional or liturgical styles, and to blend the praise and worship style with the liturgical.[7]

Because of the tendency of some blended services to accomplish little more than offending everyone present, some churches see a solution in a "split-level" approach,[8] in which one style of worship is offered on Sunday morning and another style is offered on Sunday night.

Trends

Several trends become obvious as one studies these five styles of worship. Twelve trends will be highlighted here.

Attitude. As the services move from liturgical to seeker, an attitude of open informality begins to replace that of quiet reverence. This change in attitude reflects the change in emphasis from God's transcendence to God's immanence.

Mood. Tracking the change in attitude is a change in mood. The mood becomes less solemn and more celebrational, less contemplative and more exuberant, less reflective and more expressive as the style moves from liturgical to praise and worship or seeker service.

Order. Each of these services is planned and structured carefully by ministers, although revivalist services and praise and worship services tend to be more open to spontaneity and to "the Spirit's movement."

Target Audience. The liturgical, traditional, and praise and worship styles all seek to lead Christians to worship God. The service is planned primarily with Christians in mind. The revivalist and seeker services, however, focus on non-Christians who may be in attendance.

Congregational Singing. Congregational singing is changing dramatically as worship styles move from left to right on the worship spectrum. In praise and worship and seeker services, hymnals are being discarded as words to songs are being printed in bulletins or projected onto the sanctuary wall. The traditional hymns that congregations sing in liturgical and traditional services are being augmented or replaced by gospel hymns in revivalist services and by praise choruses and scripture songs in praise and worship and seeker services. At the same time, the traditional minister of music is being augmented or replaced by a praise team in praise and worship and seeker services. In other words, many Baptist churches are choosing to worship without the use of hymnals, traditional hymns, or ministers of music.

Special Music. While choirs in most liturgical and many traditional services still sing anthems by older and modern classical composers, revivalist choirs sing gospel and hymn arrangements, and praise teams in praise and worship and seeker services sing contemporary anthems and popular Christian music arrangements. Clearly, popular music is replacing classical music as worship styles move from left to right.

Musical Instruments. While the pipe organ remains the instrument of choice in liturgical worship services, it is being augmented or replaced by the electronic organ and the piano in the traditional and revivalist services. Seeker and praise and worship services often utilize electronic organ, piano, digital synthesizer, and jazz ensemble or rock band. Taped musical accompaniment becomes more and more prominent the further one moves away from a liturgical service.

Scripture. Scripture passages are read often in the liturgical service, seldom in the revivalist service, and usually once a week in the other three services.

Offering. The reception of the offering moves from great fanfare in the liturgical service to a "soft-sell" approach in the seeker service.

Preaching. Sermons that follow the lectionary and appeal to the intellect and the social conscience characterize the liturgical service. Bible-centered, expository messages seem generally to characterize the traditional and non-charismatic praise and worship services. Evangelistic sermons, either overt or covert, characterize the revivalist and seeker services.

Public Invitation. The public invitation bears most resemblance to frontier evangelistic services in the revivalist and praise and worship traditions.

Ordinances. The Lord's Supper receives great emphasis in liturgical worship, whereas baptism receives far more emphasis in the revivalist service. The traditional and praise and worship styles have a balanced, though not frequent, emphasis on both ordinances. The seeker service does not include either ordinance.

Ends

More than anything else, the purpose of worship determines the style of worship. Once a congregation decides its reason for gathering together on the Lord's Day, the style of worship will follow. Consider these two examples. On the one hand, the purpose of liturgical worship is for Christians to offer corporate praise to the transcendent God of glory. With this controlling purpose in mind, the services are planned so that worshipers can humbly bow before their God in a spirit of reverence and awe. A formal and structured style, with appropriate attention to the fourfold pattern of adoration, confession, proclamation, and presentation, and with an offering of classical and traditional music, presents the clearest opportunity for that purpose to be met.

On the other hand, the praise and worship style looks and sounds and feels remarkably different than the liturgical style. The primary reason for the differences is that their purposes are separate and distinct. Although both styles are designed for Christians to worship God, the ways, means, and ends differ dramatically. The praise and worship style seeks to bring believers into intimate communion with the immanent Lord of love. This purpose all but requires the service to be broadly informal, outwardly celebrational, and physically expressive. Such a style, punctuated with emotionally charged special music and repetitive chorus singing, frees worshipers to be spontaneous and liberal in their praise.

In the Gospel of Matthew, Jesus referred to "the owner of a house who brings out of his storeroom new treasures as well as old" (13:52, NIV). Perhaps this brief parable has application to Baptist worship in the 1990s and into the twenty-first century. Could it be that the various styles of services in which Baptists across America are participating reflect "something old and something new" in worship? Is it possible that the creative Spirit of God is inspiring followers of Jesus Christ to offer both traditional and contemporary expressions of worship "in spirit and in truth?" Could the resurgence of interest in worship among Baptists signal a renewal of spirituality and a "hunger and thirst for righteousness?" Is it conceivable that the differences of style highlighted in this chapter are less a sign of fragmentation than of unity within diversity? What would happen if Baptists stopped judging their sisters and brothers who worship God differently than they do, instead being grateful for every expression of *weorthscipe* within the Baptist family?

May God, whose mystery and majesty demand the recognition of praise, remind us that "worship, in all its grades and kinds, is the response of the creature to the Eternal"[9] and that all of our attempts to declare the eternal worth of Father, Son, and Spirit are pleasing in the eyes of God.

Notes

[1]Ken Hemphill, "Traditional vs. non-traditional," *Facts and Trends* (July-August 1993) 5.

[2]Charles Willis, " 'Blended' worship combines traditional, contemporary" *Facts and Trends* (October 1993): 1, 6.

[3]Cf. Charles Willis' companion articles, " 'Seeker' worship style targets the unchurched" and "Praise, worship lead to God, minister of music says," *Facts and Trends* (October 1993) 6-7. Robert Webber, one of the foremost authorities on congregational worship in America, differentiates six "Contemporary Models of Worship": liturgical worship, traditional Protestant worship, praise and worship, creative worship, seeker service/believers worship, and convergence worship. See "From Jerusalem to Willow Creek," *Discipleship Journal* 70 (1992) 42-47.

[4] Charles Willis, "Traditional SBC worship: informal dignity," *The Baptist Standard* (1 September 1993), 13.

[5] Franklin M. Segler, *Christian Worship: Its Theology and Practice* (Nashville: Broadman, 1967) 4.

[6]Many Baptists also identify Rick Warren, Pastor of Saddleback Valley Community Church in Mission Viejo, California, with the seeker model. Warren, however, does not practice a true seeker service as Hybels does. Saddleback's style of worship is a creative blend of the seeker service and the praise and worship style. This reveals the difference between a "seeker-driven" service, where every aspect of the service focuses on communicating the Gospel to lost people, and a "seeker-sensitive" service, in which the goal is to lead Christians to worship God, but without the "cultural baggage" of traditional language and forms.

[7]Robert Webber, in *Signs of Wonder: The Phenomenon of Convergence in Modern Liturgical and Charismatic Churches* (Nashville: Star Song Publishing Group, 1992), describes what he calls "the phenomenon of convergence" of charismatic and liturgical worship in some evangelical churches. No doubt some Baptist churches are successfully blending the liturgical and praise and worship styles, but I do not know about them yet.

[8]This phrase comes from Timothy George, dean of Beeson Divinity School, Samford University.

[9]Evelyn Underhill, *Worship* (New York: Harper and Row, 1936) 3.

Walter Rauschenbusch on Prayer and Social Action

Philip LeMasters

Walter Rauschenbusch (1861–1918) was likely the Baptist with the most profound and widespread influence on American churches of all denominations in the twentieth century.[1] A pastor, professor of church history, author, lecturer, and social activist, Rauschenbusch was a leading figure in the social gospel movement of the late nineteenth and early twentieth centuries.[2] His various ministries focused on calling American Christians to order their lives, individually and collectively, according to the demands of God's kingdom. He understood God's reign to demand the progressive reign of love in human affairs and to grow on earth whenever social institutions became more democratic and just. Most Christian social action groups in America, such as Bread for the World and Evangelicals for Social Action, follow in Rauschenbusch's footsteps, consciously or not, in their efforts to bring American political life in line with the demands of God's kingdom.

Rauschenbusch was a complex, interesting figure. He was shaped by the evangelical piety of his German Baptist heritage, by the optimism about the course of human history shared by liberal Protestant theology and the American ethos of his day, and by his sobering encounter with the social problems associated with industrialization, urbanization, and immigration at the turn of the century in this country. Though neither a doctrinaire Marxist nor a member of a socialist party, Rauschenbusch considered himself a Christian socialist and believed that public, cooperative ownership of major industries was more in keeping with the democratic spirit of the kingdom than was capitalism.

Often a controversial figure, Rauschenbusch rose to fame in the early years of this century as an advocate of Christian social action. He died in the midst of World War I, however, a disillusioned man. The great war between "Christian" nations raised serious concerns about his optimism for the growth of God's kingdom on earth. Likewise, his German ancestry caused him to feel, perhaps for the first time, deeply alienated from the American culture about which he had been so optimistic.

The Spirituality of Justice

Rauschenbusch understood spirituality to be at the heart of the faithful Christian life. He described his *For God and the People: Prayers of the Social Awakening* as his favorite book.[3] Standing in the liberal theological tradition of Friedrich Schleiermacher, Rauschenbusch saw prayer, as well as theology, as arising from human experience.[4] He was convinced that the experience of involvement in social reform movements

> awaken[s] an almost painful compassion and longing, and these feelings are more essentially Christian than most of the fears and desires of religion in the past. Social Christianity is adding to the variety of religious experience, and is creating a new type of Christian man who bears a striking family likeness to Jesus of Galilee.[5]

In order for these "new religious emotions" to become effective in the life of the church and of society, Rauschenbusch believed that there must be new prayers, hymns, and liturgies that "enrich and purify . . . social thoughts and feelings."[6]

Such prayers would be like prayers before battle, strengthening Christians to combat the social forces of evil in the name of God. In these prayers, we open ourselves to the power of God:

> [I]f there is a center of the spiritual universe in whom our spirits join and have their being; and if the mysterious call of our souls somehow reaches and moves God, so that our longings come back from him in a wave of divine assent which assures their ultimate fulfillment—then it may mean more than any man knows to set Christendom praying on our social problems.[7]

Rauschenbusch found the model for such powerful prayer in the Lord's Prayer. He regretted that this prayer has been identified with "ecclesiastical ritual" and purely private devotion and insisted that the Lord's Prayer focuses on the great social theme of the kingdom of God. Rauschenbusch taught that the petitions for the hallowing of God's name, the coming of the kingdom, and the doing of God's will on earth

> express . . . [Jesus'] yearning faith in the possibility of a reign of God on earth in which his name shall be hallowed and his will be done. They look

> forward to the ultimate perfection of the common life of humanity on this earth, and pray for the divine revolution that is to bring that about. . . . We pray here that heaven may be duplicated on earth through the moral and spiritual transformation of humanity, both in its personal units and its corporate life.[8]

The petition for daily bread likewise had a social thrust for Rauschenbusch. As he noted,

> We sit at the common table in God's great house, and the supply of each depends on the security of all. The more society is socialized, the clearer does that fact become, and the more just and humane its organization becomes, the more will that recognition be at the bottom of all our institutions. As we stand thus in common, looking up to God for our bread, everyone of us ought to feel the sin and shame of it if he habitually takes more than his fair share and leaves others hungry that he may surfeit. It is inhuman, irreligious, and indecent.[9]

From his treatment of the above petitions, Rauschenbusch saw Jesus' model prayer as having direct, explicit social relevance. Not reflecting a purely individualistic or inward spirituality, the Lord's Prayer is first of all about how Jesus' followers, in obedience to God's reign, should treat their fellow human beings. Rauschenbusch believed that all Christian spirituality should likewise bear the fruit of socially effective love.

This concern for the social nature of the Christian life also manifests itself clearly in Rauschenbusch's comments on "Lead us not into temptation." He saw this primarily as a plea to be delivered from social situations that lead people to sin. Rauschenbusch commented that temptations

> are created largely by the social life about us. If the society in which we move is rank with sexual looseness or full of the suggestiveness and solicitations of alcoholism; if our business life is such that we have to lie and cheat and be cruel in order to live and prosper; if our political organization offers an ambitious man the alternative of betraying the public good or of being thwarted and crippled in all his efforts—then the temptations are created in which men go under, and society frustrates the prayer we utter to God. No church can interpret this petition intelligently that closes its mind to the debasing or invigorating influence of the spiritual environment furnished by society. No man can utter this petition without conscious or unconscious hypocrisy who is helping to create the temptations in which others are sure to fall.[10]

The Lord's Prayer is, then, for Rauschenbusch a plea for social righteousness before God. Those who utter its petitions are obliged to be crusaders for the earthly growth of the kingdom, the chief characteristics of which are love, mutuality, cooperation, and democracy. Rauschenbusch advocated, then, a social spirituality—or a spirituality of the kingdom—that pursues "the moral and religious transformation of mankind in all its social relations."[11] Spirituality, as all of the Christian life, falls for Rauschenbusch under the jurisdiction of the kingdom of God.

These social themes are central to the many prayers that Rauschenbusch wrote for different times and purposes. He prayed that those with authority over others would view subordinates "not as servants to our will, but as brothers equal in human dignity." Those who sleep soundly should pray for those who work at night, and "pray for thy pardon if our covetousness or luxury makes their nightly toil necessary." Grace before meals should include a petition that the strength drawn from food "may be put forward again for the common good . . . [returning] a full equivalent in useful work for the nourishment that we receive from the common store."[12] Such passages show that Rauschenbusch believed that the spirituality of the kingdom should pervade the whole of the Christian life and not be reserved for the occasional prayer for social justice. Instead, social spirituality should place our daily rest, work, and consumption of food in a new context of faithfulness to God. For Rauschenbusch, no part of the life of a Christian is beyond the reach of the kingdom, which is autonomous from the demands of true discipleship.

Since all Christians owe allegiance to the kingdom in the entirety of their lives, Rauschenbusch believed that all occupations should be pursued to the glory of God. Hence, he wrote prayers for inventors, musicians, physicians, and teachers. The kingdom of God either grows or atrophies in the workaday world where people invest their time, energies, and talents through their daily endeavors. Rauschenbusch wrote such prayers to help people see that how they lived each day had great religious significance. Far from reserving Christianity for a private or ethereal part of the self, Rauschenbusch emphasized its public, social, all-encompassing importance.

The Salvation of Society

With this integration of personal devotion and public faithfulness, Rauschenbusch stood clearly within the Reformed theological tradition of John Calvin. Though Rauschenbusch did not describe himself as a

Calvinist and disagreed with Calvin on many matters, his call for all of life to be subservient to the rule of the Sovereign bears a clear family resemblance to traditional Reformed thought. In such an approach, God requires faithfulness of both individuals and communities in both their "worldly" and "ecclesiastical" endeavors. Christianity has a direct public relevance for society as a whole, not simply for the Christian community. For both Calvin and Rauschenbusch, Christians are to participate in society's major institutions toward the end of a public righteousness that goes beyond the ministries of the institutional church.

Characteristic of such an orientation is optimism about what Christian activism may achieve in the world. In comparison with Martin Luther, for example, Calvin was more optimistic about the possibilities for good in even the worldly politics of nonbelievers. Not limited to the function of restraining sin, civil government could actually do a measure of good.[13] Rauschenbusch coupled that traditionally reserved Reformed optimism with the liberal cultural optimism of his day, which was far less restrained in its hopes for moral progress. In so doing, he spoke of social action in far more optimistic terms than Calvin ever did. Rauschenbusch viewed social improvement as "saving the social order" and building the kingdom of God. As public institutions became more democratic and just, God's kingdom grew on earth.[14] Though Rauschenbusch did not believe that human efforts would ever consummate God's reign, he did view such worldly improvements as part of salvation, as unambiguous signs of God's good rule.

Most Baptists are reluctant to speak of political progress as part of salvation. While issues of social justice are prominent throughout scripture, it departs from canonical teaching to claim that the relative improvement of a worldly political order is best described as the growth of salvation or of the kingdom of God. Very little basis is found in the New Testament and in traditional Protestant thought for speaking of salvation apart from explicit faith in Jesus Christ. Jesus proclaimed the kingdom of God in a fashion that showed great concern for just social relationships, but he never linked this kingdom with the political reform of the Roman Empire. His kingdom was something far more radical, requiring a thorough transformation of both the individual believer and of the community of disciples. Rauschenbusch's description of social reform as salvific, then, lacks solid biblical support.

At the same time, Rauschenbusch's approach embodies an extreme optimism about political affairs that—especially after the world wars, Vietnam, and Watergate—does not ring true with a sober reading of human history. Rauschenbusch believed that political reform was the growth of God's kingdom on earth. This meant that the spread of Western democracy, especially when linked with a mild form of socialism, was "saving the social order." Such a view is at odds with the inevitable ironies and failings of even the best attempts to promote political justice. For example, the French Revolution gave rise to the Reign of Terror and to Napoleon, while the defeat of Nazi Germany was linked with the rise of Stalin's Iron Curtain over Eastern Europe. America's resistance to communist tyranny in the Cold War often led to her support of military dictators, and the collapse of the European communist governments has made possible barbaric ethnic strife. American democracy often seems to be little more than a mechanism for various domestic factions to use in the pursuit of their own interests. Initiatives created with the best of intentions, such as welfare assistance, may very well in some cases perpetuate poverty and social dependence.

The point is that, given the failings and imperfections of even the best sorts of political action, Rasuchenbusch was overly optimistic about "saving the social order." Political reform is valuable and important for the sake of a relative justice in this world, but it does not reach the pure heights of salvation. It is hardly the road to anything so perfect as the kingdom of God.

A related problem in Rauschenbusch's thought is that he clearly identified a mildly socialist form of Western democracy as the way to bring salvation to society. In other words, he came very close to identifying a certain form of worldly politics with God's rule. Following his example, the uncritical affirmation, in the name of Christianity, of given political ideologies has become all too common among American believers. Many conservative Republicans and liberal Democrats alike identify certain economic and social policies with God's rule on earth. Jerry Falwell and Jesse Jackson disagree on many issues, but they are similar in their allegiance to given political agendas as the clear plan of God for America. Whether liberal or conservative, Republican or Democrat, such ideology verges on idolatry. It risks identifying God's holiness with inevitably corrupt and imperfect human agendas. This is but another way of making God in our own image, and hence of taming the radical demands of God's reign, which are far more exacting than the demands of any human kingdom.

Rauschenbusch's optimism about political action as salvific is clearly linked with this troubling aspect of his thought. If worldly politics is God's conduit for the salvation of a nation, then a given ideology must be promulgated and supported uncritically as God's will. But, when politics have a humbler and more ambiguous role in the workings of history, there is far less room for identifying any political orthodoxy with God's will. Such a chastened view of the relationship between worldly politics and the Gospel is more in keeping with the traditional Baptist emphasis on the separation of church and state, as well as with Jesus' statement on what is due God and what is due Caesar.

A related problem with Rauschenbusch's view of politics as part of salvation is that it comes very close to "works' righteousness," the Reformation term for the view that good works, apart from faith, earn salvation. Rauschenbusch risks falling into this error by suggesting that voting and reforming are actions that save the social order. In other words, salvation comes to look like a human accomplishment. Rauschenbusch could defend himself by saying that it was God who guided the course of history, enabling people to perform actions necessary for the growth of the kingdom. Nonetheless, humans gain too much credit to say that we may save society through political activism. For example, Baptist ears should be offended to hear, "I saved that man by sharing with him the good news of Jesus Christ." God, not human beings, will save us; we should never speak of salvation, whether of an individual or a society, in a way that even gives the impression that human beings themselves bring about redemption. Despite the human role in evangelism, God's role is infinitely more important. All human action pales in comparison with the salvific work of the Almighty; to blur this vital distinction is idolatrous.

To forget this point in political contexts, which are usually characterized by selfishness and the lust for power, is particularly dangerous. We may easily imagine a politician or party proclaiming "We will bring salvation, even perfect peace and justice, to America. We are God's agents in saving the nation." That sort of rhetoric lends itself to abuses of authority, for political saviors often believe that they alone may be trusted with unchecked power. We do well to remember the messianic pretensions of Soviet communism and the terrible abuses associated with it. When a party claims to be able to bring about salvation or the perfection of history, as the Soviets did, it may justify any abuse for the sake of that highest good. Such a party also has to put a good face on everything in order to show that, appearances aside, it is indeed bringing about salvation. This sort of political messianism invites hypocrisy among the rulers and cynicism among the people.

These considerations show that Rauschenbusch's idea of saving the social order leads in a number of troubling directions. Rauschenbusch gave too high a status to political action, was uncritical in his support for a certain politial ideology, and was overly optimistic about what politics could achieve in a sinful world. Nonetheless, there are important strengths in Rauschenbusch's approach to spirituality, and we may learn much even from his errors.

The Politics of Prayer

Rauschenbusch was absolutely correct to show that the Christian life, including prayer, is not primarily an insular, individualistic enterprise. Drawing from the philosophical movement of the Enlightenment and certain strands of evangelicalism, many American Christians—in both Rauschenbusch's day and ours—have emphasized the singular individual to the extent that they have forgotten the social nature of the faith. Rauschenbusch rightly challenged the view that Jesus set about simply to save individual souls for the hereafter.[15]

The New Testament clearly shows Jesus' concern that his followers form a faithful community in which members help one another pursue fidelity to the kingdom. Indeed, the very idea of a kingdom is social and political. Immediately after Jesus proclaimed the kingdom in Luke's gospel (Luke 4:31ff.), he went about his ministry in a socially symbolic way, focusing on marginalized people such as women, lepers, and those possessed by demons. Just as Moses had given the people of Israel commandments that concerned both personal piety and social justice, Jesus called Israel to a more stringent standard that concerned both how people relate to God and to one another (Matt 5-7). An important theme in Paul's writings is the communal nature of the Christian life, such that mutual edification is more important than individual glory or freedom (1 Cor 12).

From within such a social Christianity believers are to pray. We are to pray not simply for ourselves as individuals, but for God's kingdom to come and God's will to be done on earth—which would have obvious social consequences. When we pray for forgiveness of our sins, we are reminded that we must forgive those who have wronged us. Jesus also taught that his followers are to pray for those who persecute them, even as he asked forgiveness for those who crucified him. Surely, praying for our fellow Christians is part of bearing one another's burdens and of serving one another. We may conclude, then, that a prayer life that focuses exclusively on the individual who is praying falls far short of biblical teaching. Rauschenbusch rightly saw that the true Christian prayer must not focus entirely on the self.

Another important insight of Rauschenbusch on prayer was his insistence that prayer not be reserved exclusively for "private" or "inward" matters. Since God's kingdom includes every aspect of life, it would be a mistake to limit prayer simply to personal affairs. This would underwrite the assumption that social matters or public affairs would be beyond the sovereignty of God, outside the realm of God's concern. Following biblical teaching and Reformed thinking, Rauschenbusch refused to limit prayer to the private realm. He urged believers to pray for social justice, for workers, for the poor, and for themselves as they used money and political power. In other words, prayer for social problems was for Rauschenbusch a sign that all of life was accountable to God. Nothing fell outside of the rule of the Sovereign.

In encouraging such holistic prayer, Rauschenbusch stood on solid biblical grounding. The Old Testament, with its numerous laws about all aspects of social life, shows God's concern for the many varieties of human endeavor. Both the Law and the Prophets contain explicit treatments of God's concern for the poor, for fair business dealings, and for sexual morality. For the people of Israel, all of life belonged to God and was to be lived according to his direction. Likewise, Jesus stated that we must serve one master, and not pretend that certain aspects of life fall outside of God's domain. In this spirit, Jesus addressed questions of tax collection, the taking of oaths, ethnic divisions, divorce law, and giving to the poor. He also gave great importance to such tangible actions as feeding the hungry, visiting the sick and imprisoned, and clothing the naked (Matt 25:31-46).

If these "worldly" matters were of such concern to our Lord, and to the earlier faith of Israel, they are certainly fit subjects for prayer. Rauschenbusch has done us a great service by insisting that our spirituality attend to social matters and not be reserved purely for the affairs of private life.

Rauschenbusch never meant, however, for this social Christianity to exclude prayer for private matters. Neither did he intend for questions of personal salvation and faithfulness to collapse without remainder into social questions. Unfortunately, some who have responded to Rauschenbusch's plea for social ministry have reduced Christianity to social and political activism. It is not uncommon to encounter activists, usually from "mainline" denominations, for whom being a faithful Christian means essentially volunteering in a homeless shelter, donating money to Bread for the World, writing letters for Amnesty International, and voting

Democratic. I have even heard of one Baptist pastor who recommends social action as the remedy to every spiritual problem suffered by his parishoners.

Such an orientation is very close to "works' righteousness," for it makes human accomplishment the defining aspect of Christianity. This way of thinking also ignores the many pleas in the scripture for personal faithfulness that simply may not be reduced to social reform. Indeed, an overemphasis on social justice is as problematic as an overemphasis on personal piety. They both omit a vital dimension of the Christian faith, namely, God's rule over all of human life—the personal and the public.

Rauschenbusch, though he did not intend to exclude the personal dimensions of faith, sometimes wrote in a fashion that gave that impression. Recall his reading of "Lead us not into temptation." He essentially made an individual's response to temptation a function of the social environment in which he or she lived. One can easily see how that approach may collapse personal faithfulness into social activism. For example, one might say that poor people are tempted by their poverty into crime, and that the only way for them to resist that temptation is to raise them out of poverty. A problem with this line of thought is that it has little place for individual responsibility and response to the demands of the Gospel. Indeed, it defines the human being in purely economic and social terms. Clearly, Jesus did not do that. He spoke to people of different social circumstances—prostitutes, poor people, Roman officials, Jewish leaders—in a fashion that called them all to faithfulness. He did not first try to change their economic environment. While his ministry of the kingdom had obvious social implications, it may not be reduced simply to an exercise in social work. Personal faith and commitment, regardless of social circumstances, are essential to the Christian faith.

The Example of Jesus

The temptation to see Jesus primarily as "The Great Social Worker" is closely tied to a progressive, moralistic view of the kingdom of God that was dominant in the liberal Protestant theology of the nineteenth century. Rauschenbusch believed that God's reign would grow on earth through the expansion of love, cooperation, and democracy, but knew that such improvement would never amount to God's perfect rule on earth. In his estimation, Jesus' preaching of the kingdom focused on how to make the world a better place in which to live through the application of love. Jesus was our example, the human being with the greatest consciousness of God's designs for a more loving and just world. Hence, Christians should focus their lives on following Jesus' example of kingdom ministry, with a strong emphasis on social action.[16]

Rauschenbusch's approach is informed by a troubling view of God's kingdom and of Jesus. This is the case because a rough consensus has developed among biblical scholars and theologians in this century on the eschatological nature of God's kingdom that affirms that God's reign was initiated in Jesus' earthly ministry, but that it will not be fully consummated until the Parousia.[17] Hence, Jesus was not primarily concerned with social improvement in the name of building the kingdom, but with cosmic transformation that only God could consummate. Ever since Pentecost, the Spirit has enabled the church to live as a foretaste of God's kingdom, and that surely includes involvement in social ministry. The first task of the church, however, is not to join with other social institutions in making the world a better place, but rather to be a witness to the inbreaking of the coming kingdom of God, calling people to radical repentance and discipleship.

In other words, when the kingdom is understood as eschatological and transcendent over any human undertaking or worldly social order, Jesus becomes far more than a moral teacher and example. His role as risen Lord takes on crucial importance. His life, death, and resurrection become intimately intertwined with the redemption of all reality. That redemption means the subordination of all things to the ultimate purposes of God in the final consummation of history (1 Cor 15:20ff.).

This way of envisioning Jesus and the kingdom calls even the best of human culture and morality into question in a way that Rauschenbusch's eschatology and Christology do not. He has a domesticated approach in which the kingdom has so much continuity with western culture that the transcendence and otherness of God's reign are obscured. In Rauschenbusch's view, the kingdom calls us to be pious democratic socialists. Surely, the demands of God's reign are far more exacting than that. Likewise, Rauschenbusch's view of Jesus embodies the best of western culture, a sincere moral teacher and fine example of how to live. Certainly scripture goes much further and deeper in its claims about the Incarnate Word (John.1:1-18; Acts 2:32-36). Rauschenbusch's project makes Jesus and the kingdom in the image of nineteenth-century western culture, rather than boldly proclaiming that everything about humankind stands under the judgement of the one who is Alpha and Omega.

The Contribution of Social Spirituality

We have seen points of both strength and weakness in Rauschenbusch's work. Refusing to allow the relevance of Christianity to be reserved exclusively for inward and individualistic affairs, Rauschenbusch rightly emphasized public and social dimensions of Christian spirituality. Rauschenbusch forcefully made the often forgotten point that God's kingdom should reign over every dimension of our lives, including the political and economic. Nonetheless, we have seen that there are many points of weakness in his approach that will be troubling to most Baptists. Rather than therefore disregarding Rauschenbusch's work, we would do well to interpret his major contributions in ways that are consistent with biblical teaching. In other words, the challenge is to use Rauschenbusch's insights critically, reshaping them to better reflect biblical truths.

For example, Christians who distinguish clearly between salvation and social reform may be actively involved in social ministry. Though political action does not "save the social order," it has an important place in God's providential governance of the world. Likewise, believers who emphasize Jesus' identity as risen Lord should pay careful attention to Jesus' example of ministering to the impoverished. The resurrection vindicated his ministry of the kingdom, which was conspicuous for its attention to the marginalized. At the same time, a renewed focus on the eschatological nature of the kingdom may prod Christians to call into question all social orders and political ideologies, for none of them may claim to be the fulfillment of history. Many of Rauschenbusch's themes may be reinterpreted easily in ways more consistent with biblical teaching.

We may also glean some insights for pastoral ministry from our discussion of Rauschenbusch. For example, a pastor might proclaim that vital moral issues are at stake in a given political race or social controversy, without at the same time identifying one of the candidates or positions as God's unambiguous answer. Perhaps the pastor's task should be to guide the people in discerning the moral issues at stake in the controversy and then urge the people to pray for God's guidance in determining how they will respond. Likewise, a minister may encourage social ministry as a way of showing others something of the love of Jesus, while insisting that personal salvation is not the result of good works in society. Indeed, there is no contradiction between calling for personal repentance and faithfulness, while at the same time promoting efforts to feed the hungry and care for the sick.

Every theologian or preacher is, to a larger extent, a product of his or her time and culture. Rauschenbusch was clearly a thinker of his day with his optimism about society and his nineteenth-century theological liberalism. Our faith, however, is not merely a function of time and place. It is focused upon God's self-revelation in Jesus Christ, which calls into question all cultures and ways of thinking. Let our reading of Rauschenbusch, then, be shaped by that self-revelation as witnessed to in scripture and interpeted in the church. We will then be able to pursue a social spirituality in a way that is consonant with the demands of God's kingdom. Nothing less is required by the petitions: "Thy kingdom come. Thy will be done on earth as it is in heaven."

Notes

[1]Rauschenbusch's most important writings include: *Christianity and the Social Crisis* (Louisville, KY: Westminster/John Knox Press, 1992—originally published in 1907); *Christianizing the Social Order* (New York: Macmillan, 1912); *The Righteousness of the Kingdom*, Max L. Stackhouse, ed., (Nashville: Abingdon Press, 1968); and *A Theology for the Social Gospel* (Nashville: Abingdon, 1978—first published in 1917).

[2]An excellent biography of Rauschenbusch is Paul M. Minus, *Walter Rauschenbusch: American Reformer* (New York: Macmillan Publishing Company, 1988). Harlan Beckley, *Passion for Justice: Retrieving the Legacies of Walter Rauschenbusch, John A. Ryan, and Reinhold Niebuhr* (Louisville KY: Westminster/John Knox Press, 1992) provides a fine analysis of Rauschenbusch's thought. Stackhouse's introduction to *The Righteousness of the Kingdom*, "The Continuing Importance of Walter Rauschenbusch," is a helpful overview. For more critical readings of Rauschenbusch, see Stanley Hauerwas, "The Reality of the Kingdom: An Ecclesial Space for Peace," *Against the Nations* (Minneapolis MN: Winston Press, 1985), 104-21; and Janet Forsyth Fishburn, *The Fatherhood of God and the Victorian Family* (Philadelphia: Fortress Press, 1981).

[3]Walter Rauschenbusch, *For God and the People: Prayers of the Social Awakening* (Boston: Pilgrim Press, 1910). It is currently available as chapter seven of Winthrop S. Hudson, ed., *Walter Rauschenbusch: Selected Writings* (New York: Paulist Press, 1984).

[4]Schleiermacher's chief dogmatic work is available in English as *The Christian Faith* (Edinburgh: T. & T. Clark, 1986). See Richard R. Niebuhr's "Friedrich Schleiermacher," *A Handbook of Christian Theologians*, Martin Marty and Dean Peerman, eds. (Nashville: Abingdon Press, 1984) 17-35.

[5]Hudson, 209.

[6]Ibid., 209.

[7]Ibid., 210.

[8]Ibid. 212-13.

[9]Ibid. 213.

[10]Ibid, 214.

[11]Ibid., 215.

[12]Ibid., 215-22.

[13]To compare Calvin and Luther on this point, see Calvin, *Institutes of the Christian Religion* (Grand Rapids MI: Wm. B. Eerdmans Publishing Co., 1983) IV/XX; and Luther, "On Secular Authority," *Martin Luther: Selections From His Writings* (Garden City NJ: Anchor Books, 1961).

[14]See, for example, Rauschenbusch, "The Kingdom of God," in *A Theology for the Social Gospel.*

[15]Gerhard Lohfink, *Jesus and Community* (New York: Paulist Press, 1984) argues persuasively on biblical grounds against such individualism.

[16]This is also essentially the view put forward by Charles Sheldon in *In His Steps* (Springdale PA: Whitaker House, 1979), a remarkably popular novel, first published in 1897, which prompts readers to ask "What would Jesus do?" in all the circumstances that they face in life.

[17]An excellent overview of biblical and theological scholarship on the kingdom of God is Wendell Willis, ed., *The Kingdom of God in 20th-Century Interpretation* (Peabody MA: Hendrickson Publishers, 1987).

Spiritual Transcendence in the Black Experience in America

Samuel D. Proctor

The survival and viability of the African-Americans in the United States is the result of their unprecedented adaptation to an arduous existence in two worlds. W. E. B. DuBois described this double personna in *The Souls of Black Folk.*[1] When Alexis de Toqueville, the French nobleman who studied American institutions in the 1830s visited the South, he was particularly intrigued by the enslavement of so many blacks. He warned that the next crisis facing America would be the movement of these persons toward freedom and upward mobility.[2]

No doubt de Toqueville would be curious about the psychological and spiritual formula that enabled us to endure the slow passing of 244 years of slavery, and another century of apartheid. He would wonder how at the same time we appropriated the political values and institutions of America to win thirty-nine Supreme Court decisions from 1935 and 1955, and to outlast the *Dred Scott* and *Plessy* v. *Ferguson* decisions that made us faceless and nameless objects virtually with no rights.

An Amphibian Existence

The sustenance that the black people found lay in a capacity to accept and acknowledge all of the historical facts and at the same time achieve a kind of spiritual transcendence. There was no escaping the social reality, but there was the possibility of living each day like an amphibian, in two worlds. One was the world of culture and history, the other a world of release and deliverance that was only a faith hypothesis—the "substance of things hoped for and the evidence of things not seen" (Heb 11:1). The second world was not quite a present potential, but it was an image of things as they might be and a reliance on God to redeem the times at God's own moment.

Such is the testimony of our sojourn, learning how to cope in two worlds. During the Great Depression in Norfolk, Virginia, my father went to work in the Navy Yard every day. Before leaving, he ate a hearty three-course breakfast, drank a mug of coffee, gave my mother a squeeze, and boarded a used 1927 La Salle limousine in which he joined seven other riders to joke, sing, and pray their way to the Elizabeth River. All of this he did with a twelve hour growth of a salt and pepper beard covering his face. As soon as he came home in the afternoon at five o'clock he would hug Mamma and go straight to the bathroom and shave. This was his ritual, signifying that the role he played all day was one assigned to him and one that denied his intelligence, his potential, and his rights. He had to pretend to be contented all day long. He unconsciously resented his daytime identity. After he shaved, his other life began. He lived like an amphibian, in the water breathing with gills and on land breathing with lungs.

Every Wednesday night the rehearsal of the Philharmonic Glee Club was the priority. This was a singing group of about forty black males: barbers, chauffeurs, dentists, grocers, teachers, longshoremen, postal workers, coal trimmers, Pullman porters, and hotel bellhops. They were carefully selected from church choirs, and they were all well known to each other. The group was a tight brotherhood, and they sang like the sound of a great organ.

Each year the Philharmonic Glee Club presented *one* concert, a long *evening* of music from many traditions: European composers, variations on Isaac Watts' hymns, black spirituals, and rhythmic gospel and work songs. Families of the group attended but were seated in the rear. The audience was mostly white, the educated and business class. This was a moment when caste was suspended and the finest human qualities were on display. These suspensions were a part of the paradox of Christian people treating others as a sub-class without distinctions or gradations, based solely on color. Other more decent understandings that were sublimal cried out for expression. This concert was such an annual ventilation.

At the end of each concert, these golden-throated, barrel-chested, serious black men sang:

> Dawn is breaking,
> And a new day is born.
> The world is singing
> The song of the dawn.

Yesterday, the skies were gray,
But look, this morning
They are blue.
The smiling sun tells everyone,
Come! Let's start life anew.
Let's all sing *Hallelujah.* (. . . and the rafters trembled!)
For a new day is born. (The harmony shut everyone's eyes tight.)
The world is singing,
The song of the dawn.

There was no dawn and no blue skies, however—only racism, poverty, rejection, exclusion, and pain. The blacks drew heavily on the exile experience of the Hebrews in Babylon where Ezekiel saw the wheel. They often sang about the big wheel that moved by faith and the little wheel that moved by the grace of God (Ezek 1:16-21). They were moved by a valley of dry bones that came to life, reconnected, and marched like an army (Ezek 37:1-14). They were strengthened by Daniel's courage and God's protection of him (Dan 6:1-28), and they were encouraged by the three Hebrew boys who survived in the fiery furnace (Dan 3:1-30).

While these men were awaiting their own deliverance, they rejoiced in the deliverance of the Israelites in Babylon (Ezra 1:1-4) and sang songs of Zion in a strange land (Ps 137:1-4). These amphibians had left the swamps for a moment and had climbed on a rock for a breather with their lungs, like a frog or a salamander, to visit their other world. They did it with grace, with dignity, and with the kind of moral authenticity that resounds in the Sermon on the Mount (Matt 5:1-7:29).

All of this was without precedent. No other people anywhere ever attempted to last through 244 years of slavery and a hundred more of official subjugation at the hands of Christian people (adopting the language, religion, customs, and habits of their oppressors) and then stayed on the same pieces of real estate with their former masters and made a bid for inclusion and eventually full participation. The amphibians lived in two worlds.

The life of an amphibian in the long run is tenuous. Too much struggle and adaptation has to be undertaken for an amphibian merely to survive. It is, indeed, a transitional state. Ultimately, the efficiency of the amphibian will require making its home either in water *or* on land. Of course, this is where the analogy breaks down and becomes useless. African-Americans need not to be limited to a choice between only two options: either to *encapsulate ourselves* in a totally other culture by withdrawing from the mainstream of the society or to *capitulate* to the culture as it is by subscribing to its idolatry, racism, materialism, and narcissism.

A third choice is open to us because we are not animals, *living by instinct;* we are humans with imagination and awareness. We are capable of living in the subjunctive mood (not simply in the indicative and imperative moods), and we are capable of embracing goals, objectives, and new visions of our world that alter our environment. So, as we undergo the metamorphosis, we are giving up the tentative, transitional mode of existence that was imposed by slavery and its legacy. We are opting for a permanent environment that will allow us both to hold on to all that is vital, salient, and germane from our past and to participate in a modified, humanized, changed, compassionate, redefined, and redirected America. This new society reflects the ideas written in her founding charters and a higher commitment to her Jewish and Christian spiritual heritage.

The faith of blacks allowed them to envision a new America being formed one day, a new community. They leaned heavily on Paul's notion of persons becoming new creations (2 Cor 5:17), not conforming to this world (Rom 12:1-2), and yielding to the fruits of the Spirit (Gal 5:22-26). They believed in the freedom that Christ provided and trusted that such freedom would bring about a new community. African-Americans never thought of going elsewhere; they declined all invitations to leave for Africa or the Caribbean. They felt that God was able to take the awful precedent of historical slavery and the pervasive racism to bring beauty out of those ashes. They opted to remain here in America and participate in the creation of the new community.

A Sense of Belonging

In order for blacks to assert their position in American society, affirm their definition of their identity here, and work for a new community with courage and conviction, they must recognize that this is their country, that they belong here, and that the 244 years of slavery earned them the same proprietorship that anyone else had. The black contributions to the creation of the nation's enormous capital, the laying of its railroad, the tilling of its fields, the firing of its furnaces, the raising of its babies, the fighting of its wars, the nursing of its sick, and the performance of its most tedious and unpleasant tasks are unquestioned. We belong here in America.

We are blood-bound to the black Hispanics of the Caribbean; the black Catholics of South America; the Cape Verdean blacks of New Bedford and Providence; the black Puerto Ricans; the Africans scattered about the Pacific Islands and Australia; the blacks in Jericho and throughout Israel, Jordan, Kuwait, and Saudi Arabia; and the blacks of Egypt, Tunisia, Ethiopia, and all of Africa. Even though we are bound by blood and anthropology to *all* descendants of Africa, today such an identity is secondary to the identity that we have acquired as a consequence of our survival of the longest and most dehumanizing slave experience known to humankind and our coping with an amphibious existence in America for another hundred years. We may be comforted, allured, and pacified to fantasize that we are only temporary sojourners and pilgrims in this land, but our future is here—not in Nassau, Tunis, Accra, or Durban. No black or African state anywhere can absorb thirty million black Americans with our habits and appetites. Our future is here in America.

On this proposition blacks proceeded to adapt the white Anglo-Saxon culture and religion to their own needs. They continue to create their own worship style and religious idiom. They faced squarely all of the signs of rejection and applied their sense of spiritual transcendence. Black people determined to make America their home. The corollary to this affirmation is that we must take responsibility for what kind of nation this should become. We are participants, not merely spectators. We have a stake in America's success, in the efficiency of its economy, in the soundness and validity of its values, in the quality of life for all of its people, in the integrity of its government, and in its image before the world. We are not part-time Americans. We care about crime and the safety of our cities. We care about schools succeeding, about budgets getting balanced, and about children being safe from danger. We have no other home. (I for one have never even thought of surrendering my citizenship.)

It has been no small task for black Americans to assume a posture of participation and sponsorship of a new community, while fighting for simple rights and privileges, suing the government for rights that were assured in the Constitution, and struggling to find a place in the benefit system. More remarkable is that they moved in large measure without violence or vindictiveness to achieve their goals. In spite of all of this, they found themselves poised to help build a new community here.

Blacks must help America correct its faults—its accommodation of the greedy super-rich; its neglect of the chronically poor; its indifference toward the ill and indigent; its callous *disregard* of the rehabilitation of the prison population; its casual acceptance of failing public schools; its comfortable resignation to white collar, corporate crime; its sluggish response to Third World human distress, hunger, thirst, and disease; its acceptance of war and bloodshed as a *standard means* of settling international conflict; and its shameful reputation as the major gun merchant in the world.

The very thought of this should be enough to inspire the African-Americans to strive even harder to remove the stereotype, to fight for justice, to fulfill the audacious intentions of our mothers and fathers, to make this country our home, to stand tall—with heads erect, shoulders back, and hearts bursting with pride. Blacks have never thought of doing this alone, however. Their quest has never been without God. Their hope has always been that God's hand is on the throttle of history and that somehow in God's own time their change will come.

An Assumption of Responsibility

Come further and see that once we affirm that we are here to stay, the next step is to stand tall in the full dignity of a child of God, to submit our talents and potentials to God for the best and most responsible use. This means cultivating skills and abilities to offer society, eschewing the shame of parasitic dependence, being faithful stewards, counting the cost, and acquiring the discipline to become solid contributors. The deepest frustration that we experience is to see so much that needs to be done and then to be sidelined, overlooked, neutralized, and looked upon as "others."

The practice of assigning blacks to "black matters" only or to token positions is still prevalent. America has only begun to discover the full capacity of her black population. We have been appointed human relations specialists, community liaison coordinators, multicultural affairs advisors, counselors for high risk students, and urban affairs directors. The president of Howard University, for example, was offered the ambassadorship to the tiniest country in Africa, as though he could not handle any heavier traffic.

In 1947 Branch Rickey hired Jackie Robinson to play baseball for the Brooklyn Dodgers. That year I was at Graves Field in Boston and listened to the ugliest racial insults yelled at him every time he came to bat. He had a tremendous amount of "sheer guts," hearing that all over America, but what a success he initiated. Black participation in professional sports is a paradigm of what could and should happen nationwide.

Of course, we must take responsibility to prepare ourselves for the full weight of any opportunities that may come. We must further commit ourselves to create opportunities where none existed for us before. We were encouraged to do this kind of thinking before the language of separatism began to anesthetize the ambition of too many African-American youth. We thought big. Black Americans must move beyond the rhetoric and the racially chauvinistic debates in order to focus upon every aspect of our common life without arbitrary limits. The movement has only begun.

This responsibility calls for renewed emphasis on the basics that any people will have to cultivate in order not to remain marginal forever, which means that we will bring to the tasks the same quality of preparations that any others may bring. Blacks must reject the idea of claiming exemption because of our deprivation in slavery. Because of spiritual transcendence, blacks want to overcome the deficits imposed without vindictiveness. At the same time we want to see a climate that is made adaptable to our struggle for full participation. Indeed, everyone knows that blacks have suffered impediments that were not imposed on others and that we have not been treated equally. When we ask for full participation and for full rewards, however, we ask for a chance to prove that we are ready in spite of the unfair deficits imposed.

The logic of our protests must be that *we just may win our case.* When Martin Luther King, Jr., gave his immortal speech on a dream, he had in mind a dream that could become reality.[3] What if we should succeed? What if success in some areas should come sooner than in others? We simply cannot make a career out of being black. The content of our being as persons must be something plus black, something plus African-American. That something will call for the same discipline and skill refinement that anyone else would have to possess.

Therefore, the primary schools that serve our children cannot capitulate to pupils and parents who plan to wiggle in the swamps forever, resigned to a permanent pause as a long-term amphibian. We cannot surrender our secondary schools to those who fear the future and are settling for a life of poverty, crime, ignorance, dependency, and inhumanity. Parenting must take on a new seriousness. Children are *not* ready to be parents. Whatever came apart in family life must be put back together. There is no substitute for a healthful, spiritual incubator for the human infant, whatever ethnic label. If that incubator is missing, a surrogate must be invented.

I have long advocated that the present crisis has revealed to us that the poverty and poor schooling of the past hundred years has caused far more serious outcomes than we could imagine. The folks who perpetrated these misdeeds are dead, but the consequences are alive and well. We have now 1,500,000 children that are unparented and/or unsocialized who are destined to become dependent, dysfunctional, and tax burdens for a lifetime. Single parents (women especially) have done their best but have found themselves overwhelmed by poverty and neighborhoods infested with drugs and crime. Their best efforts have left them exhausted and unable to cope. These young people are the victims. We cannot blame them. What we can do is to intervene by spending $18,000 a year on them now, and later have them *pay taxes* for a lifetime rather than allow them to remain social liabilities and have to spend $40,000 a year on them for incarceration, recidivism, and other health and welfare costs for a lifetime.

My idea is a National Youth Academy, for such unparented children ages twelve through eighteen. It would embrace a program of *one third academics* with specially trained teachers and some of their parents with new training and a specially designed curricula; *one third human development*, music, swimming, mountain climbing, painting, animal breeding, flori-culture, gymnastics, and team sports; and *one third work* for pocket money and for a graduation bonus at age eighteen when they depart to work for Prudential, Gulf Oil, Merk & Co., the Air Force, or Macy's or to enter Emory, Stanford, Tuskegee, Spelman, Minnesota, Virginia Polytechnical Institute, or Rutgers or to begin their own businesses and careers in the arts, sports, and entertainment.

The National Youth Academy would be a worthy, justifiable intervention to redress a social need such as the G. I. Bill, the Marshall Plan for Europe, aid and defense for Israel, the land grant college movement of the nineteenth century, or the multi-billion dollar bailout for the savings and loan association. We are, in fact, paying for it *now*, in other fruitless ways, without the benefits. We must be willing to take the loftiest and most sublime ideas about the kingdom of God and subject them to practical application. This idea of a National Youth Academy would represent a sound effort to respect the worth of all of God's children and to apply our resources in a responsible way that gives newness and dignity to every life.

A Struggle for Justice

Perhaps the heaviest emphasis will have to be made on the necessity of continuing the fight for fairness and justice. The struggle is not over. Spiritual transcendence must not be an anesthetic or a placebo for a chronic pathology. This transcendence always keeps the real in focus even though the ideal remains a faith proposition.

The movement to erase unjust and unfair social arrangements is in accord with Jesus' resistance to patterns and practices of his day that contradicted the mandates of the kingdom. Each generation has to be educated anew on the long history of the unfair treatment of our parents and grandparents. The consequences of such treatment are some of those most indelible, negative stereotypes that have bred an endemic form of prejudice. Furthermore, a chronic poverty has resulted from the underemployment of so many of our undereducated forebears. A self-rejection has drained the few positive images that have occurred with a tried and wearied irregularity. The stubborn and effective causes of this accumulation of bad data, the marginality of an affluent society, and the social failure in a culture of success, are rooted in three centuries of chattel slavery and another hundred years of official, legal, approved, and accepted apartheid.

We have a generation in our schools and colleges today that was not born when Martin Luther King Jr., was assassinated. These students did not hear the news reports on Selma and Birmingham or the sonorous pleas of John F. Kennedy and the drawling appeals of Lyndon B. Johnson. They were not stunned by the lynch murders of young civil rights marchers like Schwerner, Chaney, and Goodman or the cold-blooded killing of a saint like Medgar Evers or the deaths of four children in a Birmingham church on a Sunday morning. They see only the packaged, slick, video televised recaps of these tragic events, but the backdrop—the social and political landscape against which these morally degenerate events occurred—are missing. Students today consequently dismiss them casually as items in history, like John Brown's raid or the Battle of Bull Run, with little or no relevance for today's decisions. They have no knowledge of the cynical ease with which blacks were denied employment outside of fixed menial categories.

My father, with an education superior to all of his superiors, drove a truck for forty-two years in the United States Navy Yard at Portsmouth, Virginia. He had been educated by Presbyterian missionaries in a small

Reconstruction school called Norfolk Mission College. He used English flawlessly, written and spoken. He played the violin, the clarinet, and the piano. He understood algebra and geometry better than all of his children, and he knew the familiar parts of the Bible by memory. He filled out tax forms and wrote obituaries for his white superiors without reluctance or resentment. He was confined to that truck, though.

All blacks of thirty-five years of age or older can recite long narratives of discrimination in the workplace, and they can point to vestiges of it today in the corporate world, in sports, foundations, hospitals, education, and industry. Of all places, the military looks better than all civilian institutions. Amazingly, there is still debate on the need for affirmative action. Persons in the majority community are the ones who have benefitted most from affirmative action because of the negative action taken against thirty million blacks to keep them out of competition by deliberate design. This meant affirmative action for those who benefitted.

The present generation hears much about merit. It has little awareness or acknowledgement of how deliberately blacks were denied a chance even to learn to read the Bible. Judge Leon Higgenbotham wrote a strong testimony to this fact in his book entitled, *In the Matter of Color.*[4] He showed how the colonies erected legal barriers of every conceivable nature to prohibit the education of blacks. Some may regard this as so distant and remote as to have no significance, but it is hard for me to forget because my grandmother was a slave. Had she been uneducated, she would have passed on a legacy of ignorance to her seven children and, hence, to her scores of grandchildren and greatgrandchildren. But—God be praised—her former owners sent her to Hampton Institute, under General Samuel C. Armstrong, where she was a schoolmate of Booker T. Washington and graduated in 1882. Consequently, seventy two of her offspring (at last count) have been college-trained with many holding professional and graduate degrees. This example simply illustrates to those who believe in *merit* how unfairly blacks were denied a chance to gain *merit* in America.

Blacks evolve out of their amphibious status and move securely to *terra firma* with celebration of the best of their heritage. They wear their racial identity with pride and dignity. They furthermore understand that the necessary concomitants will include the parallel struggles of erasing the prejudice that stains us and of securing the justice and equality for which our mothers and fathers lived and died. This will come to pass. After all, a black woman has been the head of Social Security. The Ford Foundation (the largest philanthropy in the world) and the Teachers

Insurance and Annuity Association (the largest pension plan in the world) have been headed by a black. A black quarterback has won the Super Bowl, and a black tennis player has won the Wimbledon. A black preacher is the pastor of the Riverside Church in New York City, the monument to Protestantism in America. The chairman of the Joint Chiefs of Staff has been a black general, and both the major of New York City and the governor of Jefferson's Virginia have been black. Six members of the presidential cabinet and forty members of the Congress are black. It will come to pass.

No matter what progress blacks make on the human scale, their struggle has been sustained because it was propelled and sustained by a more moral and spiritual criterion for success. The paradigm for this transcendence has been the person and the teachings of Jesus Christ, and the content of that transcendence has been the mind of Christ. Success may be manifested in temporal, material ways, but blacks have always known that they should seek first the kingdom and everything else is incidental to that quest (Matt 6:33).

Notes

[1]W. E. B. DuBois, *The Souls of Black Folk* (New York: Fawcett, 1961).

[2]Alexis de Toqueville, *Democracy in America,* 2 vols (New York: Random, 1954).

[3]Speech delivered by Martin Luther King, Jr., on 28 August 1963, at the Lincoln Memorial in Washington, D.C.

[4]Leon Higgenbotham, *In the Matter of Color* (New York: Oxford University Press, 1978).

"Holy Insecurity": The Practice of Piety and the Politics of the Spirit[1]

Barry Harvey

"To confess God as Spirit is to acknowledge that the world is not in our control, nor in that of any other creature, system, force, or thing."

—*Nicholas Lash*

Unlike Martin Luther with his ninety-five theses, I have only two to declare. The first is that Christian piety is inextricably linked with politics. More specifically, spiritual discipline is properly numbered among the practices of the church that constitute it as a political body. Any approach to spirituality that is divorced from *the politics of the Spirit* wrenches the practice of piety away from its proper context, stripping it of its integrity and purpose. Moreover, apart from the activity of the Holy Spirit in the church, and through this community to all the world, any kind of spiritual discipline whatsoever will invariably make of ourselves, as one author puts it, both "subject and object of our own quest."[2] When this happens, spirituality converts into apostasy and, ironically, into a most virulent form of impiety.

The second thesis has to do with the kind of life fostered by the Spirit. Our everyday existence as Christians begins with the acknowledgement of our vulnerability as creatures, or as the Bible refers to it, with the fear of God. This vulnerability is sanctified, made holy, when we learn to embrace and love it as given to us by the creator of all, whom we also learn to love as the one who first loved us. The love of God for creation that is manifested through the incarnation of the Word and communicated in the Spirit, therefore, defines the aim of spirituality as *holy insecurity*. In short, the goal of Christian piety is to keep open the "window of vulnerability," as Dorothee Soelle puts it, for it is the only window toward heaven that we have.[3]

The Spirit of God and the Politics of Christian Piety

The notion of spirituality is a very ambiguous one in our society, covering a wide range of techniques, images, and interests. In popular culture the term has become synonymous with self-care manuals and twelve-step programs, yet another product that is marketed as an effective way to be in harmony with the universe, cope with the stress of modern life, overcome substance abuse, or enhance one's self-esteem. This product, furthermore, may be enjoyed in the privacy of your own home, head, and heart. In effect, spirituality has become a kind of personalized "diet plan" for the soul, complete with "before" and "after" testimonies.[4]

Christian piety, on the other hand, is another matter altogether. As Rowan Williams notes, Christian faith originated in "an experience of profound contradictoriness, an experience that so questioned the religious categories of its time that the resulting reorganization of religious language was a centuries-long task." Christianity, in other words, rests on the affirmation "that all 'meaning', every assertion about the significance of life and reality, must be judged by reference to a brief succession of contingent events in Palestine." The sense and direction of all created life can only be truthfully discerned in relation to the events that revolved around one seemingly insignificant Jewish man, Jesus of Nazareth. This unlikely figure was someone who—according to his own people—came from the wrong neighborhood, an itinerant rabbi who spent his days pursuing a way of life that—while being the way of peace—moved inexorably toward confrontation and violence. Finally, his life was tragically cut short by a peculiar alliance between the mightiest and most efficient empire the world has ever known and those whom these imperial rulers had selected to administer the affairs of the Jewish people. Yet what this person accomplished so radically called into question the dominant categories and relations of any culture, that the restructuring of language and life continues to this day.[5]

So disruptive was the presence of Jesus to the normal course of events that it took his followers centuries to develop adequate ways to speak about the sense and direction of his life, death, and resurrection. In particular, they discovered that new uses had to be put to the word

"God." Without jeopardizing the mystery and simplicity of God, the church concluded that the only way to do justice to all that Jesus did and suffered was to refer to him as the incarnate Word of God. As one early church leader put it, Christ is himself "what the Father says."[6] In speaking this word, God enters into the day-to-day realities of our existence in the company of his followers, so that we might in turn share in the life-giving activity of God. God enters into history to act and suffer, live and die, as a creature, in order to reweave the tattered fabric of life according to the messianic pattern of human life. Without effacing the difference between the speaker and the spoken, then, the church confesses that *God* appears in the particular events and circumstances of this one man's life.

Spiritual discipline, insofar as it relates to Christian faith, finds its occasion and significance in the restructuring of language and life that this "experience of profound contradictoriness" sets into motion. Spirituality, Williams concludes, is properly defined in terms of the task set before each believer to make "his or her own that engagement with the questioning at the heart of faith that is so evident in the classical documents of Christian belief." Williams cautions us that he is not advocating fashionable notions about the relative nature of all human endeavors, nor entertaining romantic sentiments about the person who, while half-believing, withholds assent from all commitments in order to preserve her moral and intellectual autonomy. He insists,

> The question involved here is not our interrogation of the data, but its interrogation of us. It is the *strangeness* of the ground of belief that must constantly be allowed to challenge the fixed assumptions of religiosity; it is a *given,* whose question to each succeeding age is fundamentally one and the same. And the greatness of the great Christian saints lies in their readiness to be questioned, judged, stripped naked and left speechless by that which lies at the center of their faith.[7]

The purpose of such interrogation is ultimately not to indict and condemn, but to renew human life and all that is created, according to the form and fate of Christ, who in the midst of the present darkness has inaugurated a "counter-history of peace regained through redemptive suffering."[8] In other words, what Jesus accomplishes (or more precisely, what God accomplishes in and through Jesus' faithfulness, even to the point of the cross) is the beginning of the long-awaited reign of God, the dawning of the age to come and a new creation and with it a new covenant and a new humanity. In the person and community of Jesus the future messianic age becomes a present reality, not in some kind of private religious experience or moral ideal, but in terms of the day-to-day concerns and celebrations of life. Against the forces and powers that presently govern the course and content of life in the modern world, this counter-history extends to all the offer of an alternative pattern of life, a distinctive set of habits and relations, and a different story by which to make sense of the order of things.

The confession that God's address and agency takes flesh in Christ—a particular person who lived at a certain time and place, who said and did and suffered certain things—does not cancel or set aside the particularity of Jesus' own history. So crucial are the events that make up the life of Jesus, that a story is the only appropriate form in which the truth about him can be told. Nevertheless, when we ask about the significance of Jesus for those of us who live in a different time and place, who say and do and endure things in different circumstances that are also marked by their own particularity, we discover that this story has not come to an end, but through it the presence and power of God continue to restructure life and language according to the pattern of Jesus' life and death. When the early disciples struggled with the idea of God, they concluded that the church could not stop with the confession of Jesus as God's address, for to do so would reduce his story "to the status of an *anecdote*: a tale without enduring or universal significance."[9] The fullness of God's power and presence, they realized, is encountered in both the utterance of the Word *and* the breathing forth of the Holy Spirit.

Only in the Spirit, then, can we learn that God's address to us is ultimately a word of redemption, that life and not death is the goal of creation. The movement of God's Spirit in the world, however, is inseparable from the history of God's people, the story of both Israel and the church. The gift of God's Spirit, while it cannot be contained by any created thing, takes form within the community of faith, creating and sustaining a people who offer to the world a different kind of existence in which relations misshapen by death and sin are transfigured into patterns of life and wholeness. In short, Christian spirituality does not exist apart from the politics of the Spirit—that is, the practices and institutions of the church.

While most will regard the reference to the Holy Spirit in keeping with a book on spirituality, the idea of politics may come as a surprise to many. When one looks closely at the scriptures, however, this reaction itself seems curiously out of place, for the formative images that describe the activity of God and the response of human beings in both the Old and New Testaments are almost exclusively political images.[10] The fact that we find the dominance of political images strange is itself revealing, disclosing more about who we are and how we deal with the world than perhaps any other aspect of modern life.

It is also strange because, according to the New Testament, the place of the Spirit's activity is not the individual believer as such but the gathered community of believers. Salvation is not a matter of Christ rescuing individuals from life's traumas by recruiting them for an otherworldly existence, but of the Spirit adding to the *koinonia* (a standard term in the political vocabulary of Paul's day) of Christ's body, the church. As a result of the Spirit's labors, the church (and not heaven) stands against the world. In short, the church—the community of peace and reconciliation, the city of redemption from the powers and rulers of the present age—is the goal of God's saving work in creation. Who Christians are as individuals, therefore, is the product of our involvement in this communion, this *community*, which is the corporate body of Christ.[11]

Christian piety is, therefore, a church-centered spirituality, which sets it in firmly in a political context. While spiritual discipline has an intensely personal dimension, it is not at the outset nor in the end a private matter. The practice of Christian piety is a community affair, intersecting with every aspect and every concern of life. No field of human endeavor and inquiry stands outside the purview of spiritual discipline, because our quest for God is not one quest alongside all the others—personal relations, social policies, scientific research, literature, and art—that human beings undertake.[12] Spirituality from a biblical standpoint impinges on all these areas, not to dictate to them how to do their jobs, but to help us become attentive to the concrete ways these activities link together and direct the events that make up our day-to-day existence.

In the sense I am using it here, then, the term politics refers to "the science, art, and practice of human community, i.e., of knowing, doing, and achieving what is required for relating and interrelating individuals and groups in the art of giving shape to a society fit for being human in."[13] This definition will undoubtedly strike many as foreign, in part due to the transformation of politics in the modern world and in part owing to the popular conception of what it means to be a person, which was also invented with the rise of modernity. Whereas politics was once principally concerned about those goals called "goods" that the members of all kinds of communities—ranging in size from the extended family to empires that covered whole continents—pursued in common, it is now a formal process through which an optimum amount of coexistence among people (most of whom share little in common other than the fact they happen to live inside the borders of the same nation-state) is secured by means of the division and management of individuals through wage labor, bureaucratic controls, and economic adjustments.

Of all the techniques used to supervise those persons who live within liberal nation-states, one of the most important is the hard and fast distinction that is drawn between the public and the personal or private realms of life. Similar to the fate suffered by politics in the modern world, this distinction also serves a different purpose than it did in former years, when it was recognized as a social construct designed to provide for the development of intimacy and of the self.[14] With the emergence of the modern world, however, this distinction was reinterpreted as a way to protect and promote the latter from the unwanted and unwarranted attention of public authorities. While this seems like an innocent and even noble aim, employing the distinction in this fashion automatically compels individuals to subordinate their allegiance to whatever private concerns they might have to the public requirements of the dominant social order. Since we generally do not recognize the distinction between public and private as a social product, and therefore as the creation, instrument, and effect of political processes, we fail to notice how effectively it enforces certain political norms regarding the kinds of private concern permitted us.[15] Thus, who we are as "persons" is not determined by "what we initially, privately and 'inwardly' are," but by what the technical apparatus of modernity permits us to become.[16]

The purpose of any political body—the family, the tribe, the empires of the ancient world, the kingdoms of medieval Europe, the church, or the modern nation-state—is, therefore, essentially educational in nature. By education, however, I am not speaking primarily about the communication of information. Communities exist and function, first of all, to foster a particular style of life. In this capacity they require our complete loyalty, and they constantly seek to locate every possibility, every choice and option, within their structures. Again, this is equally true of Israel and the church—both of which exhort the believer to "love the Lord your God with all your heart, and with all your soul, and with all your might" (Deut 6:5)—and of liberal democracies such as the United States. George Will observes in this regard that

> a central purpose of America's political arrangements is the subordination of religion to the political order, meaning the primacy of democracy. The founders wished to tame and domesticate religious passions of the sort that convulsed Europe. They aimed to do so not by establishing religion, but by

> establishing a commercial republic—capitalism. They aimed to submerge people's turbulent energies in self-interested pursuit of material comforts.[17]

A liberal capitalist state, in other words, insists that we subordinate our identities as Christians to the given political and economic order, with no questions asked. In an interesting reversal of the biblical mandate, the state requires that we render to Caesar (which in our context refers to the political consortium of managerial government and corporate businesses) our first loyalty, which then permits us in his sovereign benevolence the right to religious "beliefs," which are perfectly free as long as they are perfectly private ("in the closet" of your mind or heart, so to speak).[18] Thus, many Christians in the so-called "First World" find themselves in the ironic position of refusing out of principle to force their religion on anyone, but sense nothing amiss in supporting the mandatory establishment (by any and all means available, including force of arms) of liberal democracy and its commercial republic around the globe.[19]

In order to facilitate the growth of this republic, modern culture reinterpreted the quest for God as one among many quests we were free to pursue, and then gradually defined it as a particular kind of inner experience or a preference for a distinctive set of beliefs and values. Relegating so-called "religious matters" to the margins of public life was permissible because the world, so it was believed, was perfectly capable of being dealt with *etsi deus non daretur*—as though God did not exist. So, spirituality became a purely private concern. Ironically, the more religion became a private matter confined to the individual and detached from particular communities and traditions, the more it could be kept under close scrutiny, and when necessary, called upon to support more public causes (usually various types of conflicts, both military and economic, against "them," those strange beings who inhabit other nation-states).[20]

Politics and piety, life together in the community of faith and life with God, thus go hand in hand, both for good and for evil. Nowhere is this unbreakable bond more evident than in the history of Baptists in the South. Much has been said and written about the links between the origin of the Southern Baptist Convention and the perpetuation of slavery prior to the Civil War. Equally significant, but yet to receive either the popular or scholarly attention it deserves, is the role that the development of a certain type of spirituality among Southern Baptists and other marginalized whites played both before the war and in the ensuing periods of Reconstruction and the Jim Crow era. Moreover, the effects of this impoverished spirituality continue to nourish the political climate of racism in America. This pietistic, individualisitic, literalist mode of religious faith was invaluable to the creation of the "redneck" Baptist and his imbibing an institutionalized form of religiosity distilled from a dangerous concoction of devotion and violence.[21]

When we define politics in this broader sense, we discover that it revolves about a number of core practices that constitute any community as a social body, and in which virtually all persons must participate in order to be members of that community (and therefore to be persons). By core practices I mean those activities in which at least some, and usually all, members of a community must routinely engage so as to sustain it and its distinctive way of life, and without which it would cease to exist. While these practices are never exactly the same from one community to another or from one historical period to the next, some overlap usually occurs. For example, one can almost always find in any society practices that determine who belongs to that community, facilitate the production and distribution of material goods among its members, assign social roles and responsibilities to each individual, and oversee the maintenance of just and orderly relations.

In addition to the practices themselves, a community must also develop institutional forms to sustain these practices in good order. It must also ensure that its members acquire those intellectual and moral skills that will enable them to perform adequately in these practices. While we should never confuse these institutions and skills with practices they serve, we can never separate them either. We should not, for example, confuse the institution of the hospital with the practice of medicine, and yet all the wonders of modern medicine would be inconceivable without such institutions. We also do not equate the practice of medicine with expertise in the areas of chemistry, biology, physiology, and so on, nor do we only expect physicians to exhibit moral traits such as trustworthiness, yet few of us would knowingly stay in the same room with a doctor who did not possess these qualities in good measure, along with many others.

While similarities usually exist between the practices of different societies, the goods at which a community as a whole aims distinguishes one community and its set of practices from the others. In the liberal nation-state, there is but one such good: the commercial republic as such. Please do not misunderstand me. I am *not* saying that the making and selling of commodities is the only thing that those of us who live in this society hold dear, or that money alone makes life worthwhile, or that this republic of commerce prevents individuals from doing good works of mercy and justice. Nor do I think that if somehow we could change our economic system most of our social and individual ills would eventually disappear, or that this one good will sustain a community for very long (one needs only look at the kind of society in which we now live to see the poverty of spirit that plagues it).

I *am* saying that when it comes to what governs our day-to-day lives, in public *and* in private, the commercial republic largely determines, not particular acts, but the range of possible acts available to us as individuals. The control that this form of politics exercises over us is therefore anonymous and indirect, but precisely for this reason all the more sweeping. To be a person in this society is to be a consumer, period. Virtually everything else is optional to our individuality; every option is presented as a product to be consumed (including having children and friends), and the value of every product is determined by its "market share"—that is, its ability to please the consumer. America doesn't need politics in the traditional sense to determine what goods it will pursue as a society; the structural apparatus of liberal capitalism does that for us.

The politics of the Spirit, by contrast, presupposes a very different form of community, nurtures a radically different kind of life, and tells a markedly different story about the world than those that underwrite the modern nation-state and its commercial republic. The goods that this community seeks, the moral and intellectual qualities it fosters, the institutions it develops, and most importantly of all, the practices that constitute it as the body of Christ—all work in concert to give the world a concrete and visible sign that it is ultimately ruled by one who has determined that life rather than death, community and not chaos, light rather than darkness, joy rather than despair, and solidarity rather than private property will have the final say.

Christian spirituality, as with the other practices of the church, has no purpose apart from this story. Baptism, for example, begins an individual's involvement in the politics of the Spirit as the sign of his/her induction into a new society, marking the passage from life to death and the transfer of citizenship from the realm of darkness to the kingdom of light. Immersion in the baptismal waters relativizes all previous definitions of identity based on class, ethnic or national origin, and gender, so that these matters no longer determine who we are as persons. Together with the Spirit's endowment of every member of the community with her own distinctive role (the divine *charisma*), baptism establishes a new mode of social relations within the community and forms the basis of Christian egalitarianism, a way of relating that—unlike the brand of equality prescribed by liberal democracies—does not treat us as interchangeable cogs in a giant machine.

Politics in a biblical context, William Stringfellow says, "refers comprehensively to the total configuration of relationships among humans and institutions and other principalities and the rest of created life in this world." Politics thus names both the arena of God's activity in this world to redeem it from the effects of death and sin and the impact of the divine presence and power "upon the fallen existence of this world, including the fallen life of human beings and that of the powers that be. Politics points to the militance of the Word of God incarnate, which pioneers the politics of the kingdom that is to come." Spirituality in this context thus refers to *"a reiteration of the act of creation in the Word of God* . . . renewing human life (and all of created life) in the midst of the era of the fall, or during the present darkness, in which the power of death apparently reigns."[22]

Holy Insecurity and the Politics of the Spirit

Spiritual discipline, as one of the core practices of the Christian community, begins with what scripture calls the fear of God. This disposition, says Martin Buber, comes when the whole of our existence between birth and death becomes incomprehensible and uncanny.[23] Only when we have accepted deep down that we do not hold the deed to our own lives nor to anything or anyone else in the world, can a genuine and mature piety can take root. The fear of God entails knowing that our existence is, in the basic sense of the word, a *gift*, and to accept our giftedness is to come to face to face with our contingency as creatures. "But from contingency," says Lash, "nothing follows. Here we are. This is how things are. That's it. No safety belts, no metacosmic maps or guidebooks, no mental cradles for our 'ultimate' security."[24]

The most basic and important thing we learn, as we come to terms with our contingency is that the fact of our existence resides in mystery. This is a mystery that eludes all categories of our understanding and shatters every form of security that we devise to protect ourselves from the vulnerability implied in the world's giftedness. This state of affairs "is not the relative mystery of that which is inaccessible only to the present state of human knowledge and is hence in principle discoverable. It is the essential mystery, the inscrutableness of which belongs to its very nature; it is the unknowable." Consequently, there are no experts in the knowledge of matters divine, for the God who, according to scripture, knows us in Jesus Christ is unknowable as such, "the You that in accordance with its nature cannot become an It."[25]

Spirituality's starting point presents a fundamental challenge to the prevailing ethos of liberal capitalism. Scholars give the name *instrumental rationality* to the way that most of us, most of the time, think about the world. While instrumental rationality involves very complex forms of reasoning, it is, very simply, a way of coping with the world that continually strives to subject all things, even life itself, to its control. In striving for control, instrumental reasoning recognizes no boundaries, acknowledges no limitations, encounters no mystery, and allows no exemptions from its all-embracing quest for mastery. No *thing* lies outside the scope of its calculating gaze. As we begin the long pilgrimage toward maturity and insight, therefore, we must first learn that the nature of the mystery that accounts not only for our existence as human beings, but for the world as a whole, is shrouded in impenetrable darkness. God is not an object, thing, or person that we can encounter, identify, categorize, or compare and contrast along with all the other things and persons that make up the world. *What* God is will forever remain unknown to us.

The darkness that surrounds the mystery, moreover, holds countless dangers: disease, war, hunger, cruelty, and abuse—the mere threat of which governs our daily lives in innumerable ways. Then for all things comes death, the single most determinative aspect of our contingent existence. It is therefore not surprising that Christians, along with most Americans, are tempted to bypass this first step and move straight to the comfort afforded by the Bible's affirmation of God's love.[26] As with all forms of temptation, this is one we should avoid, for both Old and New Testaments maintain that the one "who begins with the love of God without having previously experienced the fear of God, loves an idol that he himself has made, a god whom it is easy enough to love."[27] Thus we must return time and again to the Bible's scripting of piety as holy insecurity, and to that love that scripture describes as a fierce and dreadful love, a love that would have us sacrifice our lives and even our children's lives, a love that presupposes rather than replaces the fear of God as the point of departure for spirituality. But without this "gut-level" grasp of just how fragile and besieged, how insecure and out of control, human life really is, the wisdom and wholeness that characterize spiritual maturity will lie forever beyond our reach.

God's severe love also informs the New Testament's protest against spirituality without conflict—that is, God addresses us apart from the suffering of the world. Spirituality without conflict has to do with the gods of this world, not the God of Jesus Christ. A form of piety that leaves us feeling safe, sated, and secure does not partake of the politics of the Spirit, but the politics of the present age. We must never, however, confuse Christ's acceptance of suffering, nor his insistence that his disciples must follow him down this same path, with passivity in the face of it. Abuse and suffering are endured in hope of the new creation, relying on whatever God may will, "and this," says Williams, "is pre-eminently the gift of the Spirit." Our suffering is conformed to the pattern of Christ "by the presence of the same Spirit of protest, trust, and hope." The follower of Christ

> meets pain in acceptance and *hope;* he or she confronts it, identifies with those experiencing it, and then struggles through it to grow into new humanness, more capable both of pain and of love. . . . The Spirit is the "pledge," the Spirit is that which more and more conforms to Christ; and so the Spirit is that which impels us forward, which creates hope out of our cries of protest in the present. We protest because we have tasted the reality of new life.[28]

The politics of liberal democracy, by contrast, capitalizes on the power of death and sin through its own brand of spirituality, so that it might take full advantage of our vulnerability and anxiety as contingent beings and thus consolidate its hold upon our loyalty. Secular piety, in other words, corrupts the insatiable human longing for wholeness and integrity with the lure of security, the promise of safety, stability, and predictability through the eradication of tragedy. The modern quest for security and its corruption of God's creation manifests itself in a variety of ways. In some the quest for self-mastery runs roughshod over our created solidarity with each other and with all the world, as we are alternatively encouraged, enticed, and threatened to seek safety and stability by taking ownership of the people and things around us. Through the alchemy of the commercial republic we strive to transform God's gift of communion with other people and things into private property, commodities to be possessed and disposed of as it suits our needs.

In one of its most crude and violent form, the sparks of insecurity were fanned by the southern aristocracy among marginalized whites after the Civil War. These sparks erupted into the white hot flames of racism during the Jim Crow era, and its embers continue to smolder with hatred and dissension, waiting for the right moment to re-ignite. Others who are "numbed by terror and acknowledged impotence retreat into varieties of personal and moral individualism, places of private feeling and individual 'experience.' "[29] In these persons the quest for security serves to drive them further and further away from the pain and disappointment of day-to-day contact with others, in a vain attempt to carve out an inner world of safety and tranquility within themselves. As one beloved gospel song puts it, they flee to the garden to be alone with Jesus.

From the standpoint of the Spirit, however, the seemingly interminable quest for security—whether it be for ourselves, our families, our community, or our nation—is "but the desire to be rid of God, to claim for ourselves the power to determine our meaning and destiny."[30] Our pledge to Christ in baptism therefore involves, among other things, a renunciation of all idolatrous claims to security and safety. This is not something we can achieve on our own, but is the consequence of a particular form of spiritual discipline. Holy insecurity, in other words, is not strictly a human possibility, nor is it something that individuals can acquire in their own strength and solitude; it is the creation, instrument, and effect of the Spirit's activity in and through the church.

Holy insecurity, however, must be distinguished from a fatalistic acceptance of the status quo. As Buber notes, the fact that

> one accepts the concrete situation as given to him does not, in any way, mean that he must be ready to accept that which meets him as "God-given" in its pure factuality. He may, rather, declare the extremest enmity toward this happening and treat its "givenness" as only intended to draw forth his own opposing force. But he will not remove himself from the concrete situation as it actually is; he will, instead, enter into it, even if in the form of fighting against it.[31]

The hope that is ours in Christ, in other words, does not deny the darkness that casts its shroud over the present order of things, but neither does it succumb to the despair that is the worship of necessity. It does mean, however, that the ways of God in the world "can be discerned only in broken configurations of events, not in uni-linear traditions. Accordingly, obedience can never be literal but is necessarily paradigmatic."[32]

In scripture, the paradigm for this obedience is the "fatherhood" of God, but Lash warns that

> before we take this name and use it to weave comforting patterns of speculation concerning the "domestic" character of the relationship between human beings and the mystery of God, we need to remind ourselves of the context that is paradigmatic for all descriptions of ourselves as "sons" and "daughters" of him whom we call "Father." That context is Gethsemane and Calvary, where we learn what it is truthfully to stand in filial relation to the mystery of God.[33]

The cry to God as Father, echoes Williams, "is not a calm acknowledgement of a universal truth about God's abstract 'fatherhood', it is the child's cry out of the nightmare." The cries of the Christian to God are expressions of outrage, fear, and protest in face of the senseless suffering and horror of the world, yet they are not simply or exclusively protest, "but trust as well. 'Abba, Father, all things are possible to thee' (Mark 14:36). From the middle of the night, we recognize the finality of God's mercy and acceptance. Even when there is not comfort given, there may still be hope: 'not what I will, but what thou wilt' (Mark 14:36)."[34]

The fear of God, therefore, is not the end of Christian spirituality, but only its point of departure. While no natural kinship exists between the mysterious reality of God and the human mind, our ignorance in this regard is not cause for despair or resignation, as our dealings with other people demonstrate.

When we meet people for the first time, we normally begin the process of getting to know them by gathering some standard information about them: where they work, whether they are married, how many children they have, from what part of the country do they come, where they went to school, and so forth. We begin by treating them, for the most part, as one more object or thing in the world. But as we get to know them better, such information, while still a factor in the relationship, becomes less and less important as we begin to acquire a common history with each other, as the stories that form the biographies of our lives become increasingly intertwined. As this history develops, these other persons can no longer be identified by simply referring to the aforementioned list of facts; they become more complex, harder to describe, possessing a depth not seen at first. Lash writes,

> Indeed, the *closer* we are to people, and the better we understand them, the more they evade our cognitive "grasp" and the greater the difficulty that we experience in giving adequate expression to our understanding. Other people become, in their measure, "mysterious," not insofar as we *fail* to understand them, but rather in so far as, in lovingly relating to them, we succeed in doing so.[35]

The mysterious character of human relationships also extends to the relation with one's self. The better we get to know ourselves the more complex and mysterious we become, *especially* to ourselves. Anybody who has been surprised by how she responded in a moment of stress or crisis knows something of the mystery that is our sense of self.

Human relationships, embodying a mysterious nature in their own right, thus provide us with the proper image for describing our relation to God's mystery. The fear of God is therefore not a dwelling place of despair to which we are condemned, but as Buber describes it, a "dark gate" through which we move into the everyday, which is where we address the dilemmas and delights of our existence. Once the believer has stepped across this threshold, the reality of day-to-day life is

> henceforth hallowed as the place in which he has to live with the mystery. . . that the believing man who goes through the gate of dread is directed to the concrete contextual situations of his existence means just this: that he endures in the face of God the reality of lived life, dreadful and incomprehensible though it be. He loves it in the love of God, whom he has learned to love.[36]

The believer must, in other words, begin in the concreteness and vulnerability of her own existence, with all its uncertainty and uncanniness. Only then is she in a position to grasp the meaning of the biblical assertion that the divine act of creation and redemption begins in love, and that, as a consequence of the divine love, we are also able to love (1 John 4:19).

Another way to think about the fear of God is to know why the first and most basic word any human can truthfully utter about oneself is "Amen." Christian spirituality begins and ends, in other words, as a *response* to the inscrutable mystery. Only when we learn what it means to be, not just finite beings, but *creatures*, can we know the most important thing about ourselves, which is that we can never literally start "at the beginning." Beginnings and endings are God's doing, entirely outside our comprehension or control.[37] This does not condemn us to a fatalistic acceptance of what is, nor does it deny us a role in what comes between the first and the final Amen. When we begin "in the middle" we are not forced to withdraw from the tasks of life, but compelled to start with the *giftedness* of our situation.

Christian spirituality thus pertains to the day-to-day existence of all created things, to what I call the practice of everyday life. True piety, in other words, does not lead the Christian to the esoteric realm of religious experience that shuns the material and historical aspects of creation for the ecstasy of a private relationship with a resurrected-but-never-crucified Jesus, but to a world "in which people eat bread and pursue debtors, hope for power and execute subversives."[38] Secular forms of spirituality begin and end with a craving for knowledge that will increase our mastery of the things and persons around us. The practice of Christian piety, however, begins with the darkness of mystery—with an unknowing, a not-seeing—and ends with a knowledge of God that is nothing other than our involvement in the pattern of everyday life embodied by Jesus and made a continuing reality by the labor of the Spirit in the community of faith. A God who is sought, celebrated, or obeyed somewhere other than in our comings and our goings, our concerns and our celebrations, our doings and our sufferings (things that are inseparably intertwined with the lives of all those with whom we come into contact), "is a figment of our imagination destructive of our common humanity—and thereby destructive of our relations with God."[39]

Only as we know the unknown God in this way can we also truthfully know ourselves. Augustine was among the first to observe how the knowledge of God and self-knowledge, while distinct, are finally inseparable: "What I do know of myself I know because you shed your light on me; and what I do not know of myself I shall still not know until 'my darkness shall become as noonday' in the vision of Your face."[40] Spirituality is, in this sense, a discipline of self-discovery, made possible by the politics of the Spirit within the common venture of discipleship that belongs to the community of Jesus. "In a sense," write Hauerwas and William Willimon, "we follow Jesus before we know Jesus. Furthermore, we know Jesus before we know ourselves."[41]

Once we have crossed the threshold of the dark gate into the everyday, we are ready to undertake what Williams calls the discipline of "unselfing." This notion will no doubt make some uncomfortable, as it sounds all too similar to the destructive habits of self-abnegation that some persons in our world have either been persuaded or forced to accept. Unfortunately, many people have good reason to be suspicious of such ideas. The biblical images of servanthood and self-sacrifice have routinely been detached from the social practices that made the early church a subversive organization to the Romans, and reinscribed within the habits and relations of the prevailing culture and society, where they are normally reserved for certain people, especially women and minorities.

Nevertheless, to allow our reaction against such distortions to determine our response to God and the world would be foolish. Reactionary impulses do not result in freedom but continue our captivity within the structures and aims of the modern world in the form of an antithetical bondage.[42] Both forms of the quest for security—retreating within oneself and striving for mastery of self and others—take away from what God created each of us to be. Individuality within the Christian community is analogous to the growth of a vine in the vineyard, and unselfing to the pruning that is required in order to give the roots an opportunity for new and healthy growth. Unselfing, in other words, interrupts the processes of secular spirituality in order to cultivate a new selfhood within the community of Jesus, one that is not confined by its "Adamic" past but liberated for its future in the messianic kingdom. Who we are as individuals is not something that already lies within each of us, needing only to be set free from the shackles of other people's expectations. Selfhood is rather "a task to be perfected in grace" within the body of Christ.[43]

In keeping with its trinitarian context, the process of unselfing takes the form of a story—not just any story, however, and not a story that each of us gets to write for ourselves according to our own individual tastes. The idea that each of us is free to write our own stories is perhaps the most deceptive aspect of modern society. What was advertised as a quest toward freedom turned out to be "an adventure that held the seeds of its own destruction within itself, within its attenuated definition of human nature and its inadequate vision of human destiny. What we got was not self-freedom but self-centeredness, loneliness, superficiality, and harried consumerism."[44] The result of our impiety has not been the freedom we were promised, but confusion, frustration, cynicism, despair, and alienation. The sweet savor of liberty for which we longed has left the bitter taste of falsehood in our mouths. The more vigorously we sought our freedom, the more thoroughly we enslaved ourselves, our neighbors, and the whole of creation within the techniques and structures that we devised to facilitate our emancipation.

The narrative of unselfing is the story of a journey with a fellow group of travelers that radically reconstructs the sense and direction of our lives. If spirituality is "that engagement with the questioning at the heart of faith that is so evident in the classical documents of Christian belief," the form that this interrogation takes is the rewriting of our autobiographies that occurs within the communion, the *community*, of the Spirit. Spiritual discipline has basically to do with each believer becoming an active participant in, and thus a co-author of, the story of Jesus—a story with a multitude of characters, countless twists in the plot, and numerous confrontations with the present order of things. As we move through the often traumatic process from self-possession to self-giving, and from unrestrained desire and acquisitiveness to maturity and wholeness, our individual stories find their meaning and purpose in the history of the Spirit with God's people.

In modern culture, unselfing involves divesting ourselves of the illusion that "I" exist apart from creation, apart from history, apart from a community and a tradition, apart from the habits and relations that comprise my dealings with others. The discipline of unselfing is thus a process of de-mythologizing the fundamental axioms of modern life, namely, that each of us is free to make up our own story, that our lives belong to us rather than being a gift. A leading motif in the modern myth is the claim that each of us already possesses in the privacy of our inner selves a "fixed point of certainty and unshakable reassurance in our most unstable and insecure world."[45] In short, we have been enchanted by a picture of ourselves as gods, unconstrained by the material forces and historical relations of the created order, "spectators of a distanced spectacle."[46]

The moral consequences of this illusion have been devastating, not only for the world of human beings, but for all of God's creation. The origins of modern science can be traced to the desire to subject nature to our control, so that we might safeguard ourselves from its many menaces and manage its resources for our benefit. When we picture ourselves in timeless caprice as lords and masters of the physical world, rather than recognizing our place within it, God's creation "becomes something manipulable for the sake of the values we have chosen. It becomes the stock of resources on hand for the fulfillment we value."[47] As the modern world struggles with pollution, waste, and squandered resources, we are shocked to discover that the knowledges we so proudly developed to secure our freedom from nature's menace now enslave us along with the physical world. In effect, we traded away our spiritual birthright for the promise of security and self-determination, and we received instead a new and more pervasive form of bondage in return.

As Luther knew so well, the discipline of unselfing begins in accepting God's judgment: "He who judges himself and confesses his sin justifies God and affirms his truthfulness, because he is saying about himself what God is saying about him."[48] As with the fear of God, judgment is not finally a cause for despair or hopelessness. The Spirit judges us in Christ not by uttering words of condemnation but through complex processes of interaction that "force to the light hidden directions and dispositions that would otherwise never come to view, and thus make the conflicts of goals and interests between people a *public* affair." The politics of the Spirit takes the

> dramatic event of Jesus' interaction with his people—set out in a series of ritual, quasi-legal disputations, and transforms it into an event of judgment in that it gives the persons involved definitions, roles to adopt, points on which to stand and speak. They are invited to "create" themselves in finding a place within this drama—an improvisation in the theater workshop, but one that purports to be about a comprehensive truth affecting one's identity and future.[49]

Judgment is therefore a necessary precondition for conversion, when one shifts his/her allegiance from one set of powers to another and from one measure of reality to another, namely, "the reality of God that has become manifest in Christ in the reality of the world."[50] The politics of the Spirit strives "to make explicit what is at stake in particular human decisions or policies, individual and collective, and in this sense bring in the event of judgment, the revaluation of identities."[51] In contrast, the impiety fostered by liberal capitalism reconfirms the prevailing habits and relations of the world, which constitutes a *de facto* legitimation of the status quo. Such politics is in the end non-judgmental, in both the popular and biblical sense of that term, and is therefore incapable of displaying God's love for the world incarnated in the crucified one.

Judgment does not bring condemnation, but the possibility of genuine freedom joined with a new capacity and direction for love.[52] As we shed the vanity that is the quest for security, the world's grip upon us also starts to relax. The freedom of holy insecurity thus

> takes the form of dispossession, letting go, surrendering the title-deeds we forged. . . . Emancipation, letting things and people go from our grasp. . . is how life in the Spirit is to be lived; which is to say: it is how we are to die. What occurs in death is, in the last resort, the same for all of us: we are deprived of all possessions, "even of ourselves." To learn to die (which is, of course, the way that finite creatures learn to live) is, therefore, to learn to relate to each and every person, thing, disease, event, delight, that we encounter, neither as enemy nor as possession but as gift, as friend.[53]

Spiritual maturity conveys a radically new sense of freedom, one that is very different from modern conceptions. Most people, if asked to define freedom, usually will do so as freedom *from* something or someone. Freedom is, essentially, the opportunity (and the right) to be one's own tyrant. A few will add that freedom must eventually be the freedom *for* someone or something if it is to persist, and so link it with the idea of responsibility. Yet neither of these prepositions—*from* or *for*—really begins to address the freedom that is ours in Christ. Both are still mired in the picture of the self as someone who in the essence of one's being is unfettered by relations with fellow creatures, and those relations into which one does enter are, and always will be, personal choice.

In the church, by contrast, we learn through spiritual discipline to live—literally, out of control—emancipated from the promise of self-mastery with which the modern world lures us and yet that it will never allow us to achieve. Contemplation, which forms the basis of the practice of piety, is not an esoteric preoccupation but, as Williams says, "a deeper appropriation of the vulnerability of the self in the midst of the language and transactions of the world."[54] We learn through a contemplative way of life to give back our habits, our relations, our attempts at knowledge, our very lives. In the process we acquire patience and divest ourselves of our feeble and vain attempts at security, "sometimes in darkness not unlike Gethsemane."[55] The freedom that is the Spirit (2 Cor 3:17) is thus signified by another preposition, the freedom *of*—more specifically, the freedom of our adoption as the daughters and sons of God, the freedom of servanthood within the household of Christ. Within this household, freedom is a gift that can never be possessed and a power that can never become ours; yet it is a gift and power in which we share in the Spirit through our participation in the *koinonia* of the people of God.

The freedom of the Spirit, therefore, has nothing to do with that ghost that modernity calls the human ego, an apparition which only haunts its body but really does not belong to it. Human beings only begin to know what freedom is when we learn what it means to be some*body*—that is, when we know *viscerally* that human life is vested in, and is nothing apart from, our bodies, and that our bodies are inextricably woven into the social and material fabric of God's creation. Freedom thus depends upon our relations with others—parents, relatives, neighbors, even the institutions of culture—and with all created things. The freedom of Christ involves even our enemies, for only as the follower of Jesus is liberated to love those who seek to do harm does he/she have assurance that he/she is making progress on the journey toward the freedom that is the future reign of God. The life of freedom thus requires intense and rigorous schooling within the context of the messianic community and its distinctive skills and institutions.

The freedom that is realized through spiritual discipline takes form in the practices of baptism and the eucharist. Through our participation in these practices we come to understand that emancipation is the gift and effect of becoming a character in a true story that transfigures our fate as finite beings into our destiny as creatures of God. The realization of this destiny, however, does not take place apart from confrontation and conflict. The sacraments are always situated in the Bible in the context of Jesus' death and resurrection, and thus in the context of the faithfulness of Christ being met time and again by the infidelity of friend and foe alike. These practices thus nurture what Johann Baptist Metz calls the memory of suffering, in the light of which "it is clear that social power and political domination are not simply to be taken for granted but that they continually have to justify themselves in view of actual suffering."

The way of everyday life practiced by Christians, linked by God's activity in Jesus to the victims of suffering and oppression, thus challenges the world to justify itself in light of the human cost that it exacts, but at the same time this way of being in the world also extends the divine offer of new life in the messianic community, the historical sign of God's peaceable kingdom.[56]

To be buried and raised with Christ in baptism, therefore, not only begins the process of acknowledging our vulnerability before God, but also makes explicit our role in the tragic dimension of the biblical story. The sharing of bread and the cup within the family of God is likewise never simply a fellowship meal, but concretely embodies the divine summons, in the words of Dietrich Bonhoeffer, "to share in God's sufferings at the hands of a godless world."[57] The origins of this meal are invariably set in the context of Jesus' betrayal by his disciples on the night before his death. The story of the eucharist, then *and* now, does not ignore the tragic suffering associated with everyday life, nor does it cover over our complicity in this tragedy, but incorporates these within its costly solidarity with the world.

As with baptism, the Lord's Supper also affirms and proclaims God's vindication of suffering, both Christ's and ours, in the community of the crucified. Consequently, this feast "always and necessarily operates between the two poles of Maundy Thursday and Easter Sunday, between Gethsemane and Emmaus, between the Upper Room before the crucifixion and the Upper Room to which the risen Jesus comes." Our participation in God's sufferings, appropriated through contemplation, takes concrete form in the celebration of the bread and the cup, signifying the restoration of a fellowship continually broken by our unfaithfulness, hence "the wounded body and the shed blood are inescapably present."[58]

Finally, while the practice of Christian piety rejects the quest for security that holds the world in its grip, the believer is not left adrift in chaotic waters without a sense of direction or assistance. In that community where humans live by "the conviction of things not seen" (Heb 11:1), relying on the grace of the one who subjects the world to God's will by his weakness and suffering, we learn to discriminate between the fraudulent offer of security, which is forever beyond our reach, and the kind of certitude that develops through our continuing faithfulness to Christ, who accepted our vulnerability as his own, who on the cross was the most vulnerable of all.[59]

This means, however, that spirituality is a venture that carries with it the element of risk—an unavoidable aspect of being a creature rather than the creator. We have no alternative to risk on our part, and the calculating cynicism cultivated by many in our culture, as they seek to preserve their autonomy by describing all commitments as self-interested pursuits, is but "the irresponsible dilettantism which we call 'bad faith.' "[60] For "those who are called, both Jews and Greeks," the discipline of following Christ with one's brothers and sisters is "the power of God and the wisdom of God" (1 Cor 1:24).

Notes

[1]This chapter is dedicated to the "Gospel Tigers," my irreverently spiritual Sunday School class at Calvary Baptist Church in Waco, Texas.

[2]Harold Bloom, *The American Religion: The Emergence of the Post-Christian Nation* (New York: Simon & Schuster, 1992) 217.

[3]Dorothee Soelle, *The Window of Vulnerability: A Political Spirituality* (Minneapolis MN: Fortress Press, 1990) xi. I take the term *holy insecurity* from Nicholas Lash, who uses it to describe the perspective of Martin Buber.

[4]A good example of the marketing of spirituality is Thomas Moore's recent best-seller, *Care of the Soul: A Guide for Cultivating Depth and Sacredness in Everyday Life* (New York: Harper Collins Publishers Inc., 1992).

[5]Rowan Williams, *The Wound of Knowledge*, 2d ed. (Boston: Cowley Publications, 1990) 1.

[6]Ignatius of Antioch, *Epistle to the Romans* 8.

[7]Williams, 1.

[8]John Milbank, "The Second Difference: For a Trinitarianism without Reserve," *Modern Theology* 2 (1986): 227.

[9]Nicholas Lash, *Easter in Ordinary: Reflections on Human Experience and the Knowledge of God* (Charlottesville VA: University Press of Virginia, 1988) 282.

[10]See Paul L. Lehmann, *Ethics in a Christian Context* (New York: Harper & Row, 1963) 90-91, 95.

[11]In the course of struggling against corrupt institutions and practices, Baptists took for granted, but then lost sight of, what the early followers of Christ clearly recognized and Scripture consistently affirms, namely, that the church—including its institutional features and practices—is not our creation but the Spirit's. Moreover, as Stanley

Hauerwas notes, "what God did at Pentecost he continues to do to renew and to sustain the presence of the church so that the world might know there an alternative to Babel." Stanley Hauerwas, *Christian Existence Today: Essays on Church, World, and Living In Between* (Durham NC: The Labyrinth Press, 1988) 54.

[12]Nicholas Lash, *Theology on the Way to Emmaus* (London: SCM Press Ltd., 1986) 8-12.

[13]Paul Lehmann, "Piety, Power, and Politics: Church and Ministry between Ratification and Resistance," *Journal of Theology for Southern Africa* 44 (1983): 58.

[14]Stanley Hauerwas, *Truthfulness and Tragedy* (Notre Dame IN: University of Notre Dame Press, 1977) 2.

[15]Therefore, the Branch Davidians who died at the end of the siege at their "compound" outside of Waco in April, 1993, are routinely labelled as "fanatics," because "normal" persons do not die for something as insignificant as "religious beliefs." The fact that many Christians echo this sentiment only demonstrates how far we have strayed toward the distinctive type of polytheism in American culture and away from our own heritage, which asks us to make the most extraordinary sacrifice of all, to take up the cross and follow Jesus down the path of martyrdom. As Hauerwas says in connection with the similar tragedy at Jonestown: "What went wrong—is not that people died for what they believed but that they died for false beliefs and a false god." Hauerwas, *Against the Nations: War and Survival in a Liberal Society* (San Francisco: Harper and Row, 1985) 92.

[16]Lash, *Easter in Ordinary*, 86.

[17]George Will, "Scalia Missed Point But Made Right Argument on Separation of Religion," as cited in Stanley Hauerwas, *After Christendom? How the Church is to Behave if Freedom, Justice, and a Christian Nation are Bad Ideas* (Nashville: Abingdon Press, 1991) 30. What Will cannot quite bring himself to say, but which is implied in his statement, is that the institution of wage-labor is not primarily a mode of freedom, but of social discipline. Note, in addition, that one does not have a choice about these matters: They are obligatory, and the liberal nation-state will not hesitate to use its considerable coercive powers—all derived ultimately from the power of death—against those who do not "freely choose" this particular order of things.

[18]Cf. 1 Peter 2:17.

[19]Modern, moderate Southern Baptists have often confused the historic Baptist commitment to uncoerced belief, or liberty of conscience, which is strictly a negative principle (i.e., do not do such-and-so), with a positive objective of liberal capitalism, namely, to create the social conditions in which it is possible (and then necessary) for each to "choose" to believe or not. Not only does such confusion cede to secular authorities the privilege of defining what constitutes Christian faith, it also helps to secure very subtly (but which is no less coercive for all its subtlety) the fate of every individual within the politics of consumer markets and nation-states.

[20]See John Milbank, *Theology and Social Theory: Beyond Secular Reason* (Cambridge: Basil Blackwell, Inc., 1990) 109, 128.

[21]See Will D. Campbell, "The World of the Redneck," *Katallagete* 5 (1974): 34-40; James Silver, *Confederate Morale and Church Propaganda* (Tuscaloosa AL: Confederate Publishing Co., 1957); and H. Shelton Smith, *In His Image, But . . .: Racism in Southern Religion, 1780-1910* (Durham NC: Duke University Press, 1972).

[22]William Stringfellow, *The Politics of Spirituality* (Philadelphia: Westminster Press, 1984) 25f, 30.

[23]Martin Buber, *The Eclipse of God: Studies in the Relation Between Religion and Philosophy*, trans. Maurice S. Friedman, Eugene Kamenka, Norbert Guterman, and I. M. Lask (Atlantic Highlands: Humanities Press International, Inc., 1952, 1988) 36.

[24]Nicholas Lash, *Believing Three Ways in One God: A Reading of the Apostles' Creed* (Notre Dame IN: University of Notre Dame Press, 1993) 39.

[25]Buber, *Eclipse of God*, 36; Martin Buber, *I and Thou*, trans. Walter Kaufman (New York: Charles Scribner's Sons, 1970) 123.

[26]"The essence of the American," writes Harold Bloom, "is the belief that God loves her or him, a conviction shared by nearly nine out of ten of us, according to a Gallup poll." *The American Religion*, 17.

[27]Buber, *Eclipse of God*, 36.

[28]Williams, 12.

[29]Lash, *Easter in Ordinary*, 85.

[30]Stanley Hauerwas, *Against the Nations*, 196.

[31]Buber, *Eclipse of God*, 37f.; see also Lash, *Believing Three Ways in One God*, 108.

[32]Paul Lehmann, *Ideology and Incarnation: A Contemporary Ecumenical Risk* (Geneva: The John Knox Association, 1962) 6.

[33]Lash, *Theology on the Way to Emmaus*, 14.

[34]Williams, 12.

[35]Lash, *Easter in Ordinary*, 236.

[36]Buber, *Eclipse of God*, 36f.

[37]The recognition of our creaturehood depends, as Hauerwas notes, upon a particular story of God as creator, a story "that requires more significant knowledge of our humanity than simply that we are finite. For both the notions of creature and sinner require that we find ourselves constituted by narratives that we did not create." Hauerwas, *After Christendom?* 109. If Baptists better understood what it means to say "Amen" with reference to both the beginning and the end, we would soon learn to read the books of Genesis and Revelation in a far more intelligible and truthful fashion than we presently do.

[38]John Howard Yoder, *Priestly Kingdom: Social Ethics as Gospel* (Notre Dame IN: University of Notre Dame Press, 1984) 62.

[39]Lash, *Easter in Ordinary*, 181.

[40]Augustine of Hippo, *Confessions* 10.5.

[41]Stanley Hauerwas and William H. Willimon, *Resident Aliens: Life in the Christian Colony* (Nashville: Abingdon Press, 1989) 55.

[42]Lash, *Theology on the Way to Emmaus*, 55f. Reactionary bondage is particularly troublesome for Baptists, as we have often made a virtue of defining ourselves and our practices by what we are not.

[43]Williams, 21.

[44]Hauerwas and Willimon, 50.

[45]Lash, *Easter in Ordinary*, 18.

[46]William H. Poteat, *Polanyian Meditations: In Search of a Post-Critical Logic* (Durham: Duke University Press, 1985) 267.

[47]Joseph Rouse, *Knowledge and Power* (Ithaca NY: Cornell University Press, 1987) 66.

[48]Martin Luther, *Luther's Works*, ed. Hilton C. Oswald, vol. 11, *First Lectures on the Psalms II: Psalms 76-126* (Saint Louis: Concordia Publishing House, 1976) 93.

[49]Rowan Williams, "Postmodern Theology and the Judgment of the World," *Postmodern Theology*, ed. Frederic B. Burnham (San Francisco: Harper & Row, 1989) 96f.

[50]Dietrich Bonhoeffer, *Ethics*, ed. Eberhard Bethge (New York: Macmillan Publishing Co., Inc., 1955) 197.

[51]Williams, "Postmodern Theology and the Judgment of the World," 97.

[52]The love of Christ should not be confused with the genuine but aimless compassion that first allows us to think that we can solve all the world's problems, and then drives us to despair and cynicism when we discover that this is impossible.

[53]Lash, *Believing Three Ways in One God*, 103.

[54]Rowan Williams, "Theological Integrity," *New Blackfriars* 72 (1991): 148.

[55]Lash, *Believing Three Ways in One God*, 81. Incidentally, this is why the church has long affirmed that martyrdom, taking up one's cross and following Christ, is not an unfortunate accident that some Christians are forced to endure, but the natural outcome of a life of love and service.

[56]Johann Baptist Metz, *Faith in History and Society: Toward a Practical Fundamental Theology*, trans. David Smith (New York: Seabury Press, 1980) 115.

[57]Dietrich Bonhoeffer, *Letters and Papers from Prison*, enlarged ed., trans. R. H. Fuller, John Bowden, and others, (New York: Macmillan Publishing Company, 1971) 361.

[58]Rowan Williams, *Resurrection: Interpreting the Easter Gospel*, (New York: Pilgrim Press, 1984) 40.

[59]My thanks to Dorothee Soelle for drawing my attention to the subtle yet substantial difference between spiritual security and spiritual certitude.

[60]Lash, *Believing Three Ways in One God*, 19.

Postscript

The great heritage of Christian spirituality offers many models for individual and corporate spiritual discipleship. As Baptists today struggle in the face of theological and institutional dissension to reformulate the meaning of personal and corporate life, Baptist spirituality is a path that invites a dialogue with the larger Christian heritage.

We have sought to broaden that dialogue and to shift the internal dialogue within the Baptist family into some fresh directions.

First, if there is no total agreement about Baptist theology or Baptist norms, at least we see that certain recurring features and preoccupying themes do characterize Baptist devotion. As Jim McClendon observed, keeping these distinctives while accommodating the ongoing work of the spirit is a strenuous challenge.

Second, Baptist spirituality is stronger in its concrete expressions than its observers are in clarifying them. For most Baptists, stress is greater in living out the Christian life than being able to think clearly about it. Theology is inextricable from worship, community, prayer, and practice. In the Catholic tradition, however, ways have been found to incorporate both the intellectual and the affective. As educational levels and modern change force Baptists to grapple with new concerns, this challenge to integrate ourselves will grow larger.

Third, we find that Baptists see strength and value in diversity. For Baptists, this diversity not only means "pluralism" as it is often understood today, but rather a genuine confidence in truth that both accommodates all truths and enlarges our comprehension of the truth as we meet it. The task for Baptists today is just the opposite from what seems to many to be *the* problem. Our task is not to safeguard community through "circled wagons" and stifling conformity, but to welcome diversity without losing ourselves. Mature freedom assumes a certain gracious humility about one's own cherished interpretations. Much reflection is needed on how freedom can be sustained and encouraged without the loss of genuine community.

Fourth, more work is needed to unearth what Glenn Hinson has called "those ordinary saints scratching around in the soil of our souls." One particularly needed addition to this work is to tell the stories (in less "denominationally-glowing" terms) of Baptist women, lay leaders, local churches, and mission endeavors. One particular need is for truth-telling about the painful but also promising story of ethnic minorities among Baptists. People who have endured our disdain and still clung to our convictions can often tell us something that is right about us that either we never knew or conveniently forgot.

We hope that these essays will stimulate others in the Baptist family to enter into this search. A question confronts Baptists, however, as they examine this larger heritage and the countless practices, forms and structures that have been tried before us. The question is not, as might be thought in turbulent times, "Are there any options?" but "Which ones are most appropriate for this time?"

These are troubling times, but they are also times that are producing an unprecedented amount of writing, debate and theological activity. Out of our own despair may come new patterns of Christian faithfulness.

Baptists have a heritage, the streams of which draw not only from revivals in Kentucky and Georgia, but from the real lives of believers in ancient times. Baptist waters connect, not just in a trail of blood, but in the same glad river in which Jesus and John stood. This river flowed through martyrs and monks, nuns and priests, scribes and common mystics. It is a delightfully sloppy, meandering, and murky river that defies easy categories—but then, the biblical God seems to particularly delight in confounding human expectations.

The old ship of Baptist denominationalism will steer its own course. More important than maintaining institutional loyalty and financial solvency is the acceptance by Baptists of the frightening freedom implied in our convictions in our personal lives and our local congregations. There we will rediscover that God will lead us, and ultimately, if our center is Christ, we will not be forsaken. New ways will be made. That *is* the Baptist way.

Contributors

William Loyd Allen, is professor and head of the department of Religion and Philosophy at Mississippi College. Prior to assuming his present position he taught at the Southern Baptist Theological Seminary (1989–1992). He holds degrees from the University of Montevallo (B.A.) and the Southern Baptist Theological Seminary (M.Div., Ph.D.).

Paul Basden has been a pastor and interim pastor of churches in Texas, Georgia, and Alabama. From 1990–1994 he was university minister at Samford University. He is currently pastor of Brookwood Baptist Church, Birmingham, Alabama. Paul is a graduate of Baylor University (B.A.) and Southwestern Baptist Theological Seminary (M.Div., Ph.D.).

Curtis W. Freeman is associate professor of Christianity and Philosophy at Houston Baptist University where he has taught theology and ethics since 1987. He is also pastor of the West End Baptist Church in the inner city of Houston. Freeman is a graduate of Baylor University (B.A., Ph.D.) and Southwestern Baptist Theological Seminary (M.Div.).

Gary A. Furr is pastor of the Vestavia Hills Baptist Church in Birmingham, Alabama. He has served churches in Georgia, Texas, and North Carolina. Furr holds degrees from Baylor University (Ph.D.), Southeastern Baptist Theological Seminary (M.Div.), and Carson Newman College (B.A.). He has completed the Academy for Spiritual Formation.

Barry Harvey teaches in the department of Religion at Baylor University. He holds degrees from Duke University (Ph.D.), the Southern Baptist Theological Seminary (M.Div.), and the University of Colorado (B.Mus.Ed. and M.Mus.Ed.).

Randy Hatchett is assistant professor of Philosophy at Houston Baptist University. Before coming to Houston he taught at Williams Baptist College. He is a graduate of Southwestern Baptist Theological Seminary (M. Div., Ph.D.) and Dallas Baptist University (B.A.).

E. Glenn Hinson is professor of Spirituality, Worship, and Church History at Baptist Theological Seminary at Richmond, Virginia. He has held teaching positions at the Southern Baptist Theological Seminary (1959–1991) and Wake Forest University (1982–1984). He is a graduate of the Southern Baptist Theological Seminary (B.D., Th.D.), Oxford University (D.Phil.), and Washington University (B.A.). He has written and lectured extensively on Christian spirituality.

Philip LeMasters is assistant professor of Philosophy and Religion at Northeast Missouri State University and previously taught ethics in the Religion department at Wake Forest University. He holds degrees from Duke University (Ph.D.), Rice University (M.A.), and Baylor University (B.A.).

Bill J. Leonard is professor and chair of the Religion department at Samford University and taught at the Southern Baptist Theological Seminary (1975-1991). He is a graduate of Boston University (Ph.D.), Southwestern Baptist Theological Seminary (M.Div.), and Texas Wesleyan College, Fort Worth (B.A.). He did post-doctoral work at Yale and is a widely-quoted writer in Baptist life.

James William McClendon, Jr., is writer-in-residence at Fuller Theological Seminary. He has held teaching positions at the Church Divinity School of the Pacific and Graduate Theological Union in Berkeley, the University of San Francisco, and Golden Gate Baptist Theological Seminary. McClendon is a graduate of Princeton Theological Seminary (Th.M.), Southwestern Baptist Theological Seminary (B.D., Th.D.), and the University of Texas (B.A.). He is currently completing a three-volume work on systematic theology.

Samuel D. Proctor is professor emeritus at Rutgers University and pastor emeritus of Abyssinian Baptist Church of New York City. He is currently professor at the Divinity School of Duke University. He earned a Th.D. from Boston University and is a graduate of Virginia Union University and Crozer Theological Seminary. He is widely recognized as an authority of theology and spirituality in African-American Christianity.

James E. Reed is associate pastor and administrator of the First Baptist Church in Dothan, Alabama. He previously held teaching positions at New Orleans Baptist Theological Seminary and Mississippi College. He holds degrees from Princeton Theological Seminary (Th.M.), New Orleans

Baptist Theological Seminary (M.Div., Ed.D.), and Samford University (B.S.).

Robert Reid is associate professor of Music at Houston Baptist University. He also serves as minister of music at the Memorial Drive Baptist Church of Houston, Texas. He is a graduate of the University of Texas (D.M.A.) and Baylor University (B.M.E., M.M.).

Thomas E. Turner is the minister of Spiritual Direction for Pilgrims Rest Retreat Center in Nashville, Tennessee. He is a graduate of Vanderbilt Divinity School (M.Div.) and Furman University (B.A.). He has done doctoral study in Christian spirituality at the Graduate Theological Union. He has experience in pastoral ministry with churches in Tennessee, South Carolina, and California.